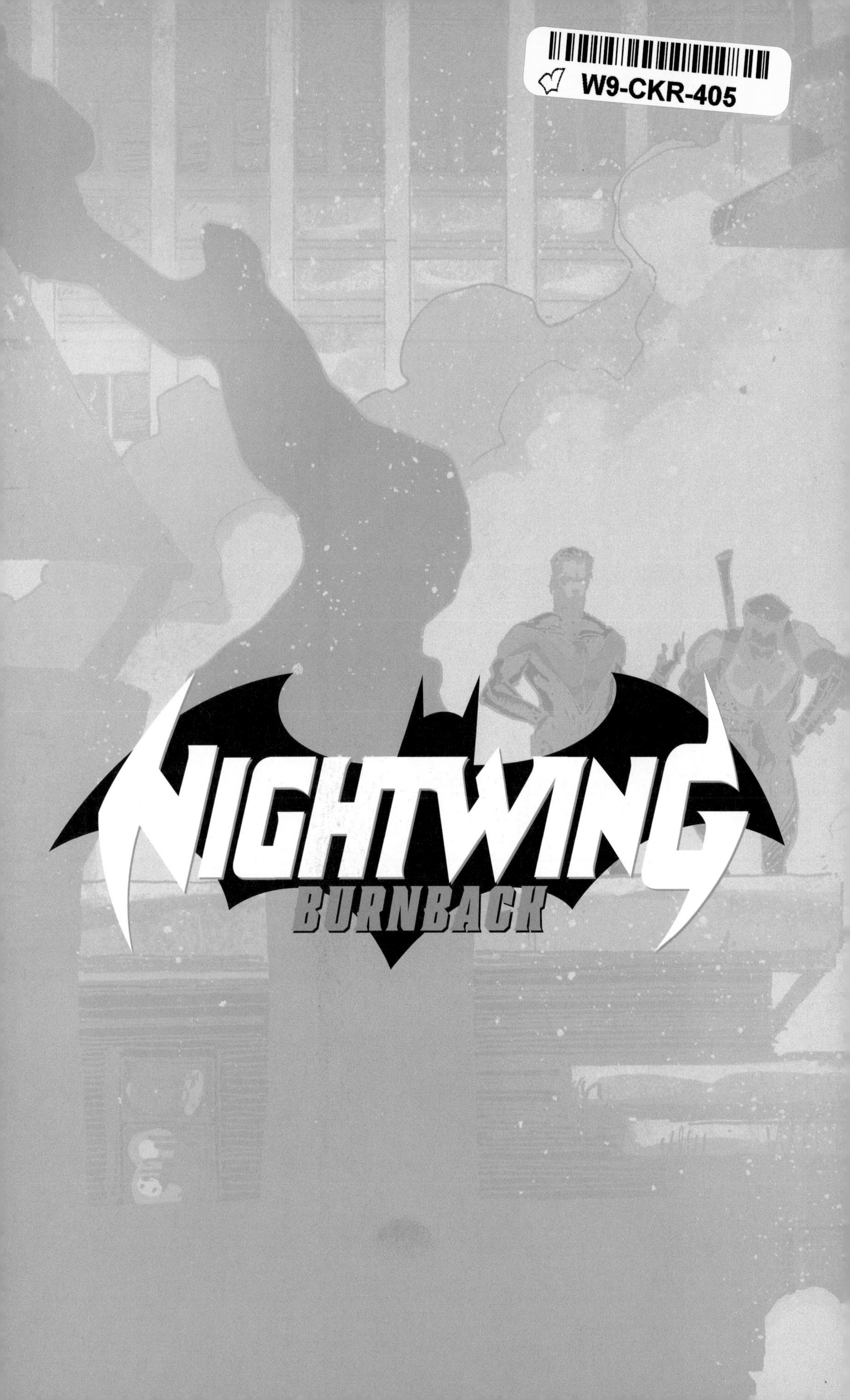
NIGHTWING
BURNBACK

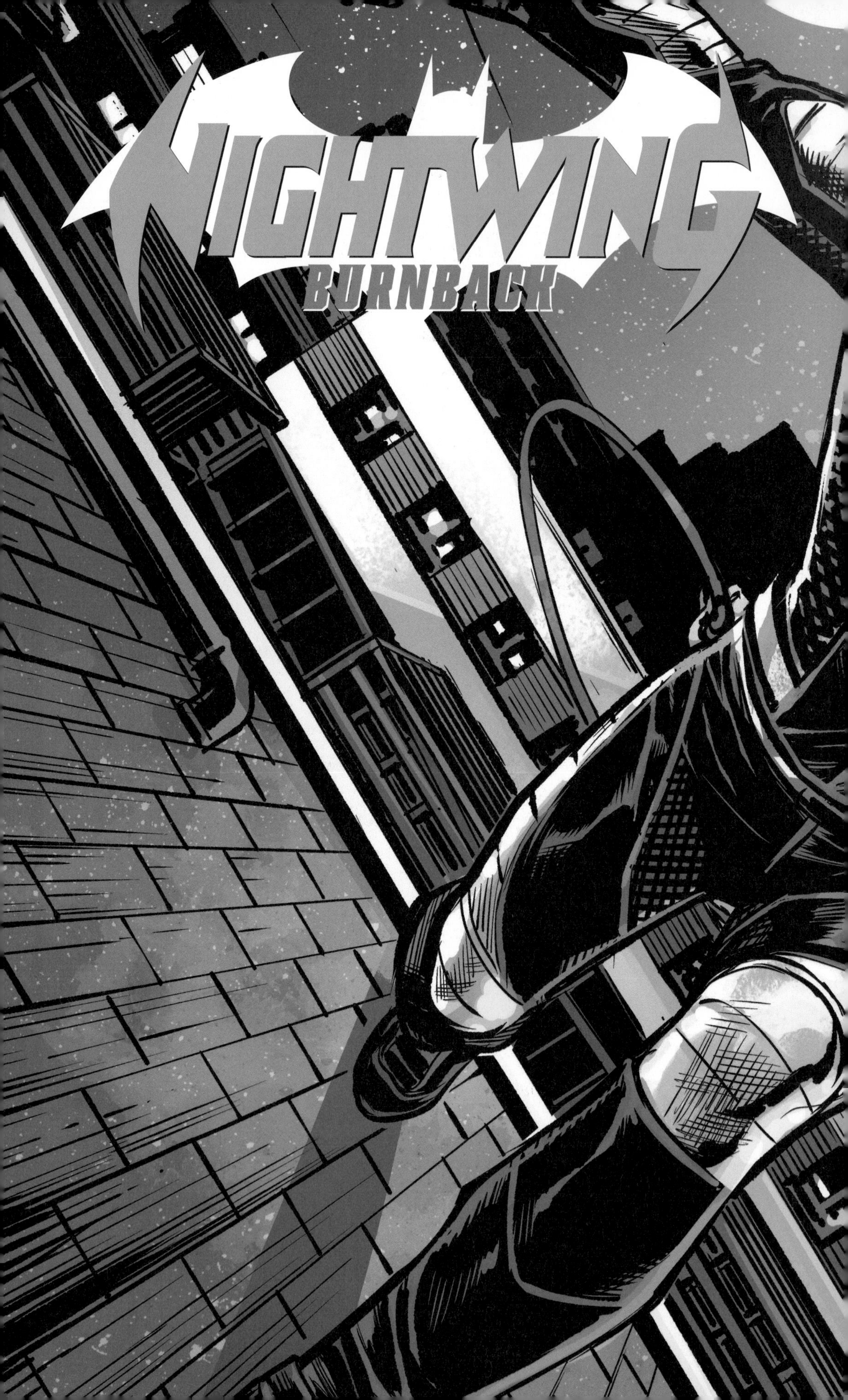
NIGHTWING
BURNBACK

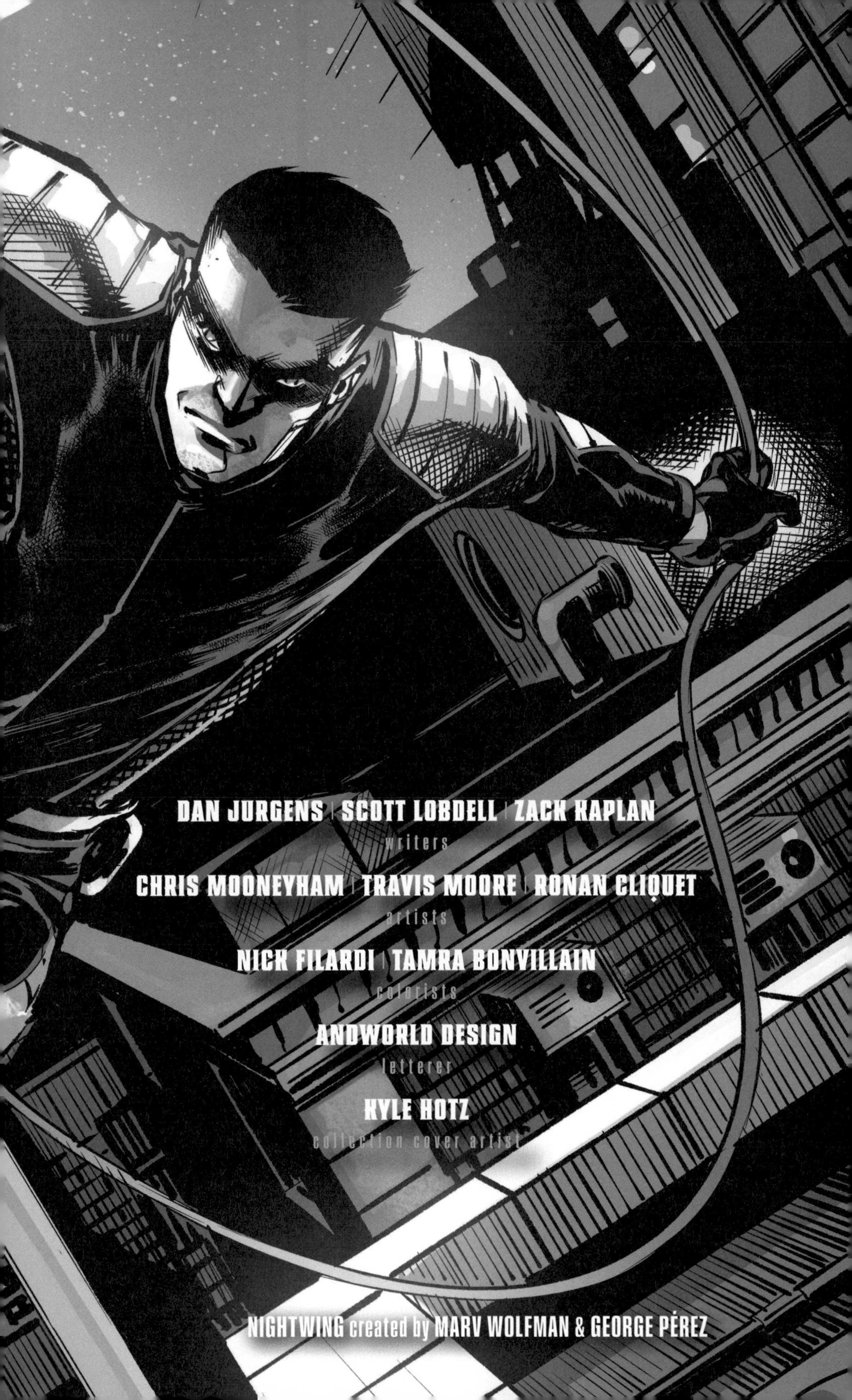

DAN JURGENS | SCOTT LOBDELL | ZACK KAPLAN
writers

CHRIS MOONEYHAM | TRAVIS MOORE | RONAN CLIQUET
artists

NICK FILARDI | TAMRA BONVILLAIN
colorists

ANDWORLD DESIGN
letterer

KYLE HOTZ
collection cover artist

NIGHTWING created by **MARV WOLFMAN & GEORGE PÉREZ**

KATIE KUBERT, MOLLY MAHAN   Editors – Original Series
HARVEY RICHARDS   Associate Editor – Original Series
DAVE WIELGOSZ   Assistant Editor – Original Series
JEB WOODARD   Group Editor – Collected Editions
ERIKA ROTHBERG   Editor – Collected Edition
STEVE COOK   Design Director – Books
MEGEN BELLERSEN   Publication Design
DANIELLE DIGRADO   Publication Production

BOB HARRAS   Senior VP – Editor-in-Chief, DC Comics
PAT McCALLUM   Executive Editor, DC Comics

DAN DiDIO   Publisher
JIM LEE   Publisher & Chief Creative Officer
BOBBIE CHASE   VP – New Publishing Initiatives & Talent Development
DON FALLETTI   VP – Manufacturing Operations & Workflow Management
LAWRENCE GANEM   VP – Talent Services
ALISON GILL   Senior VP – Manufacturing & Operations
HANK KANALZ   Senior VP – Publishing Strategy & Support Services
DAN MIRON   VP – Publishing Operations
NICK J. NAPOLITANO   VP – Manufacturing Administration & Design
NANCY SPEARS   VP – Sales
MICHELE R. WELLS   VP & Executive Editor, Young Reader

NIGHTWING: BURNBACK

DC Comics, 2900 West Alameda Ave., Burbank, CA 91505
Printed by LSC Communications, Owensville, MO, USA. 10/4/19. First Printing.
ISBN: 978-1-4012-9458-8

Library of Congress Cataloging-in-Publication Data is available.

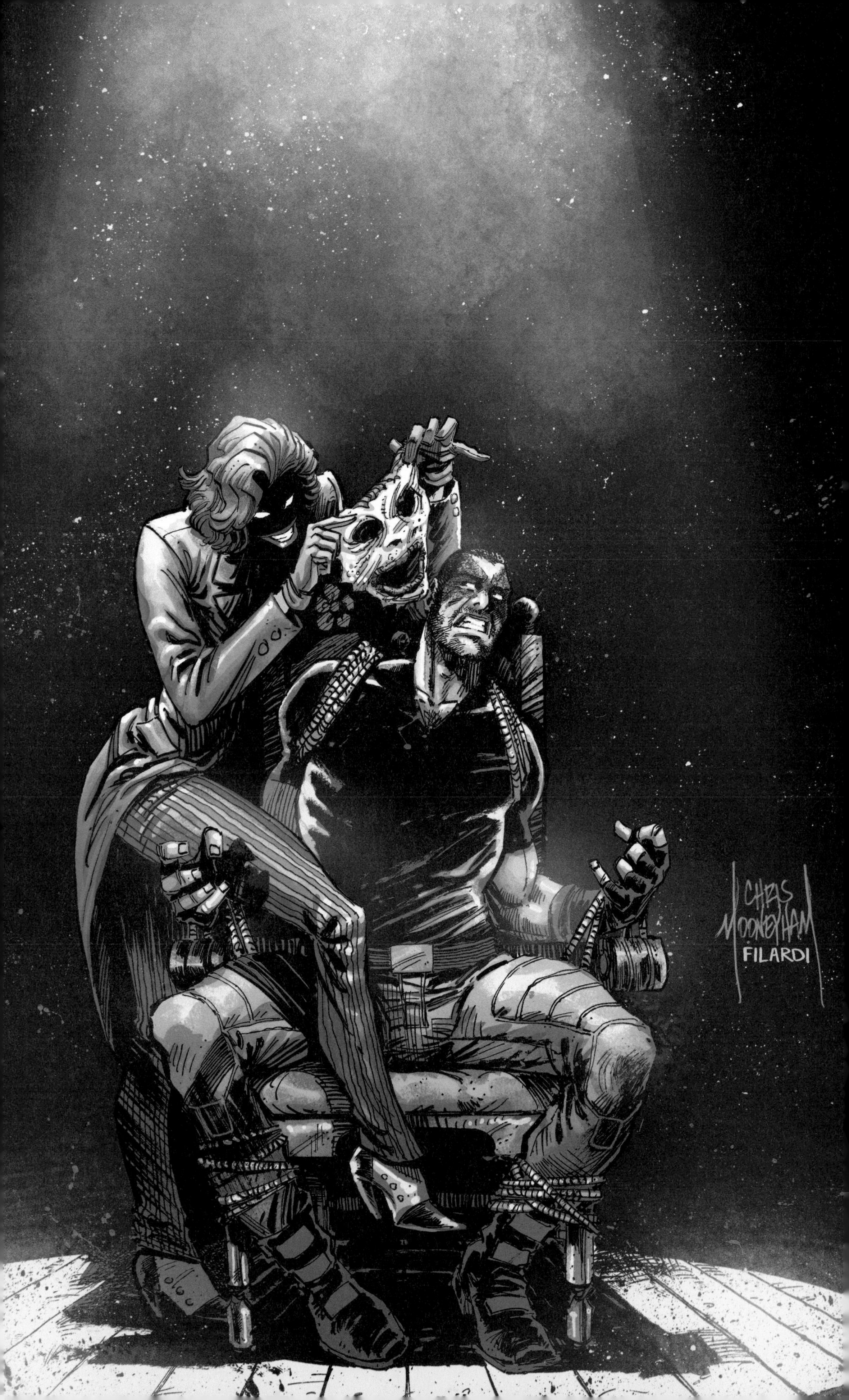
CHRIS
MOONEYHAM
FILARDI

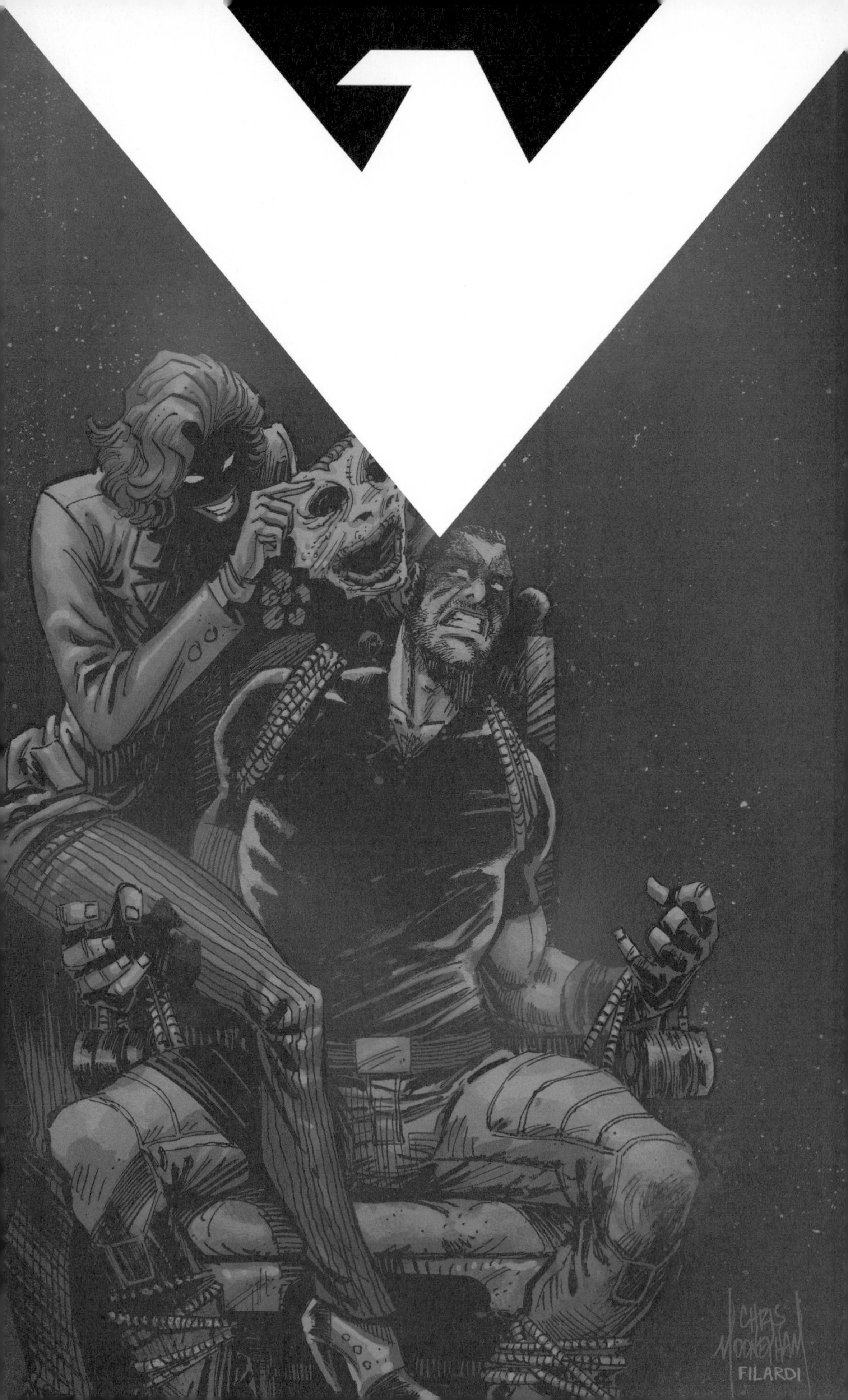
CHRIS
FILARDI

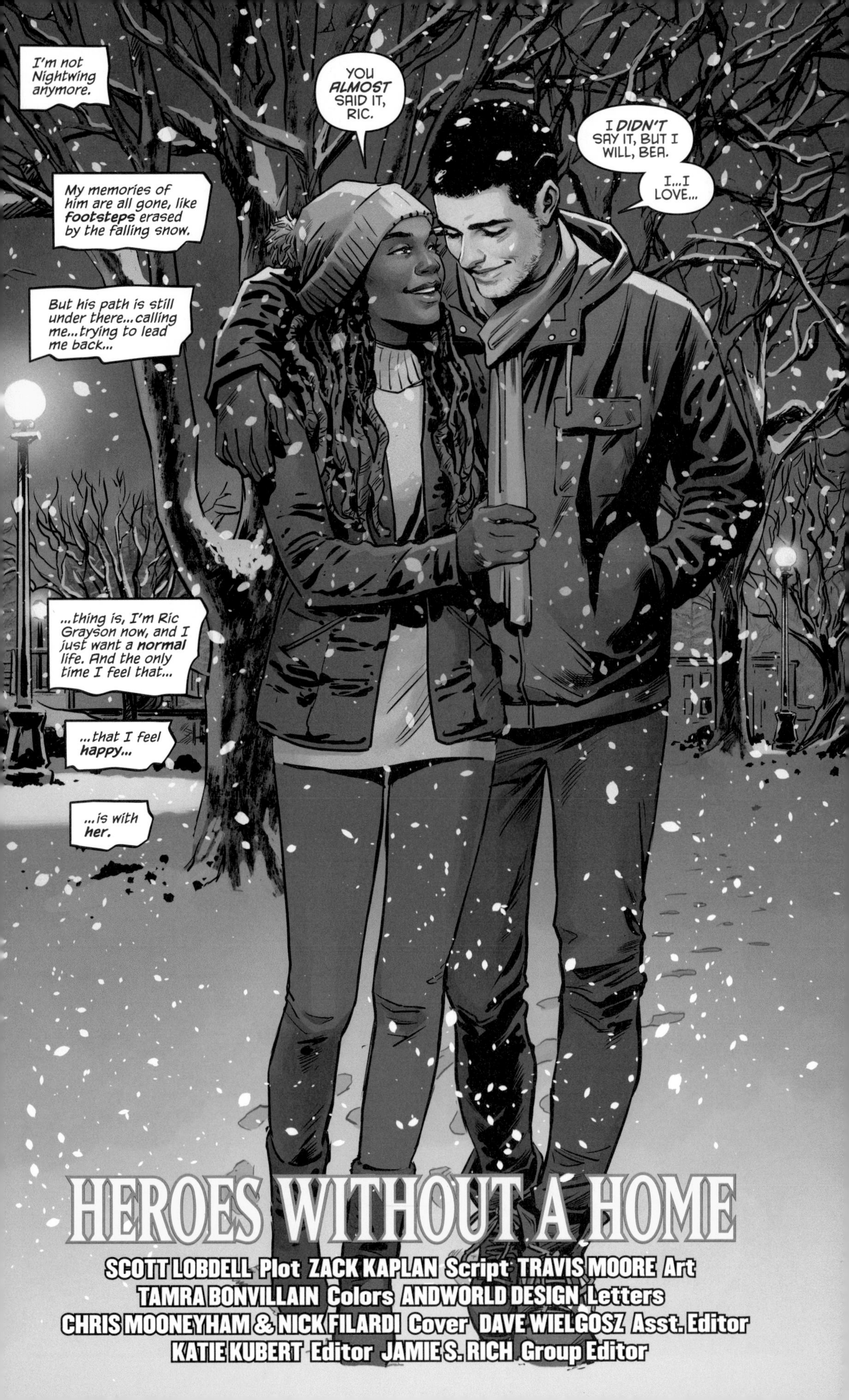
I'm not Nightwing anymore.
YOU ALMOST SAID IT, RIC.
I DIDN'T SAY IT, BUT I WILL, BEA.
I...I LOVE...
My memories of him are all gone, like footsteps erased by the falling snow.
But his path is still under there...calling me...trying to lead me back...
...thing is, I'm Ric Grayson now, and I just want a normal life. And the only time I feel that...
...that I feel happy...
...is with her.
HEROES WITHOUT A HOME
SCOTT LOBDELL Plot ZACK KAPLAN Script TRAVIS MOORE Art
TAMRA BONVILLAIN Colors ANDWORLD DESIGN Letters
CHRIS MOONEYHAM & NICK FILARDI Cover DAVE WIELGOSZ Asst. Editor
KATIE KUBERT Editor JAMIE S. RICH Group Editor

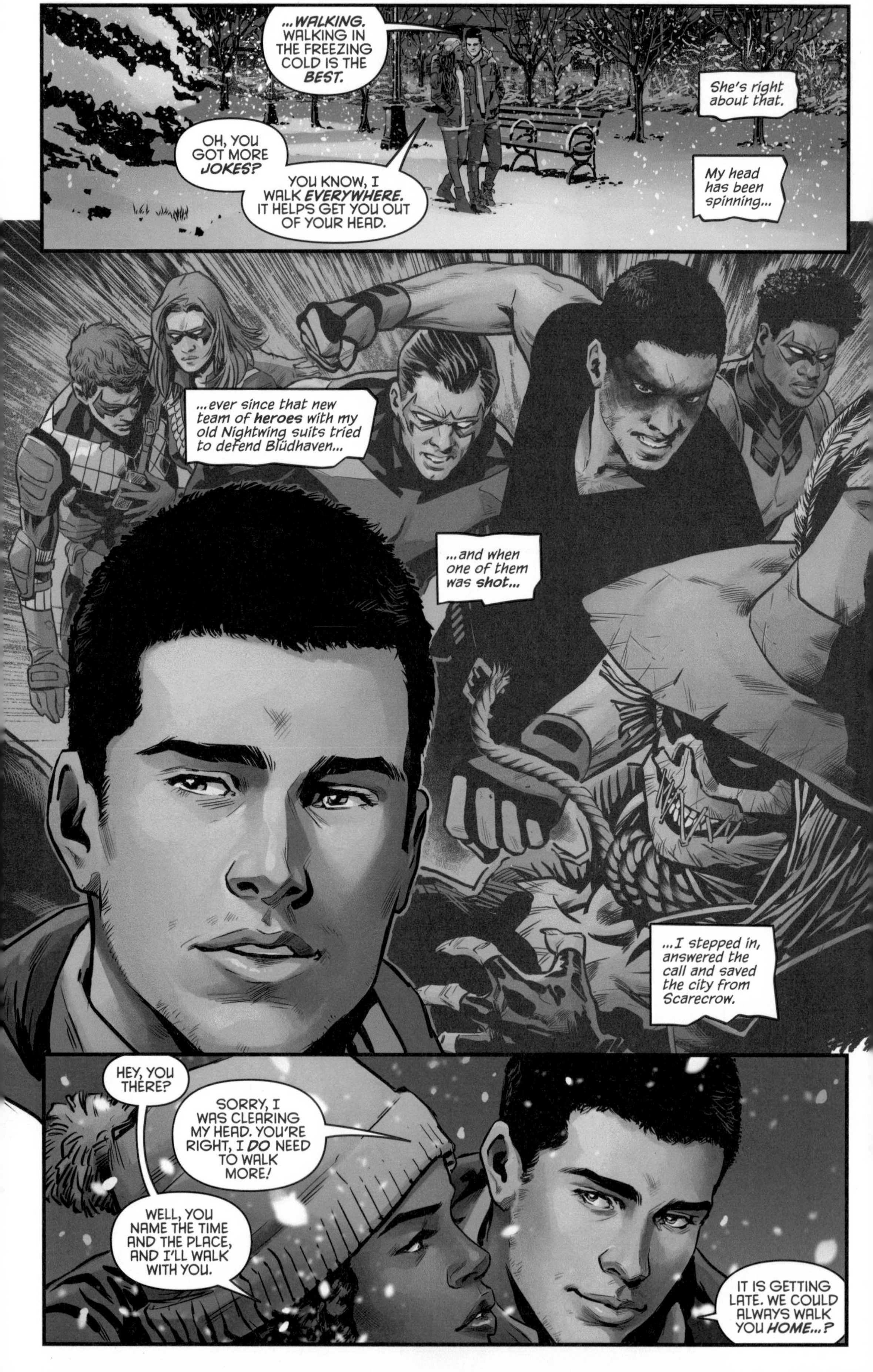
...WALKING. WALKING IN THE FREEZING COLD IS THE BEST.
OH, YOU GOT MORE JOKES?
YOU KNOW, I WALK EVERYWHERE. IT HELPS GET YOU OUT OF YOUR HEAD.
She's right about that.
My head has been spinning...
...ever since that new team of heroes with my old Nightwing suits tried to defend Blüdhaven...
...and when one of them was shot...
...I stepped in, answered the call and saved the city from Scarecrow.
HEY, YOU THERE?
SORRY, I WAS CLEARING MY HEAD. YOU'RE RIGHT, I DO NEED TO WALK MORE!
WELL, YOU NAME THE TIME AND THE PLACE, AND I'LL WALK WITH YOU.
IT IS GETTING LATE. WE COULD ALWAYS WALK YOU HOME...?

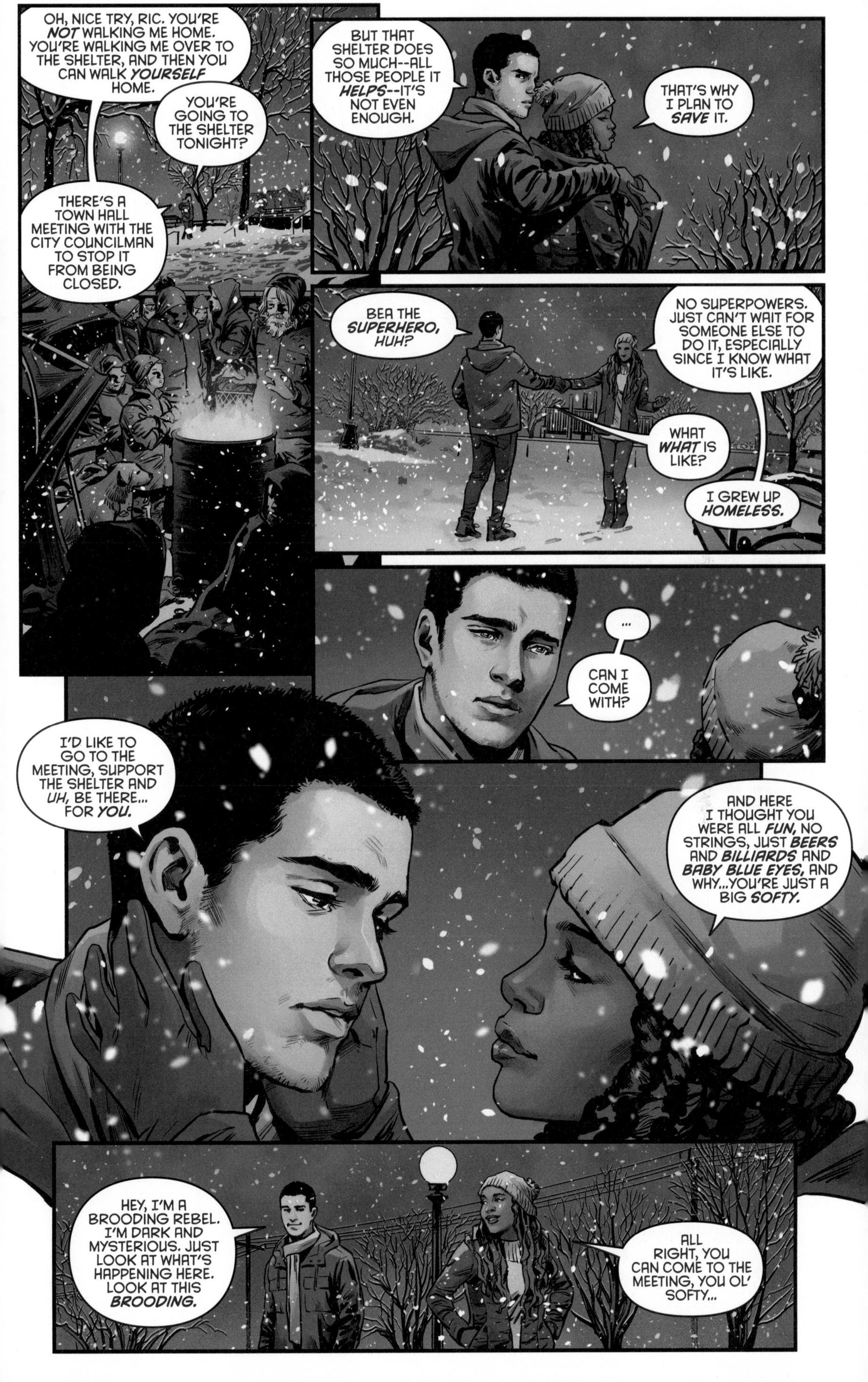
OH, NICE TRY, RIC. YOU'RE NOT WALKING ME HOME. YOU'RE WALKING ME OVER TO THE SHELTER, AND THEN YOU CAN WALK YOURSELF HOME.
YOU'RE GOING TO THE SHELTER TONIGHT?
THERE'S A TOWN HALL MEETING WITH THE CITY COUNCILMAN TO STOP IT FROM BEING CLOSED.
BUT THAT SHELTER DOES SO MUCH--ALL THOSE PEOPLE IT HELPS--IT'S NOT EVEN ENOUGH.
THAT'S WHY I PLAN TO SAVE IT.
BEA THE SUPERHERO, HUH?
NO SUPERPOWERS. JUST CAN'T WAIT FOR SOMEONE ELSE TO DO IT, ESPECIALLY SINCE I KNOW WHAT IT'S LIKE.
WHAT WHAT IS LIKE?
I GREW UP HOMELESS.
...
CAN I COME WITH?
I'D LIKE TO GO TO THE MEETING, SUPPORT THE SHELTER AND UH, BE THERE... FOR YOU.
AND HERE I THOUGHT YOU WERE ALL FUN, NO STRINGS, JUST BEERS AND BILLIARDS AND BABY BLUE EYES, AND WHY...YOU'RE JUST A BIG SOFTY.
HEY, I'M A BROODING REBEL. I'M DARK AND MYSTERIOUS. JUST LOOK AT WHAT'S HAPPENING HERE. LOOK AT THIS BROODING.
ALL RIGHT, YOU CAN COME TO THE MEETING, YOU OL' SOFTY...

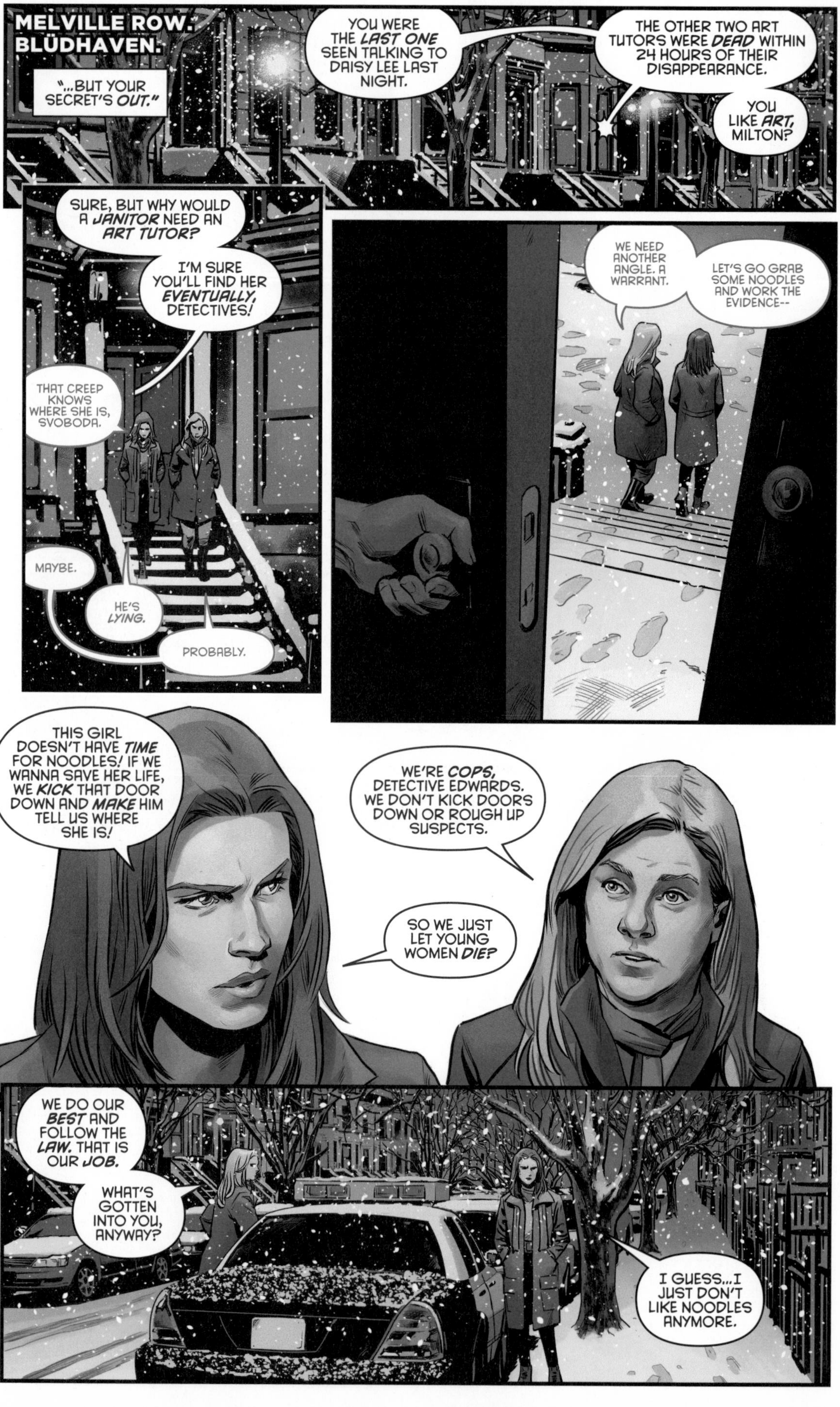
MELVILLE ROW. BLÜDHAVEN.
"...BUT YOUR SECRET'S OUT."
YOU WERE THE LAST ONE SEEN TALKING TO DAISY LEE LAST NIGHT.
THE OTHER TWO ART TUTORS WERE DEAD WITHIN 24 HOURS OF THEIR DISAPPEARANCE.
YOU LIKE ART, MILTON?
SURE, BUT WHY WOULD A JANITOR NEED AN ART TUTOR?
I'M SURE YOU'LL FIND HER EVENTUALLY, DETECTIVES!
THAT CREEP KNOWS WHERE SHE IS, SVOBODA.
MAYBE.
HE'S LYING.
PROBABLY.
WE NEED ANOTHER ANGLE. A WARRANT.
LET'S GO GRAB SOME NOODLES AND WORK THE EVIDENCE--
THIS GIRL DOESN'T HAVE TIME FOR NOODLES! IF WE WANNA SAVE HER LIFE, WE KICK THAT DOOR DOWN AND MAKE HIM TELL US WHERE SHE IS!
WE'RE COPS, DETECTIVE EDWARDS. WE DON'T KICK DOORS DOWN OR ROUGH UP SUSPECTS.
SO WE JUST LET YOUNG WOMEN DIE?
WE DO OUR BEST AND FOLLOW THE LAW. THAT IS OUR JOB.
WHAT'S GOTTEN INTO YOU, ANYWAY?
I GUESS...I JUST DON'T LIKE NOODLES ANYMORE.

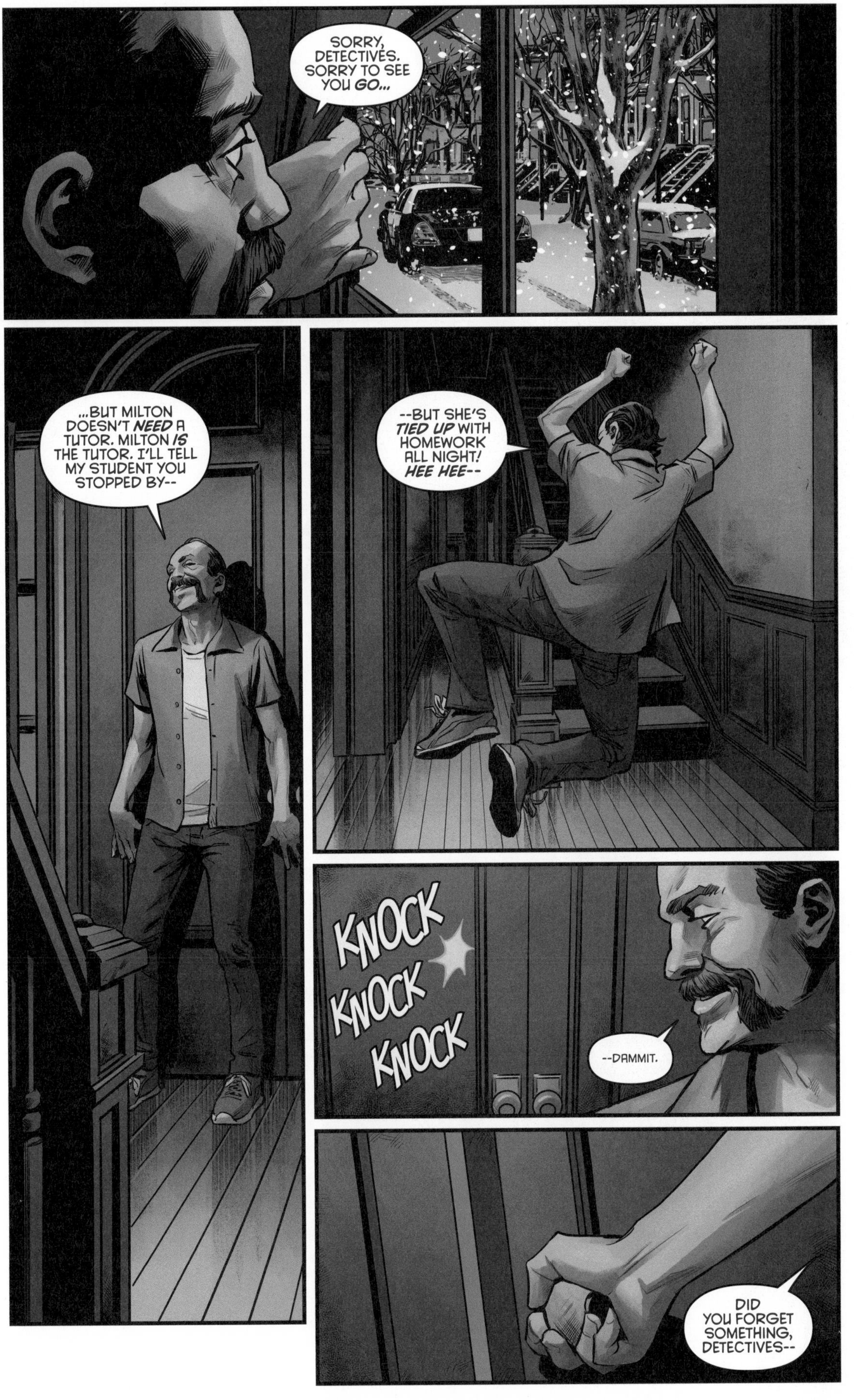
SORRY, DETECTIVES. SORRY TO SEE YOU GO...
...BUT MILTON DOESN'T NEED A TUTOR. MILTON IS THE TUTOR. I'LL TELL MY STUDENT YOU STOPPED BY--
--BUT SHE'S TIED UP WITH HOMEWORK ALL NIGHT! HEE HEE--
KNOCK KNOCK KNOCK
--DAMMIT.
DID YOU FORGET SOMETHING, DETECTIVES--

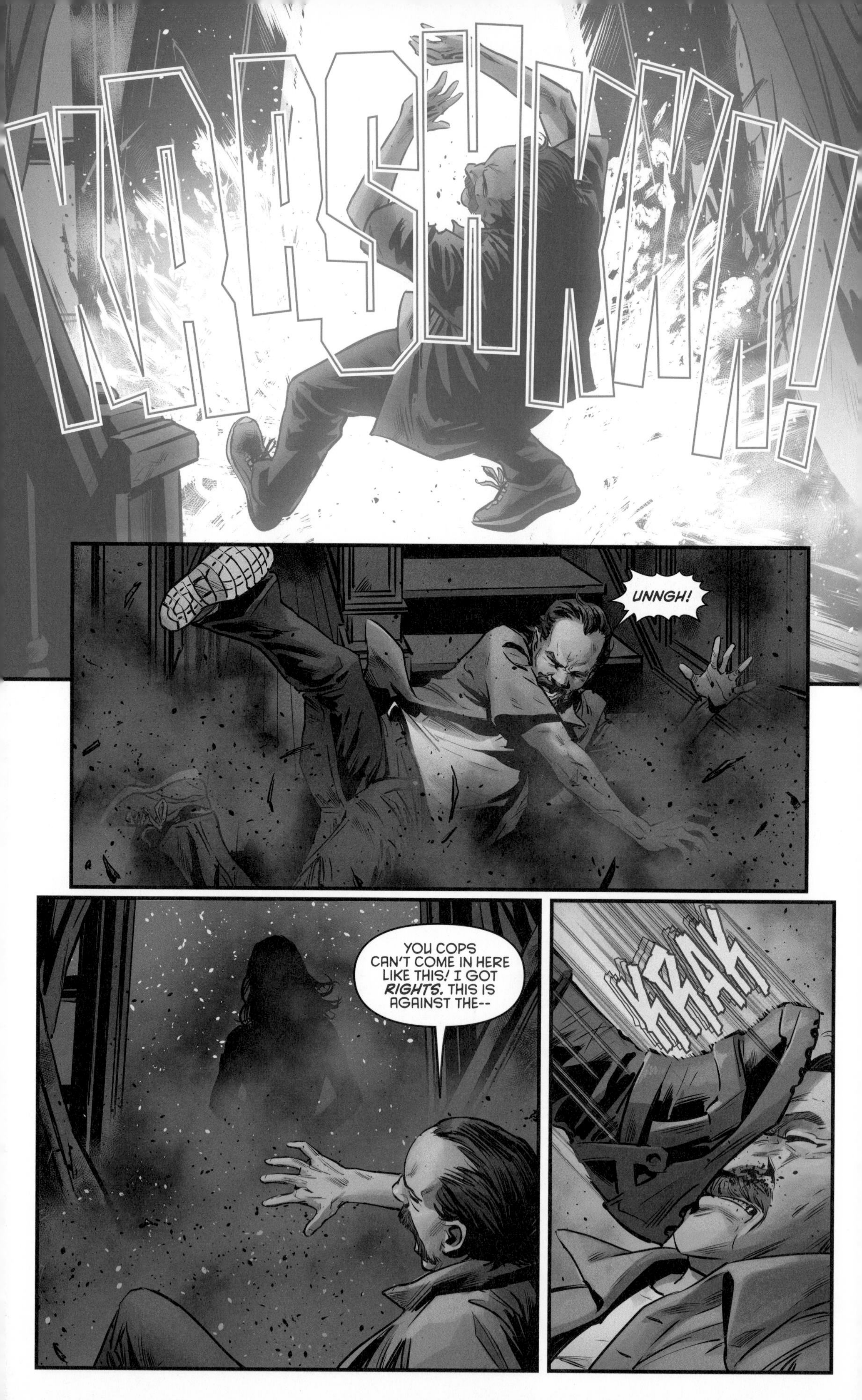
UNNGH!
YOU COPS CAN'T COME IN HERE LIKE THIS! I GOT **RIGHTS.** THIS IS AGAINST THE--
KRAK

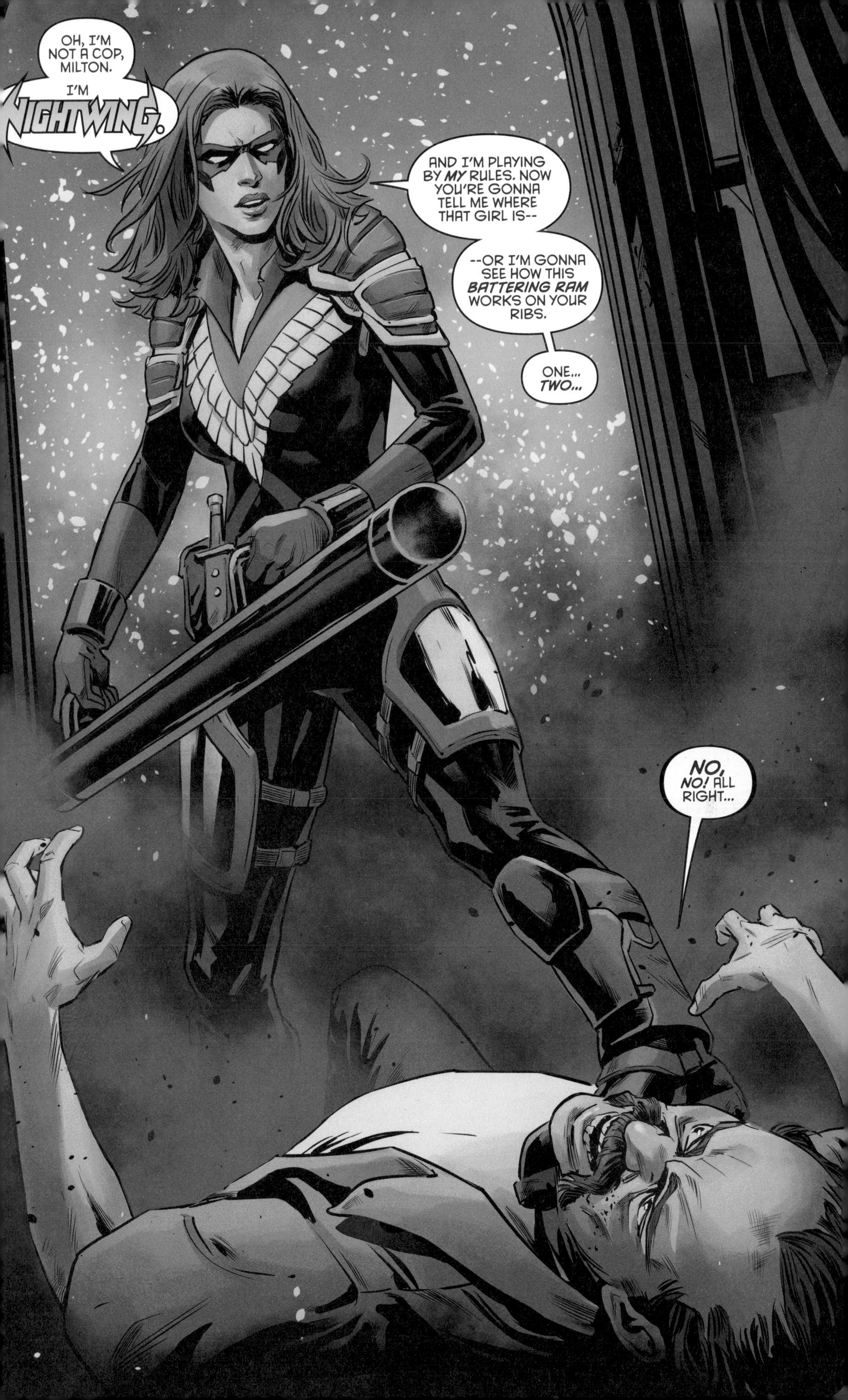
OH, I'M NOT A COP, MILTON.
I'M NIGHTWING.
AND I'M PLAYING BY MY RULES. NOW YOU'RE GONNA TELL ME WHERE THAT GIRL IS--
--OR I'M GONNA SEE HOW THIS BATTERING RAM WORKS ON YOUR RIBS.
ONE... TWO...
NO, NO! ALL RIGHT...

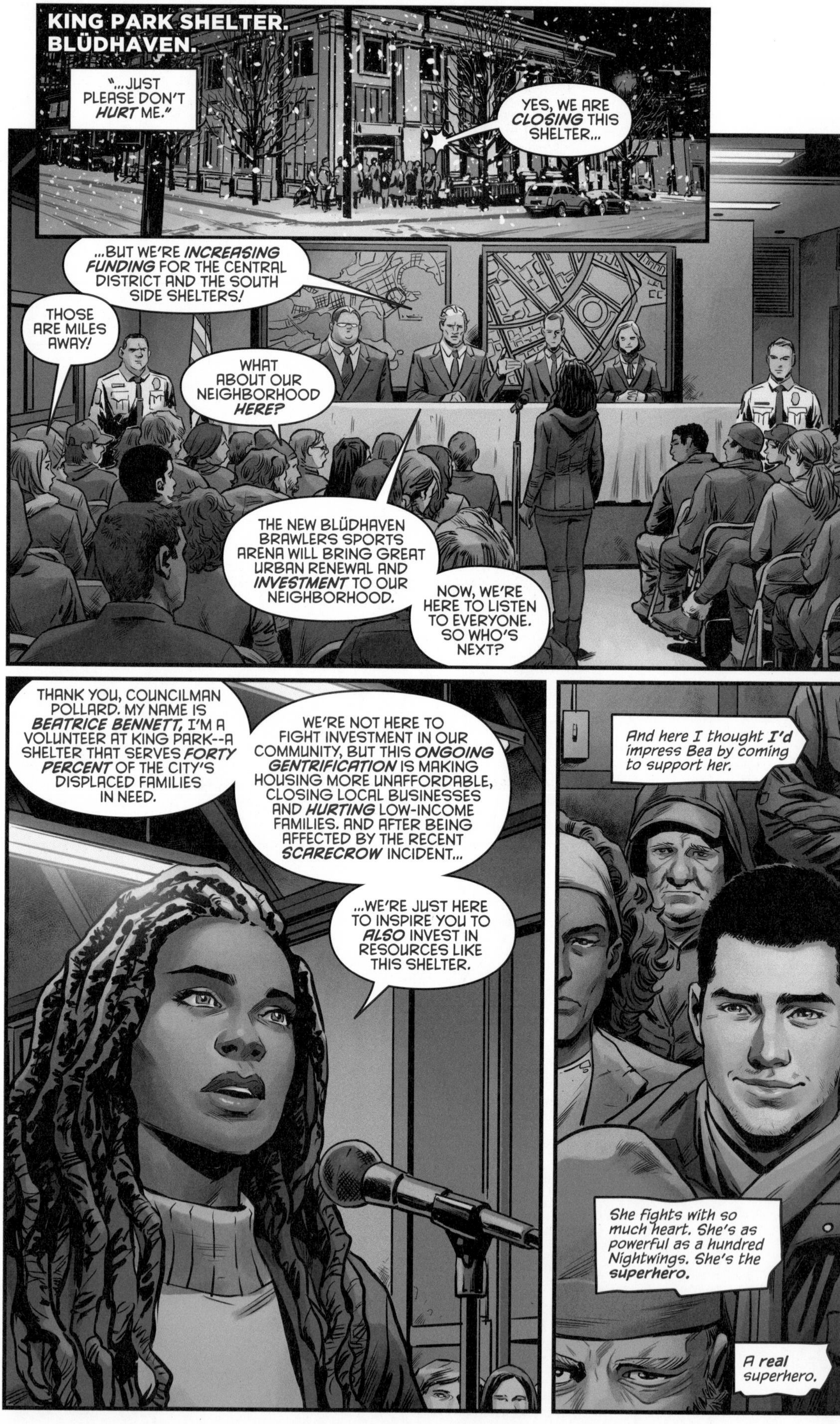
KING PARK SHELTER. BLÜDHAVEN.
"...JUST PLEASE DON'T HURT ME."
YES, WE ARE CLOSING THIS SHELTER...
...BUT WE'RE INCREASING FUNDING FOR THE CENTRAL DISTRICT AND THE SOUTH SIDE SHELTERS!
THOSE ARE MILES AWAY!
WHAT ABOUT OUR NEIGHBORHOOD HERE?
THE NEW BLÜDHAVEN BRAWLERS SPORTS ARENA WILL BRING GREAT URBAN RENEWAL AND INVESTMENT TO OUR NEIGHBORHOOD.
NOW, WE'RE HERE TO LISTEN TO EVERYONE. SO WHO'S NEXT?
THANK YOU, COUNCILMAN POLLARD. MY NAME IS BEATRICE BENNETT, I'M A VOLUNTEER AT KING PARK--A SHELTER THAT SERVES FORTY PERCENT OF THE CITY'S DISPLACED FAMILIES IN NEED.
WE'RE NOT HERE TO FIGHT INVESTMENT IN OUR COMMUNITY, BUT THIS ONGOING GENTRIFICATION IS MAKING HOUSING MORE UNAFFORDABLE, CLOSING LOCAL BUSINESSES AND HURTING LOW-INCOME FAMILIES. AND AFTER BEING AFFECTED BY THE RECENT SCARECROW INCIDENT...
...WE'RE JUST HERE TO INSPIRE YOU TO ALSO INVEST IN RESOURCES LIKE THIS SHELTER.
And here I thought I'd impress Bea by coming to support her.
She fights with so much heart. She's as powerful as a hundred Nightwings. She's the superhero.
A real superhero.

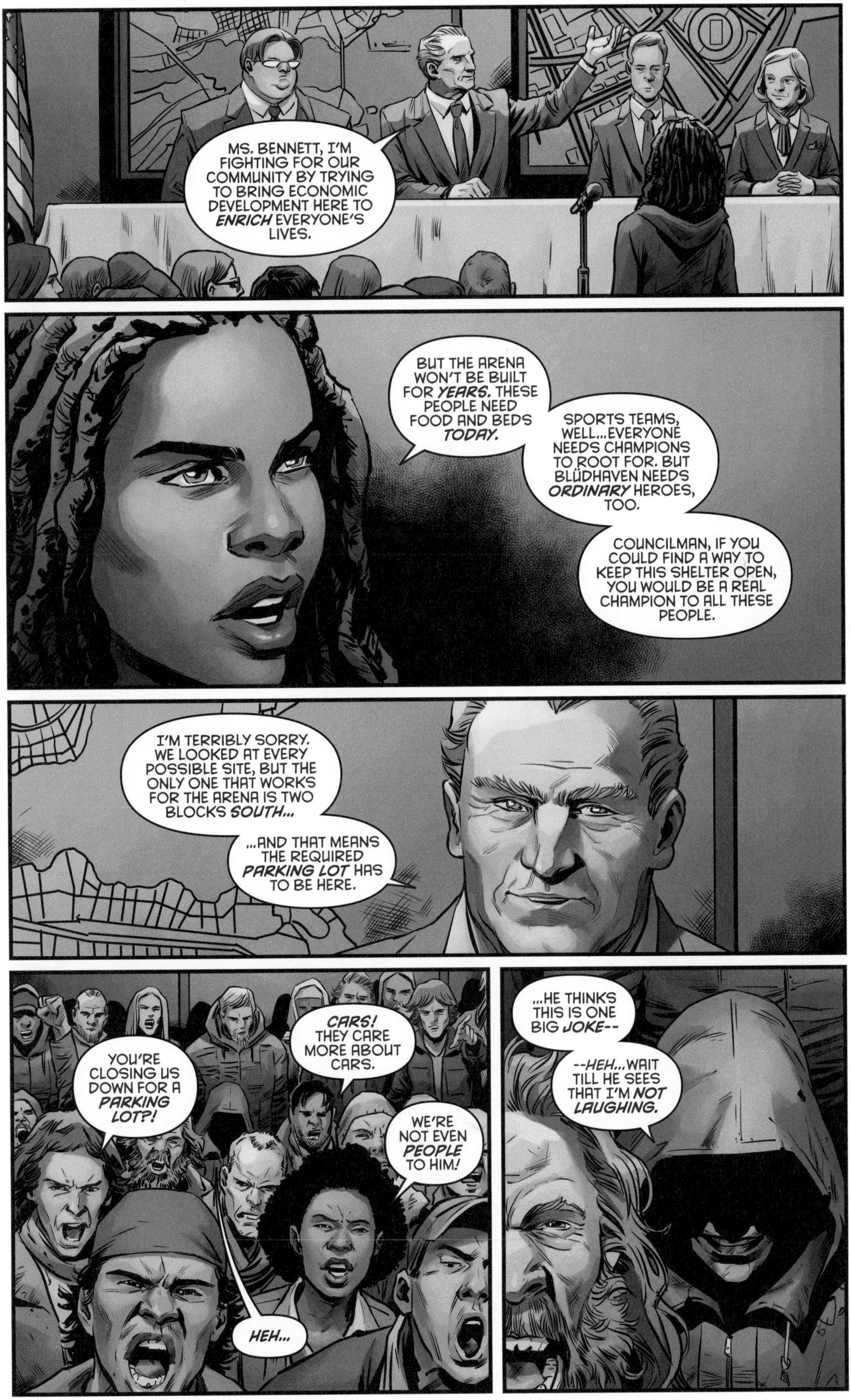
MS. BENNETT, I'M FIGHTING FOR OUR COMMUNITY BY TRYING TO BRING ECONOMIC DEVELOPMENT HERE TO *ENRICH* EVERYONE'S LIVES.
BUT THE ARENA WON'T BE BUILT FOR *YEARS.* THESE PEOPLE NEED FOOD AND BEDS *TODAY.*
SPORTS TEAMS, WELL...EVERYONE NEEDS CHAMPIONS TO ROOT FOR. BUT BLÜDHAVEN NEEDS *ORDINARY* HEROES, TOO.
COUNCILMAN, IF YOU COULD FIND A WAY TO KEEP THIS SHELTER OPEN, YOU WOULD BE A REAL CHAMPION TO ALL THESE PEOPLE.
I'M TERRIBLY SORRY. WE LOOKED AT EVERY POSSIBLE SITE, BUT THE ONLY ONE THAT WORKS FOR THE ARENA IS TWO BLOCKS *SOUTH...*
...AND THAT MEANS THE REQUIRED *PARKING LOT* HAS TO BE HERE.
YOU'RE CLOSING US DOWN FOR A *PARKING LOT?!*
CARS! THEY CARE MORE ABOUT CARS.
WE'RE NOT EVEN *PEOPLE* TO HIM!
HEH...
...HE THINKS THIS IS ONE BIG *JOKE--*
*--HEH...*WAIT TILL HE SEES THAT I'M *NOT LAUGHING.*

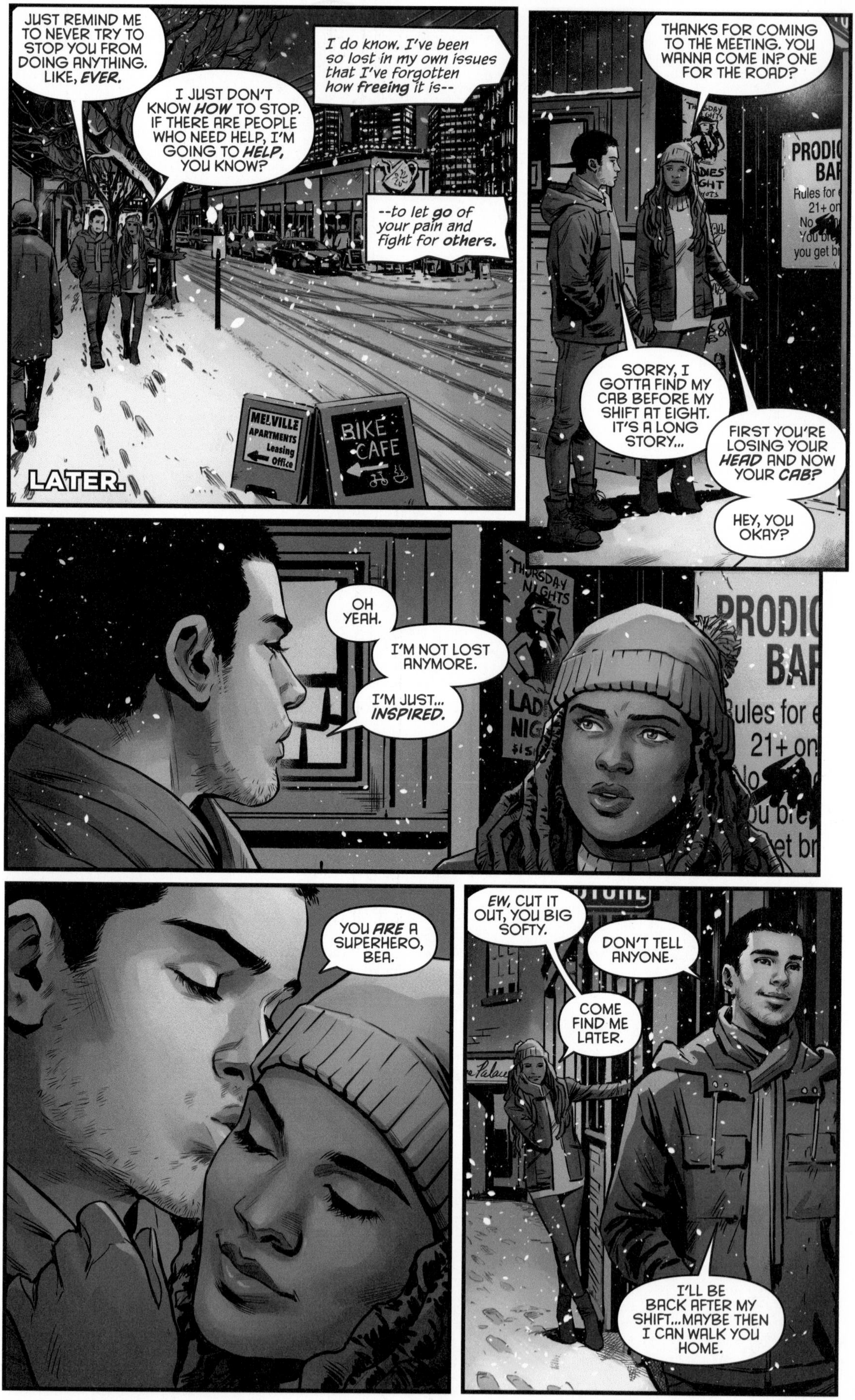
JUST REMIND ME TO NEVER TRY TO STOP YOU FROM DOING ANYTHING. LIKE, EVER.
I JUST DON'T KNOW HOW TO STOP. IF THERE ARE PEOPLE WHO NEED HELP, I'M GOING TO HELP, YOU KNOW?
I do know. I've been so lost in my own issues that I've forgotten how freeing it is--
--to let go of your pain and fight for others.
MELVILLE APARTMENTS Leasing Office
BIKE CAFE
LATER.
THANKS FOR COMING TO THE MEETING. YOU WANNA COME IN? ONE FOR THE ROAD?
SORRY, I GOTTA FIND MY CAB BEFORE MY SHIFT AT EIGHT. IT'S A LONG STORY...
FIRST YOU'RE LOSING YOUR HEAD AND NOW YOUR CAB?
HEY, YOU OKAY?
THURSDAY NIGHTS
OH YEAH.
I'M NOT LOST ANYMORE.
I'M JUST... INSPIRED.
YOU ARE A SUPERHERO, BEA.
EW, CUT IT OUT, YOU BIG SOFTY.
DON'T TELL ANYONE.
COME FIND ME LATER.
I'LL BE BACK AFTER MY SHIFT...MAYBE THEN I CAN WALK YOU HOME.

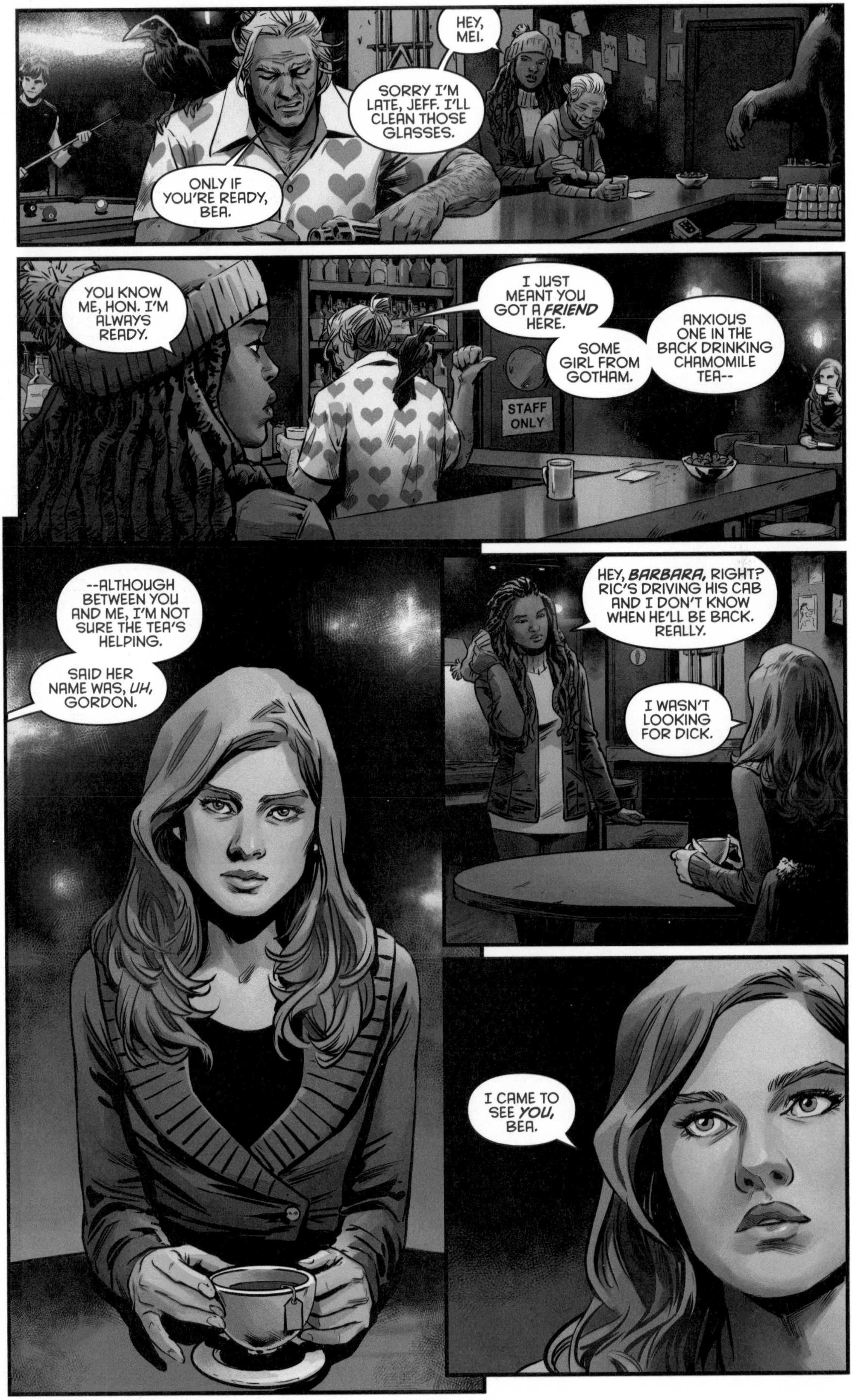
HEY, MEI.
SORRY I'M LATE, JEFF. I'LL CLEAN THOSE GLASSES.
ONLY IF YOU'RE READY, BEA.
YOU KNOW ME, HON. I'M ALWAYS READY.
I JUST MEANT YOU GOT A *FRIEND* HERE.
SOME GIRL FROM GOTHAM.
ANXIOUS ONE IN THE BACK DRINKING CHAMOMILE TEA--
STAFF ONLY
--ALTHOUGH BETWEEN YOU AND ME, I'M NOT SURE THE TEA'S HELPING.
SAID HER NAME WAS, *UH,* GORDON.
HEY, *BARBARA,* RIGHT? RIC'S DRIVING HIS CAB AND I DON'T KNOW WHEN HE'LL BE BACK. REALLY.
I WASN'T LOOKING FOR DICK.
I CAME TO SEE *YOU,* BEA.

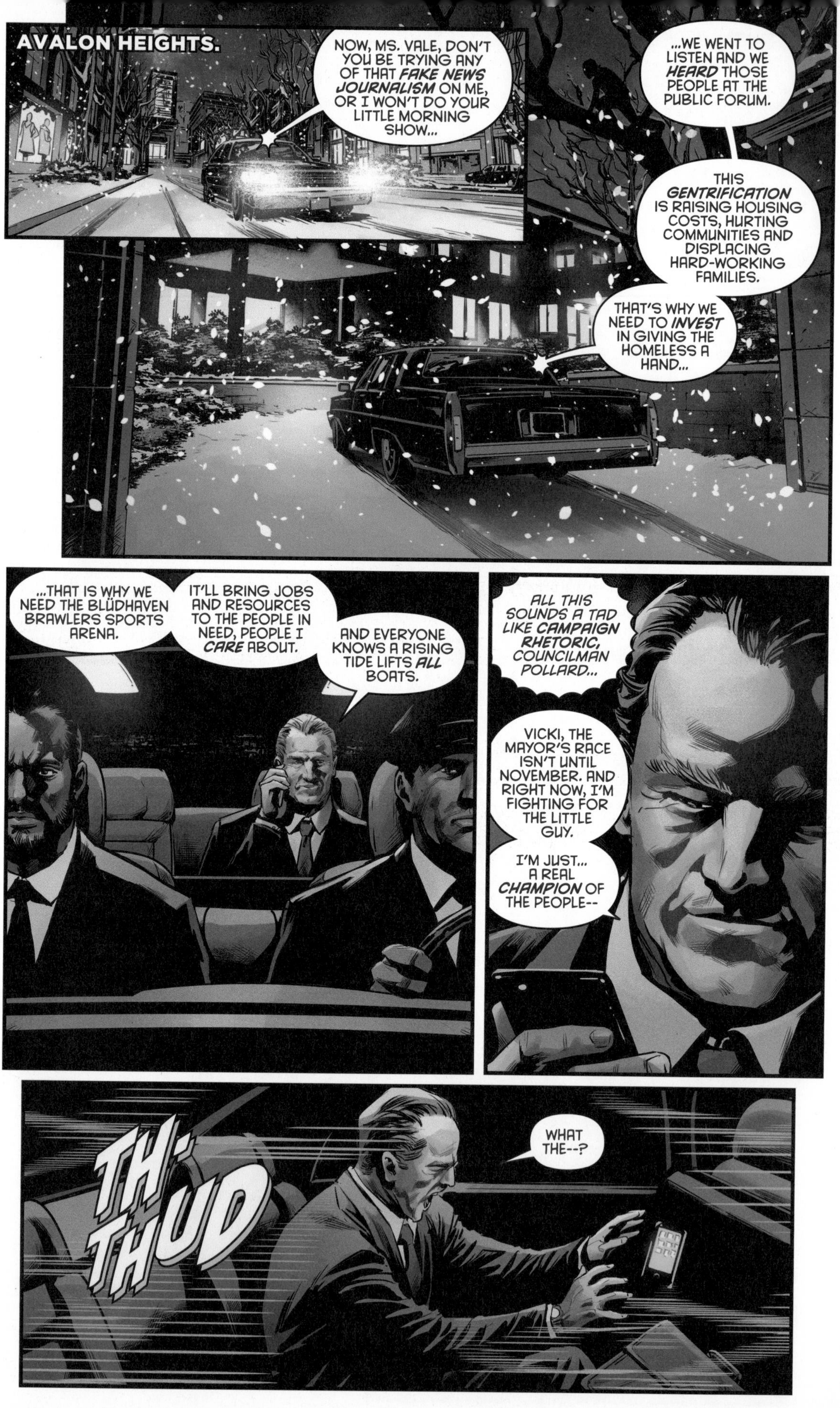
AVALON HEIGHTS.
NOW, MS. VALE, DON'T YOU BE TRYING ANY OF THAT FAKE NEWS JOURNALISM ON ME, OR I WON'T DO YOUR LITTLE MORNING SHOW...
...WE WENT TO LISTEN AND WE HEARD THOSE PEOPLE AT THE PUBLIC FORUM.
THIS GENTRIFICATION IS RAISING HOUSING COSTS, HURTING COMMUNITIES AND DISPLACING HARD-WORKING FAMILIES.
THAT'S WHY WE NEED TO INVEST IN GIVING THE HOMELESS A HAND...
...THAT IS WHY WE NEED THE BLÜDHAVEN BRAWLERS SPORTS ARENA.
IT'LL BRING JOBS AND RESOURCES TO THE PEOPLE IN NEED, PEOPLE I CARE ABOUT.
AND EVERYONE KNOWS A RISING TIDE LIFTS ALL BOATS.
ALL THIS SOUNDS A TAD LIKE CAMPAIGN RHETORIC, COUNCILMAN POLLARD...
VICKI, THE MAYOR'S RACE ISN'T UNTIL NOVEMBER. AND RIGHT NOW, I'M FIGHTING FOR THE LITTLE GUY.
I'M JUST... A REAL CHAMPION OF THE PEOPLE--
TH-THUD
WHAT THE--?

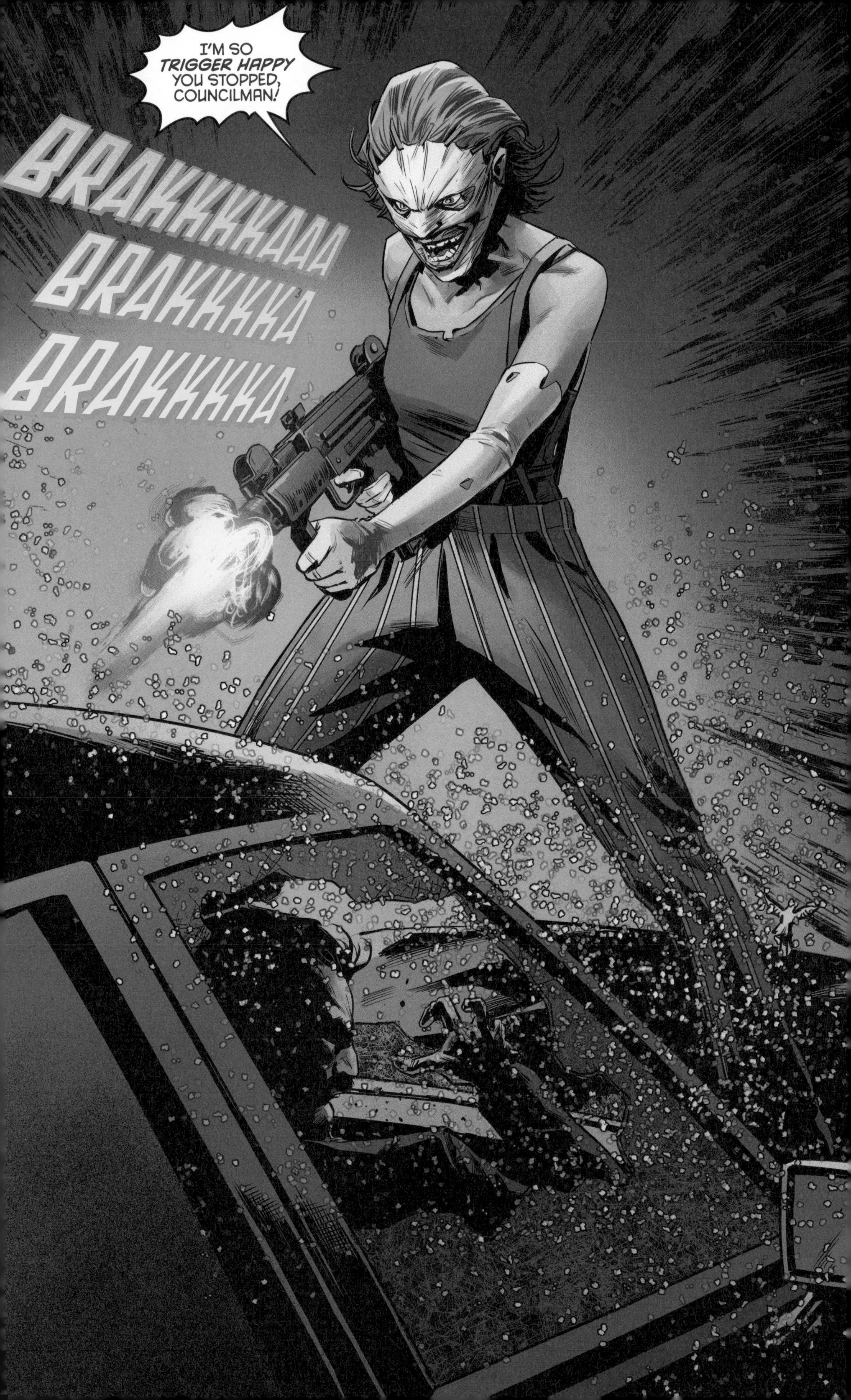
I'M SO TRIGGER HAPPY YOU STOPPED, COUNCILMAN!
BRAKKKKKAAA
BRAKKKKA
BRAKKKKA

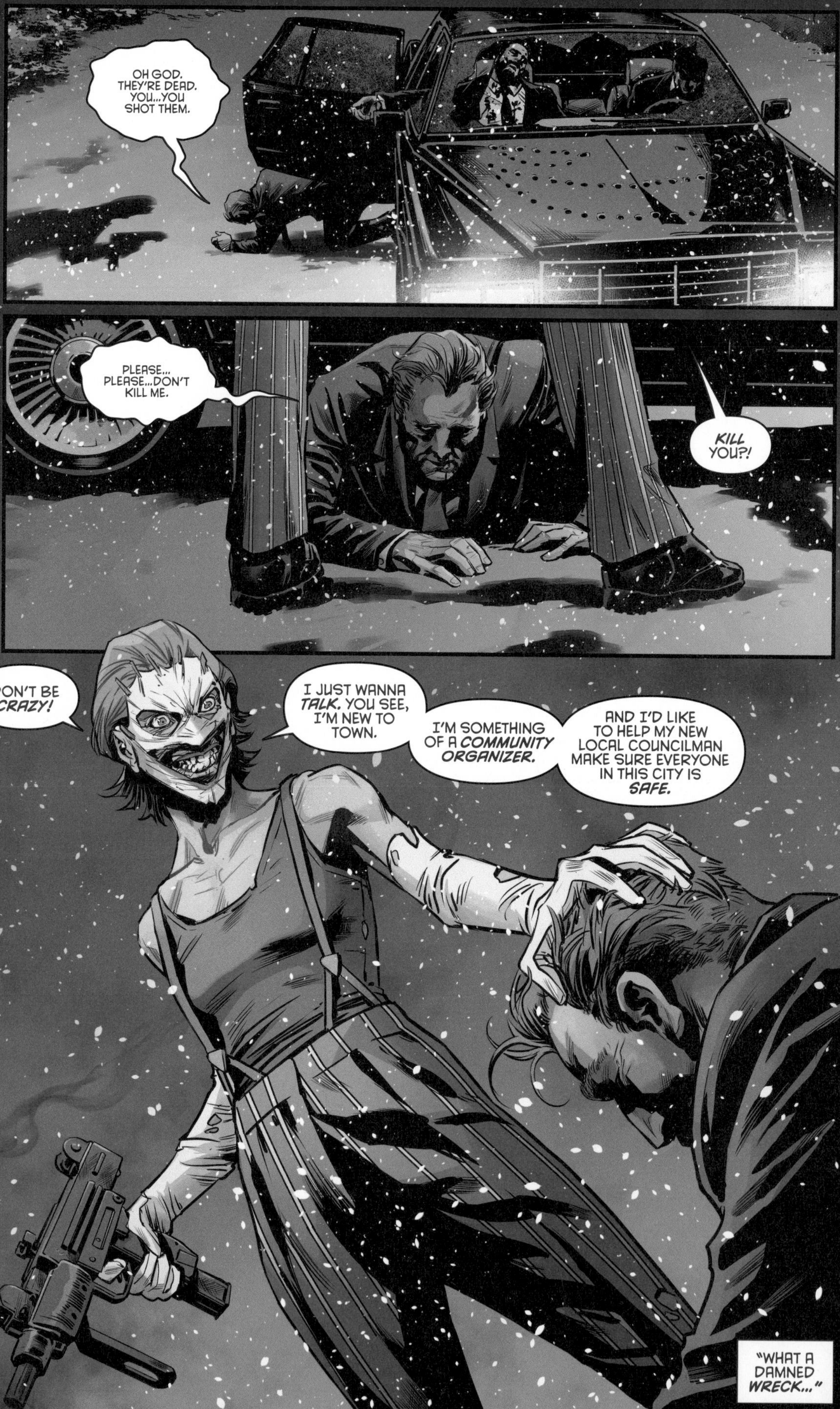
OH GOD. THEY'RE DEAD. YOU...YOU SHOT THEM.
PLEASE... PLEASE...DON'T KILL ME.
KILL YOU?!
DON'T BE CRAZY!
I JUST WANNA TALK. YOU SEE, I'M NEW TO TOWN.
I'M SOMETHING OF A COMMUNITY ORGANIZER.
AND I'D LIKE TO HELP MY NEW LOCAL COUNCILMAN MAKE SURE EVERYONE IN THIS CITY IS SAFE.
"WHAT A DAMNED WRECK..."

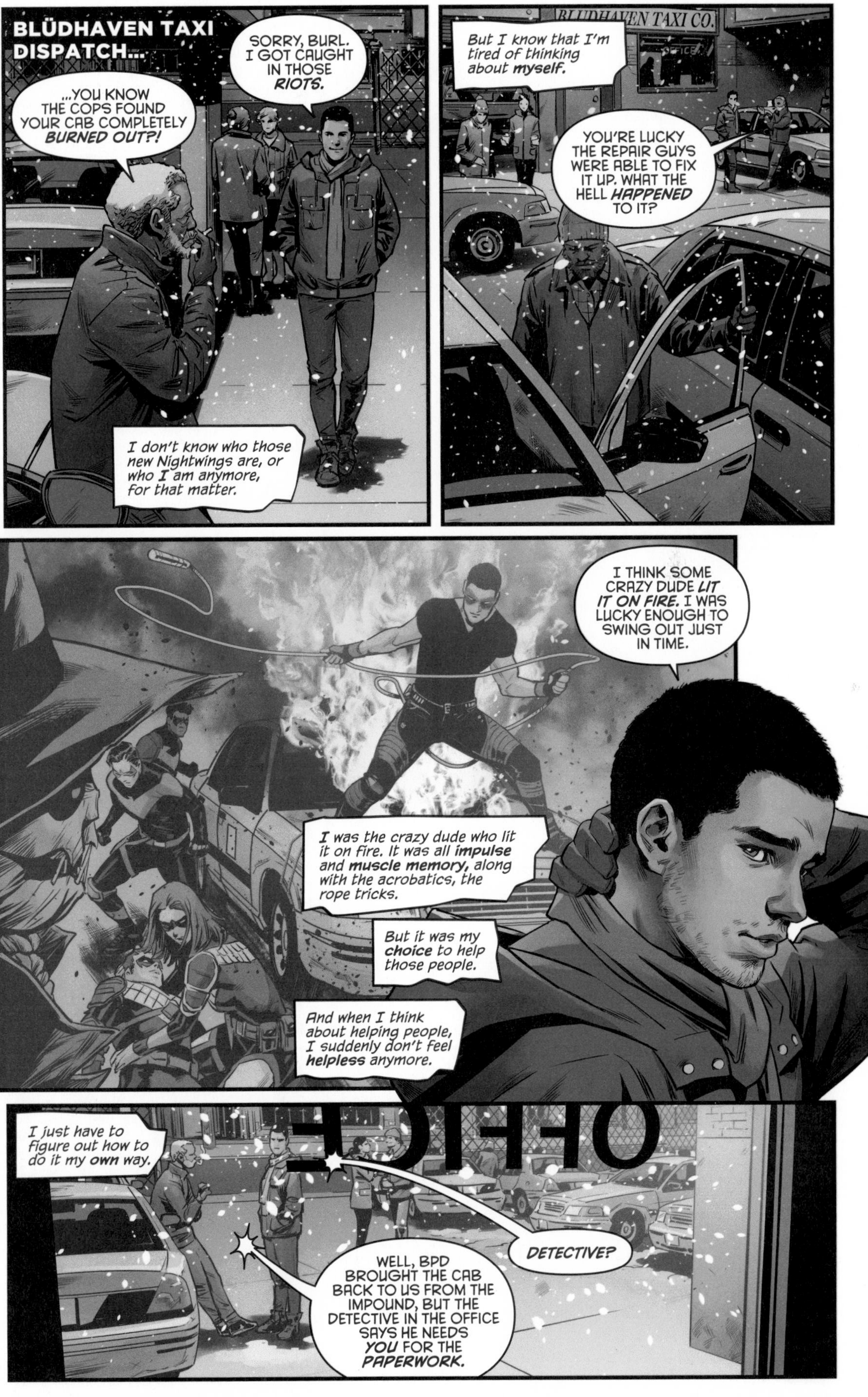
BLÜDHAVEN TAXI DISPATCH...
...YOU KNOW THE COPS FOUND YOUR CAB COMPLETELY BURNED OUT?!
SORRY, BURL. I GOT CAUGHT IN THOSE RIOTS.
I don't know who those new Nightwings are, or who I am anymore, for that matter.
BLÜDHAVEN TAXI CO.
OFFICE
But I know that I'm tired of thinking about myself.
YOU'RE LUCKY THE REPAIR GUYS WERE ABLE TO FIX IT UP. WHAT THE HELL HAPPENED TO IT?
I THINK SOME CRAZY DUDE LIT IT ON FIRE. I WAS LUCKY ENOUGH TO SWING OUT JUST IN TIME.
I was the crazy dude who lit it on fire. It was all impulse and muscle memory, along with the acrobatics, the rope tricks.
But it was my choice to help those people.
And when I think about helping people, I suddenly don't feel helpless anymore.
I just have to figure out how to do it my own way.
DETECTIVE?
WELL, BPD BROUGHT THE CAB BACK TO US FROM THE IMPOUND, BUT THE DETECTIVE IN THE OFFICE SAYS HE NEEDS YOU FOR THE PAPERWORK.

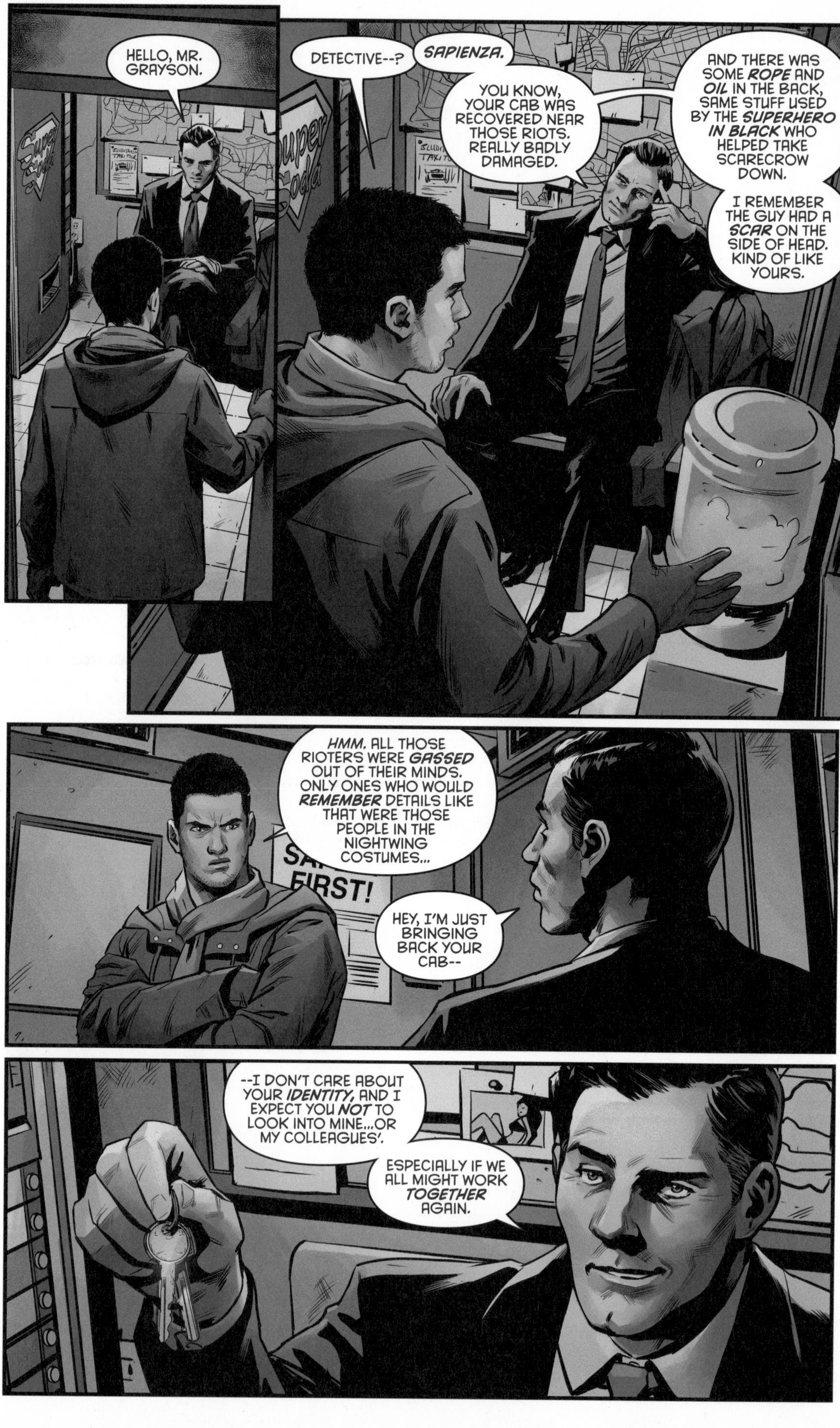
HELLO, MR. GRAYSON.
DETECTIVE--?
SAPIENZA.
YOU KNOW, YOUR CAB WAS RECOVERED NEAR THOSE RIOTS. REALLY BADLY DAMAGED.
AND THERE WAS SOME ROPE AND OIL IN THE BACK, SAME STUFF USED BY THE SUPERHERO IN BLACK WHO HELPED TAKE SCARECROW DOWN.
I REMEMBER THE GUY HAD A SCAR ON THE SIDE OF HEAD. KIND OF LIKE YOURS.
HMM. ALL THOSE RIOTERS WERE GASSED OUT OF THEIR MINDS. ONLY ONES WHO WOULD REMEMBER DETAILS LIKE THAT WERE THOSE PEOPLE IN THE NIGHTWING COSTUMES...
HEY, I'M JUST BRINGING BACK YOUR CAB--
--I DON'T CARE ABOUT YOUR IDENTITY, AND I EXPECT YOU NOT TO LOOK INTO MINE...OR MY COLLEAGUES'.
ESPECIALLY IF WE ALL MIGHT WORK TOGETHER AGAIN.

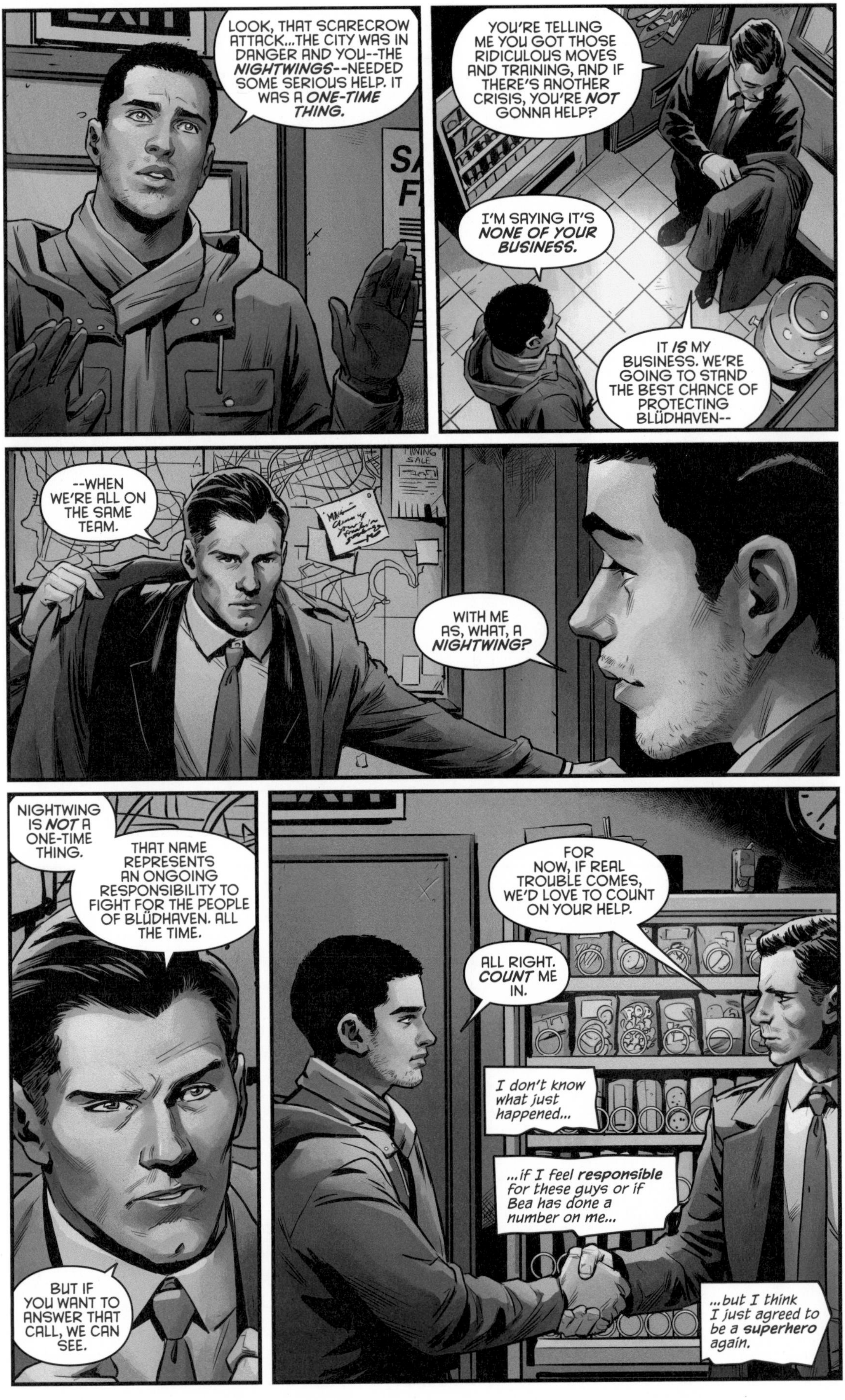
LOOK, THAT SCARECROW ATTACK...THE CITY WAS IN DANGER AND YOU--THE NIGHTWINGS--NEEDED SOME SERIOUS HELP. IT WAS A ONE-TIME THING.
YOU'RE TELLING ME YOU GOT THOSE RIDICULOUS MOVES AND TRAINING, AND IF THERE'S ANOTHER CRISIS, YOU'RE NOT GONNA HELP?
I'M SAYING IT'S NONE OF YOUR BUSINESS.
IT IS MY BUSINESS. WE'RE GOING TO STAND THE BEST CHANCE OF PROTECTING BLÜDHAVEN--
--WHEN WE'RE ALL ON THE SAME TEAM.
WITH ME AS, WHAT, A NIGHTWING?
NIGHTWING IS NOT A ONE-TIME THING.
THAT NAME REPRESENTS AN ONGOING RESPONSIBILITY TO FIGHT FOR THE PEOPLE OF BLÜDHAVEN. ALL THE TIME.
BUT IF YOU WANT TO ANSWER THAT CALL, WE CAN SEE.
FOR NOW, IF REAL TROUBLE COMES, WE'D LOVE TO COUNT ON YOUR HELP.
ALL RIGHT. COUNT ME IN.
I don't know what just happened...
...if I feel responsible for these guys or if Bea has done a number on me...
...but I think I just agreed to be a superhero again.

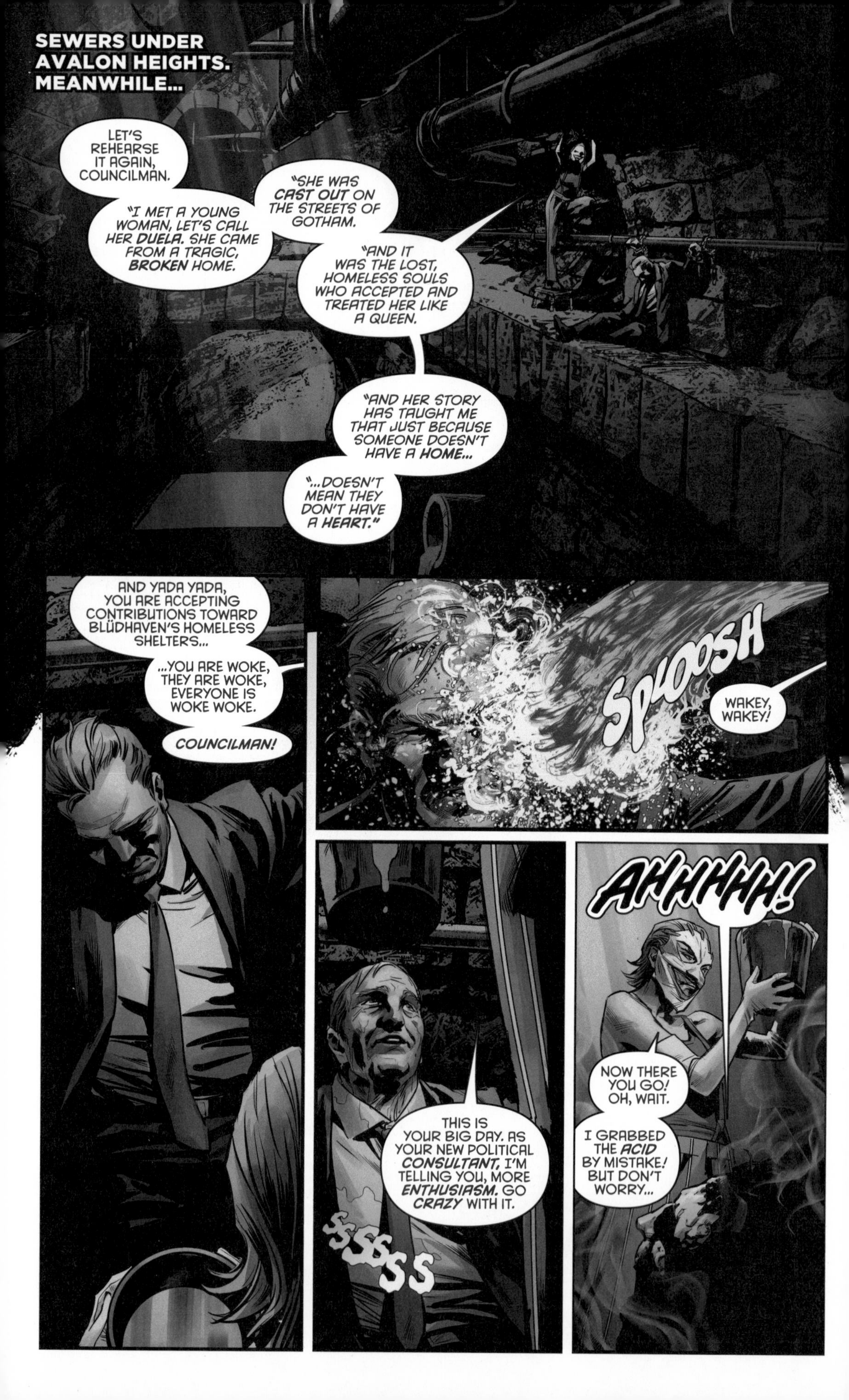
SEWERS UNDER AVALON HEIGHTS. MEANWHILE...
LET'S REHEARSE IT AGAIN, COUNCILMAN.
"I MET A YOUNG WOMAN, LET'S CALL HER DUELA. SHE CAME FROM A TRAGIC, BROKEN HOME.
"SHE WAS CAST OUT ON THE STREETS OF GOTHAM.
"AND IT WAS THE LOST, HOMELESS SOULS WHO ACCEPTED AND TREATED HER LIKE A QUEEN.
"AND HER STORY HAS TAUGHT ME THAT JUST BECAUSE SOMEONE DOESN'T HAVE A HOME...
"...DOESN'T MEAN THEY DON'T HAVE A HEART."
AND YADA YADA, YOU ARE ACCEPTING CONTRIBUTIONS TOWARD BLÜDHAVEN'S HOMELESS SHELTERS...
...YOU ARE WOKE, THEY ARE WOKE, EVERYONE IS WOKE WOKE.
COUNCILMAN!
SPLOOSH
WAKEY, WAKEY!
THIS IS YOUR BIG DAY. AS YOUR NEW POLITICAL CONSULTANT, I'M TELLING YOU, MORE ENTHUSIASM. GO CRAZY WITH IT.
SSSSSS
AHHHHH!
NOW THERE YOU GO! OH, WAIT.
I GRABBED THE ACID BY MISTAKE! BUT DON'T WORRY...

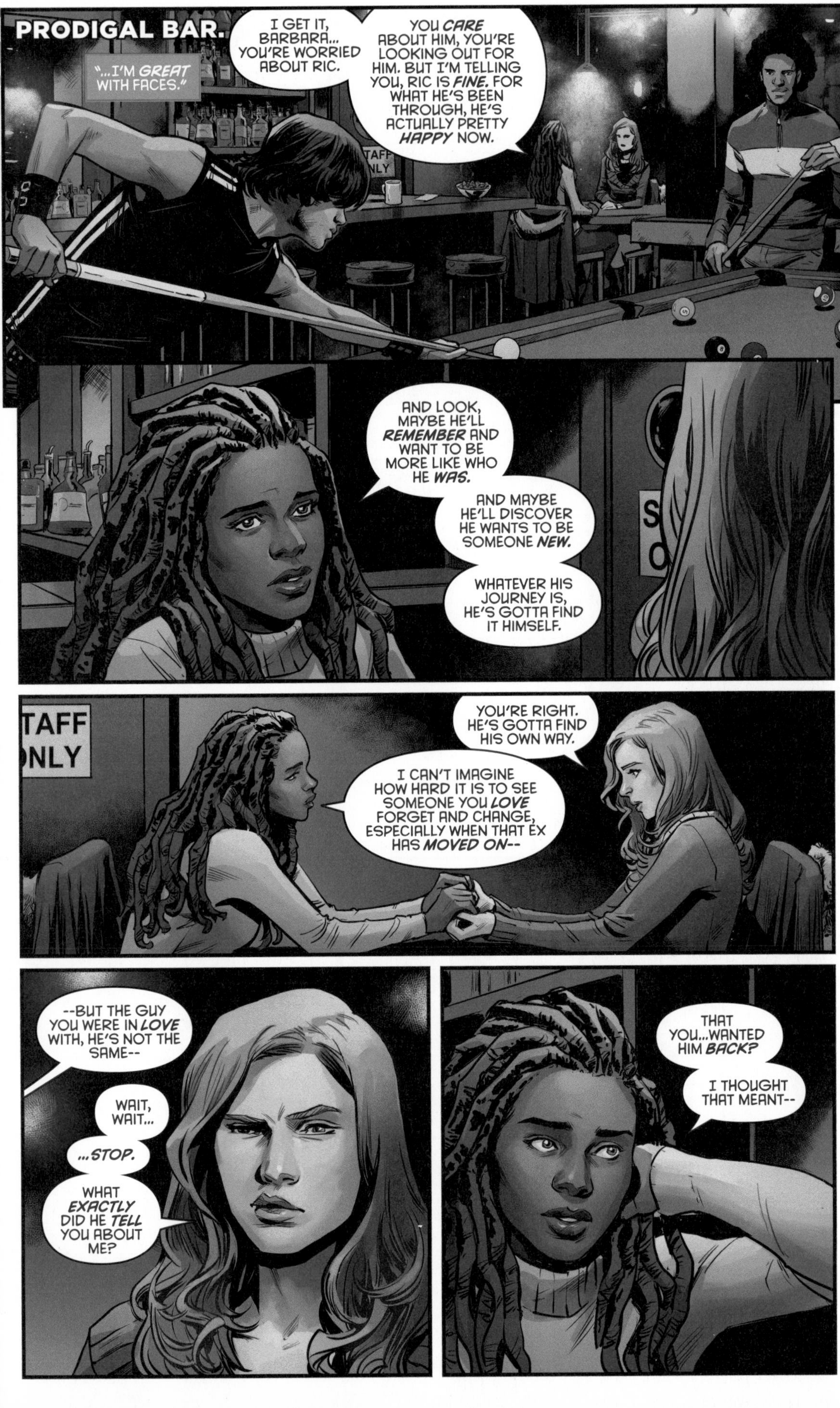
PRODIGAL BAR.
"...I'M GREAT WITH FACES."
I GET IT, BARBARA... YOU'RE WORRIED ABOUT RIC.
YOU CARE ABOUT HIM, YOU'RE LOOKING OUT FOR HIM. BUT I'M TELLING YOU, RIC IS FINE. FOR WHAT HE'S BEEN THROUGH, HE'S ACTUALLY PRETTY HAPPY NOW.
STAFF ONLY
AND LOOK, MAYBE HE'LL REMEMBER AND WANT TO BE MORE LIKE WHO HE WAS.
AND MAYBE HE'LL DISCOVER HE WANTS TO BE SOMEONE NEW.
WHATEVER HIS JOURNEY IS, HE'S GOTTA FIND IT HIMSELF.
YOU'RE RIGHT. HE'S GOTTA FIND HIS OWN WAY.
I CAN'T IMAGINE HOW HARD IT IS TO SEE SOMEONE YOU LOVE FORGET AND CHANGE, ESPECIALLY WHEN THAT EX HAS MOVED ON--
--BUT THE GUY YOU WERE IN LOVE WITH, HE'S NOT THE SAME--
WAIT, WAIT...
...STOP.
WHAT EXACTLY DID HE TELL YOU ABOUT ME?
THAT YOU...WANTED HIM BACK?
I THOUGHT THAT MEANT--

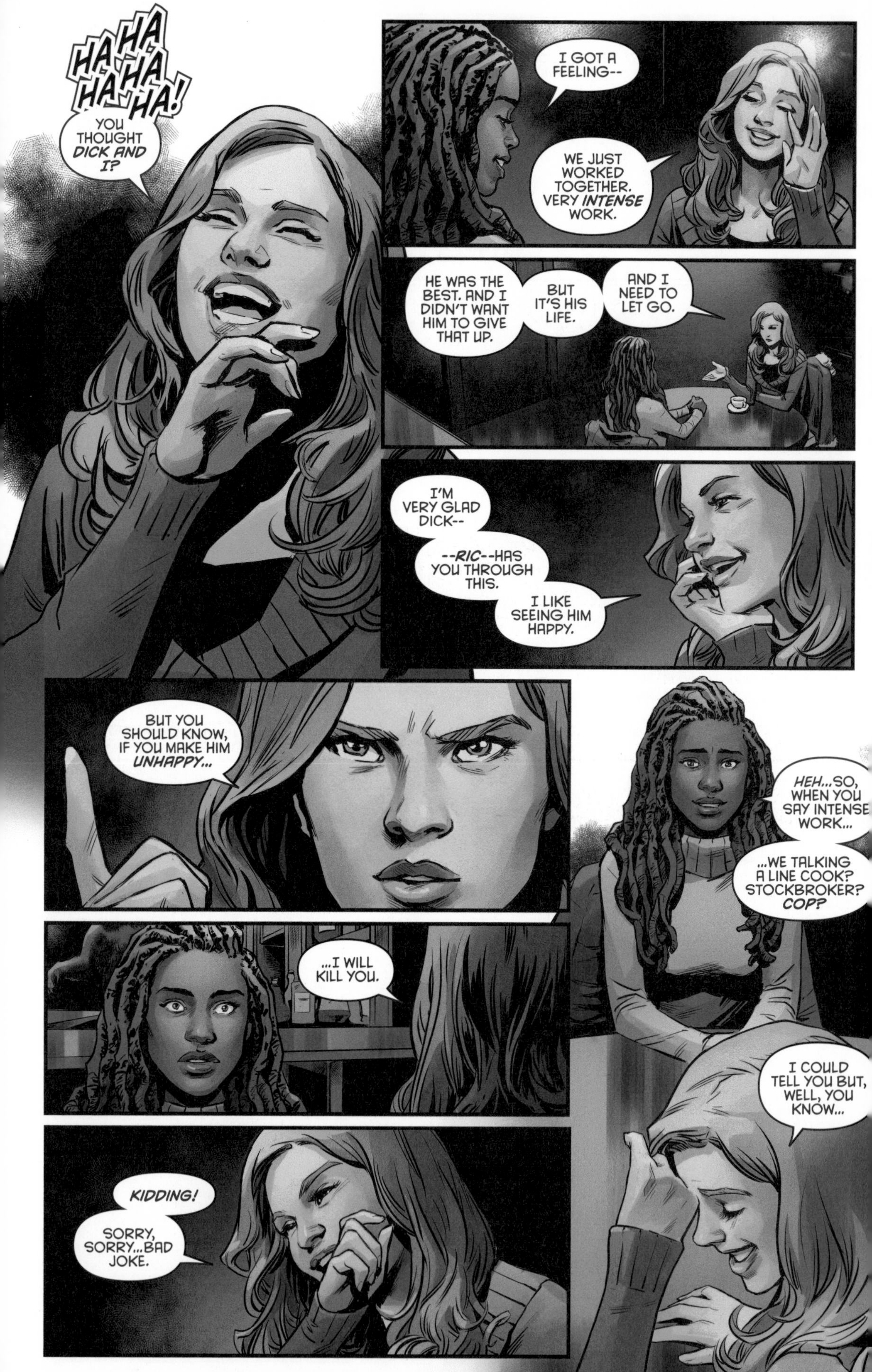
HA HA HA HA HA HA!
YOU THOUGHT DICK AND I?
I GOT A FEELING--
WE JUST WORKED TOGETHER. VERY INTENSE WORK.
HE WAS THE BEST. AND I DIDN'T WANT HIM TO GIVE THAT UP.
BUT IT'S HIS LIFE.
AND I NEED TO LET GO.
I'M VERY GLAD DICK--
--RIC--HAS YOU THROUGH THIS.
I LIKE SEEING HIM HAPPY.
BUT YOU SHOULD KNOW, IF YOU MAKE HIM UNHAPPY...
...I WILL KILL YOU.
KIDDING!
SORRY, SORRY...BAD JOKE.
HEH...SO, WHEN YOU SAY INTENSE WORK...
...WE TALKING A LINE COOK? STOCKBROKER? COP?
I COULD TELL YOU BUT, WELL, YOU KNOW...

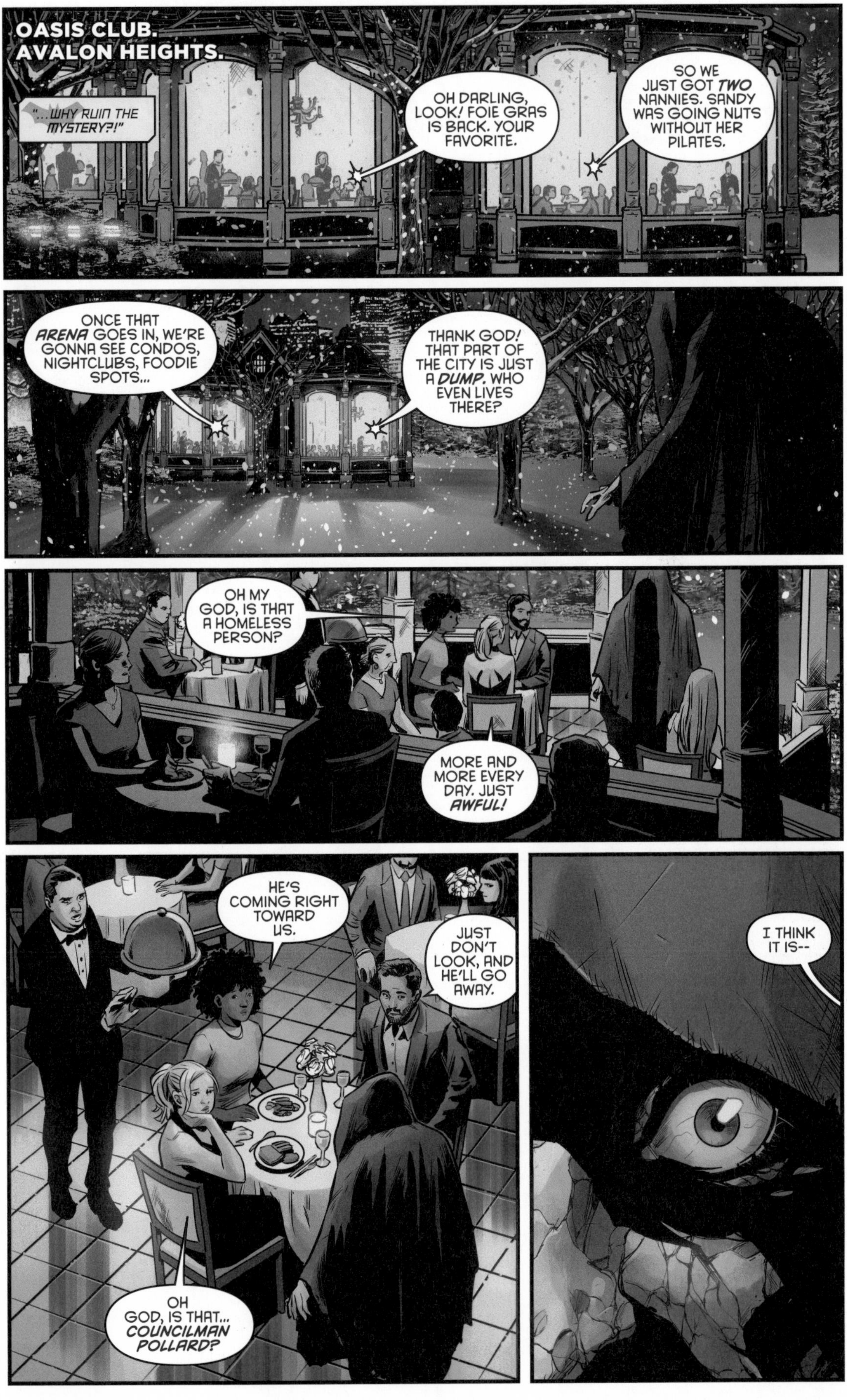
OASIS CLUB. AVALON HEIGHTS.
"...WHY RUIN THE MYSTERY?!"
OH DARLING, LOOK! FOIE GRAS IS BACK. YOUR FAVORITE.
SO WE JUST GOT TWO NANNIES. SANDY WAS GOING NUTS WITHOUT HER PILATES.
ONCE THAT ARENA GOES IN, WE'RE GONNA SEE CONDOS, NIGHTCLUBS, FOODIE SPOTS...
THANK GOD! THAT PART OF THE CITY IS JUST A DUMP. WHO EVEN LIVES THERE?
OH MY GOD, IS THAT A HOMELESS PERSON?
MORE AND MORE EVERY DAY. JUST AWFUL!
HE'S COMING RIGHT TOWARD US.
JUST DON'T LOOK, AND HE'LL GO AWAY.
OH GOD, IS THAT... COUNCILMAN POLLARD?
I THINK IT IS--

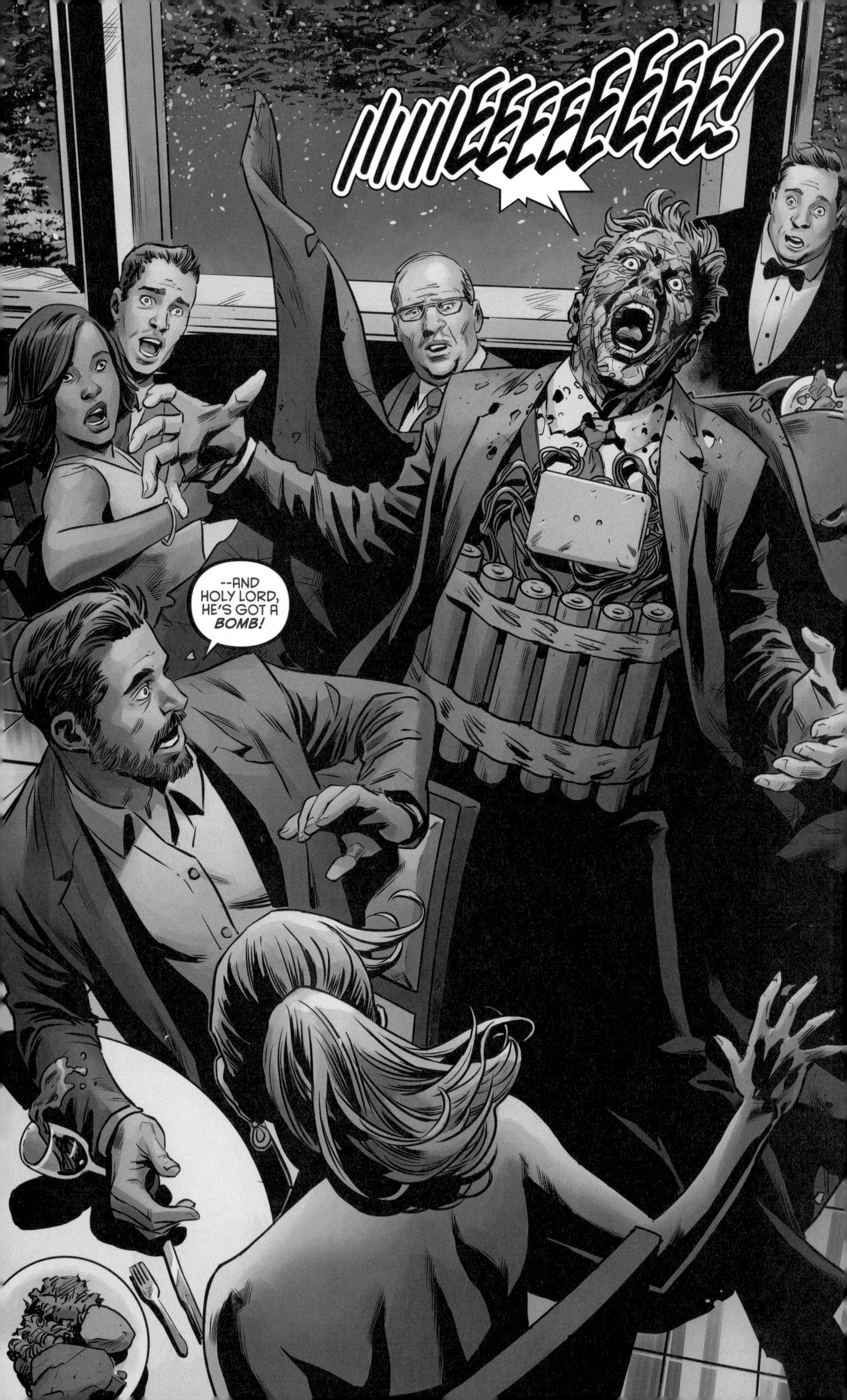
IIIIIEEEEEEEE!
--AND HOLY LORD, HE'S GOT A BOMB!

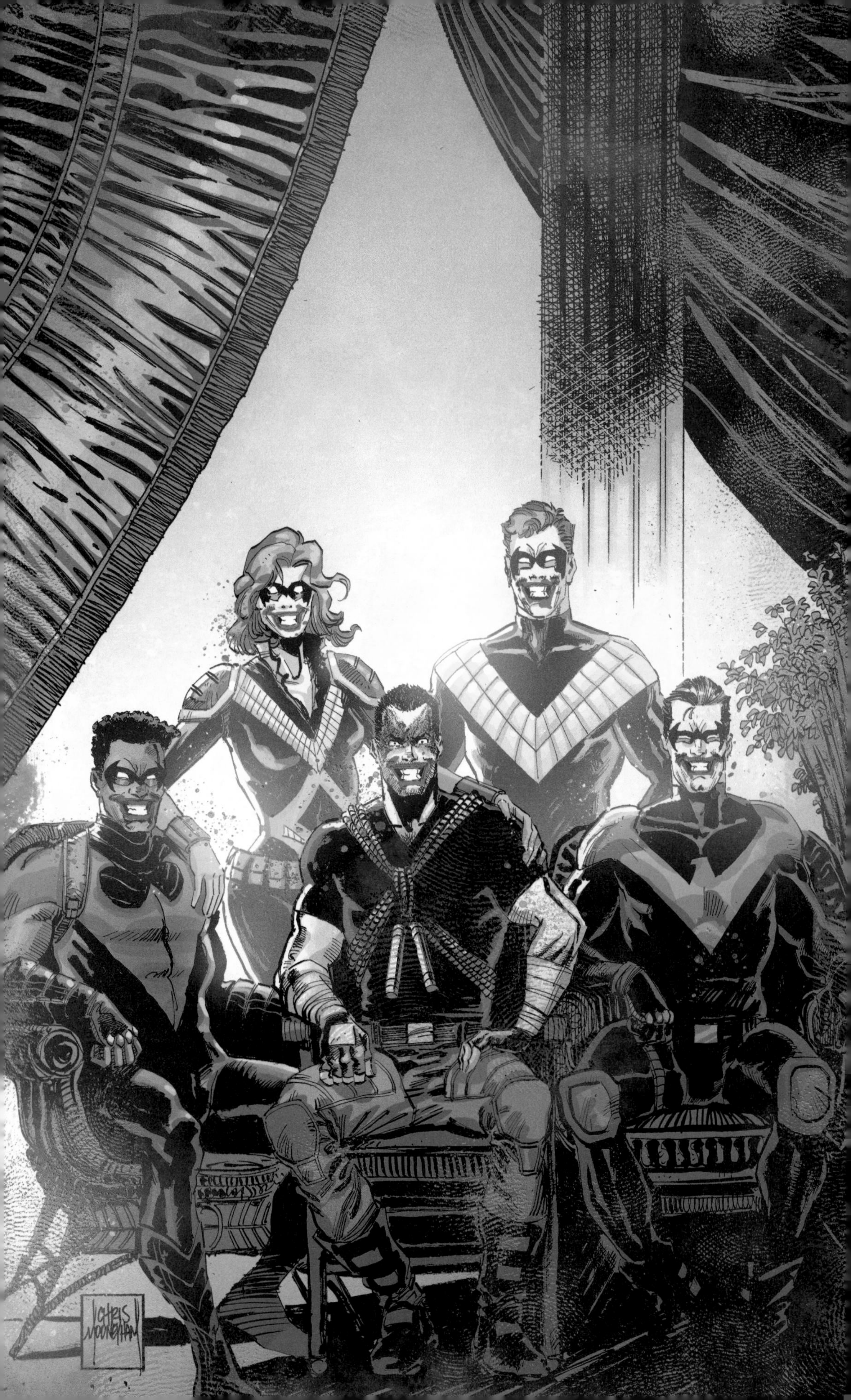
CHRIS MOONEYHAM

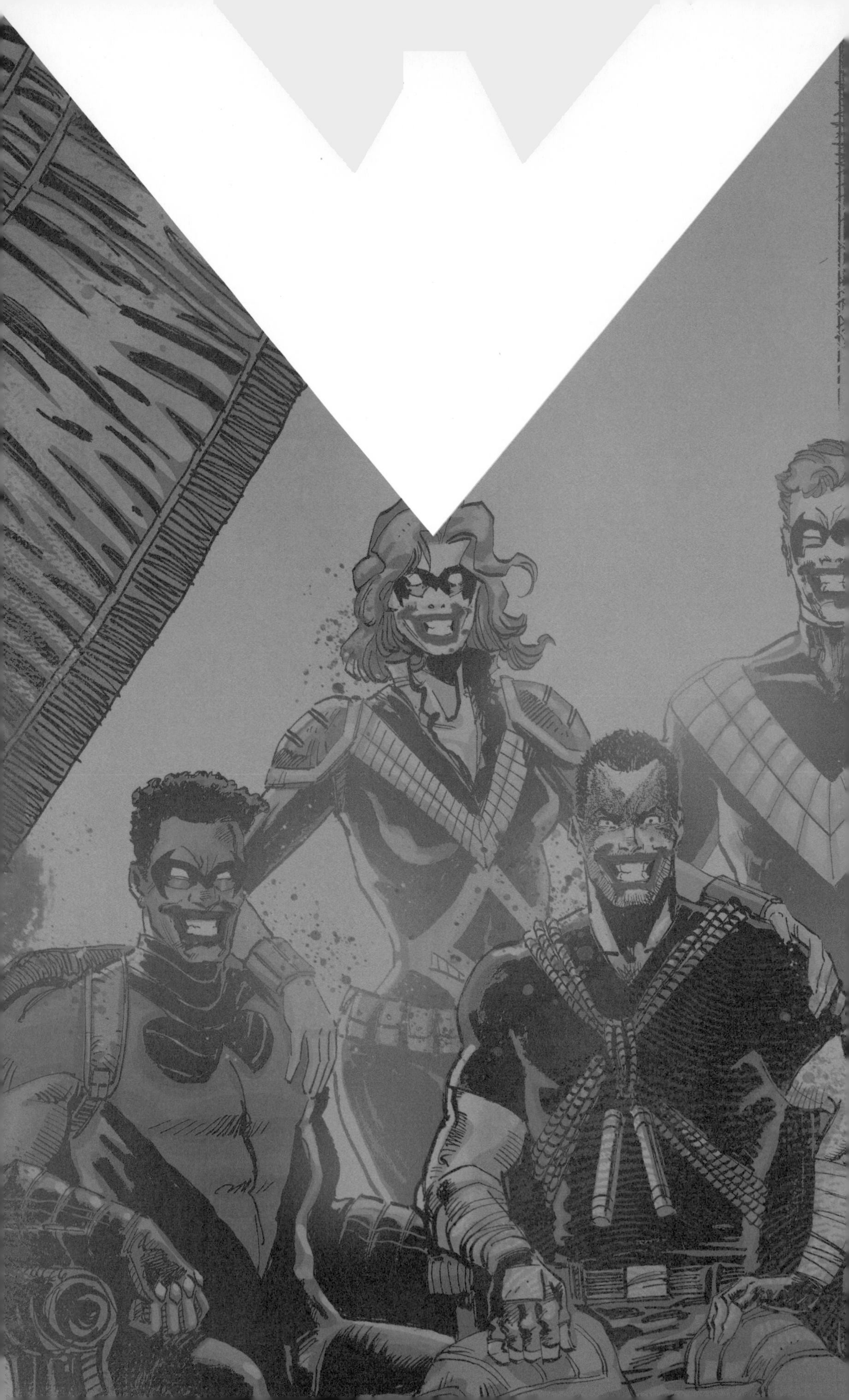

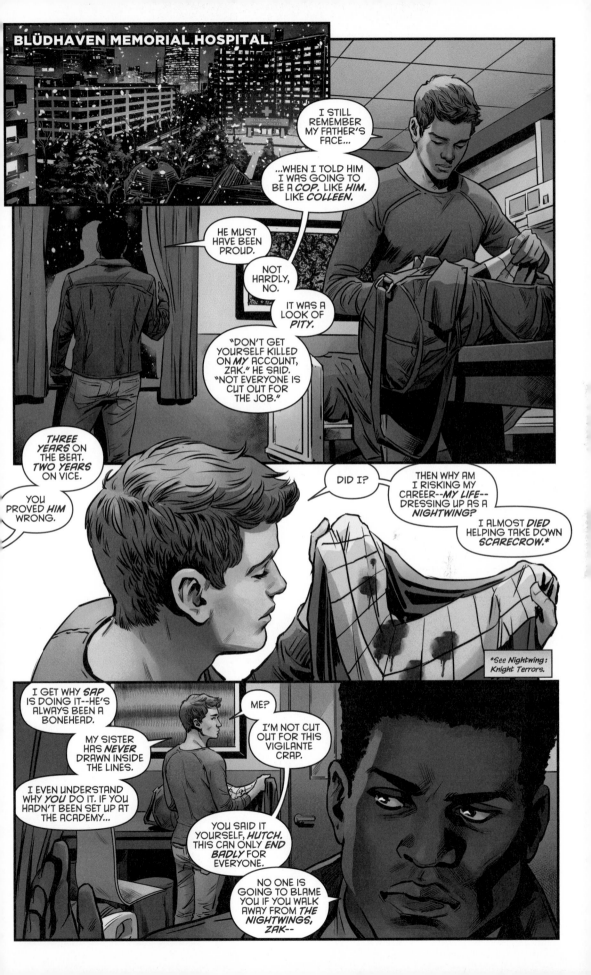

BLÜDHAVEN MEMORIAL HOSPITAL.

I STILL REMEMBER MY FATHER'S FACE...

...WHEN I TOLD HIM I WAS GOING TO BE A *COP*. LIKE *HIM*. LIKE *COLLEEN*.

HE MUST HAVE BEEN PROUD.

NOT HARDLY, NO.

IT WAS A LOOK OF *PITY*.

"DON'T GET YOURSELF KILLED ON *MY* ACCOUNT, ZAK." HE SAID. "NOT EVERYONE IS CUT OUT FOR THE JOB."

THREE YEARS ON THE BEAT. *TWO YEARS* ON VICE.

YOU PROVED *HIM* WRONG.

DID I?

THEN WHY AM I RISKING MY CAREER--*MY LIFE*-- DRESSING UP AS A *NIGHTWING*?

I ALMOST *DIED* HELPING TAKE DOWN *SCARECROW*.*

*See Nightwing: Knight Terrors.

I GET WHY *SAP* IS DOING IT--HE'S ALWAYS BEEN A BONEHEAD.

MY SISTER HAS *NEVER* DRAWN INSIDE THE LINES.

I EVEN UNDERSTAND WHY *YOU* DO IT. IF YOU HADN'T BEEN SET UP AT THE ACADEMY...

ME?

I'M NOT CUT OUT FOR THIS VIGILANTE CRAP.

YOU SAID IT YOURSELF, *HUTCH*. THIS CAN ONLY *END BADLY* FOR EVERYONE.

NO ONE IS GOING TO BLAME YOU IF YOU WALK AWAY FROM *THE NIGHTWINGS*, ZAK--

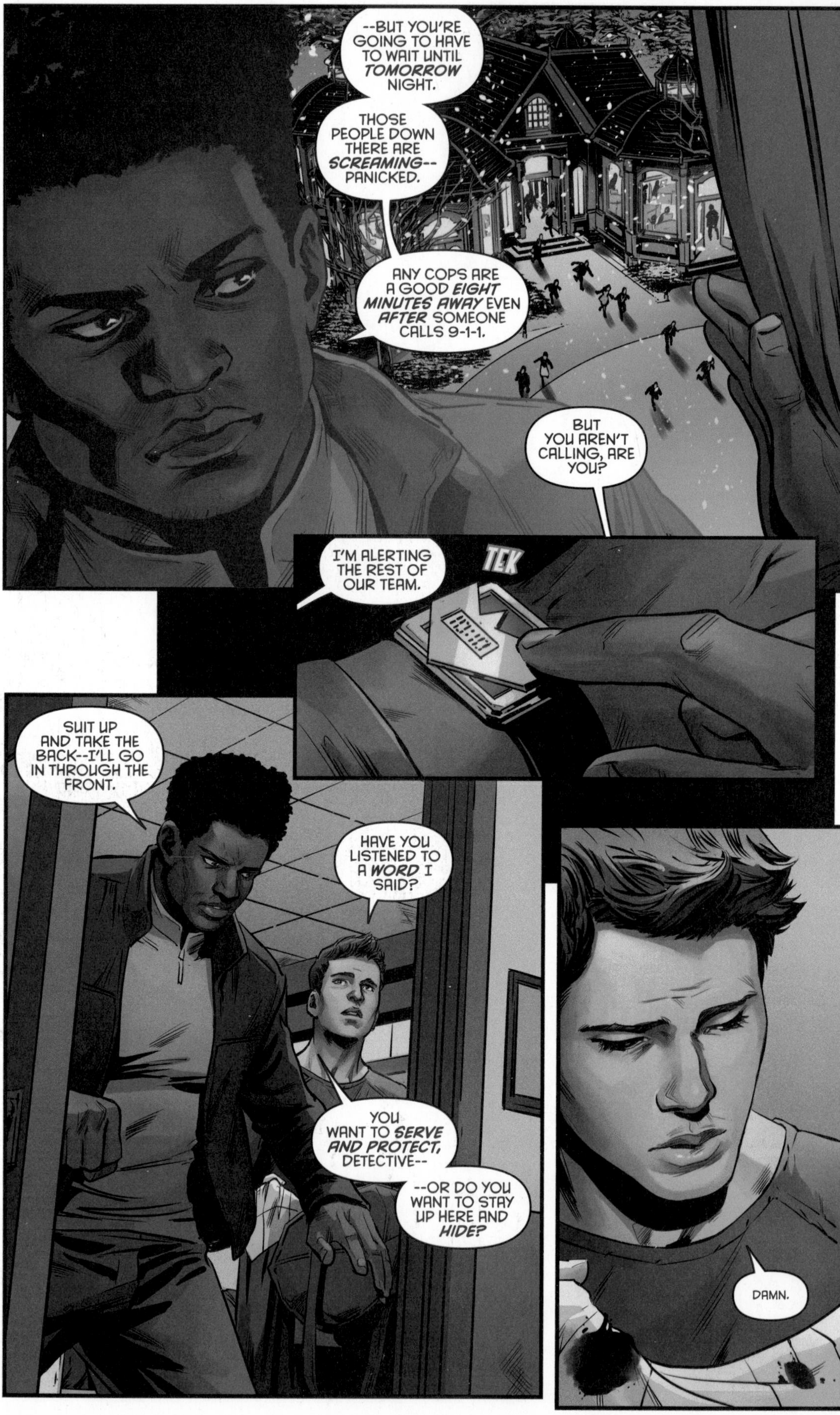
--BUT YOU'RE GOING TO HAVE TO WAIT UNTIL *TOMORROW* NIGHT.
THOSE PEOPLE DOWN THERE ARE *SCREAMING*-- PANICKED.
ANY COPS ARE A GOOD *EIGHT MINUTES AWAY* EVEN *AFTER* SOMEONE CALLS 9-1-1.
BUT YOU AREN'T CALLING, ARE YOU?
I'M ALERTING THE REST OF OUR TEAM.
TEK
SUIT UP AND TAKE THE BACK--I'LL GO IN THROUGH THE FRONT.
HAVE YOU LISTENED TO A *WORD* I SAID?
YOU WANT TO *SERVE AND PROTECT,* DETECTIVE--
--OR DO YOU WANT TO STAY UP HERE AND *HIDE?*
DAMN.

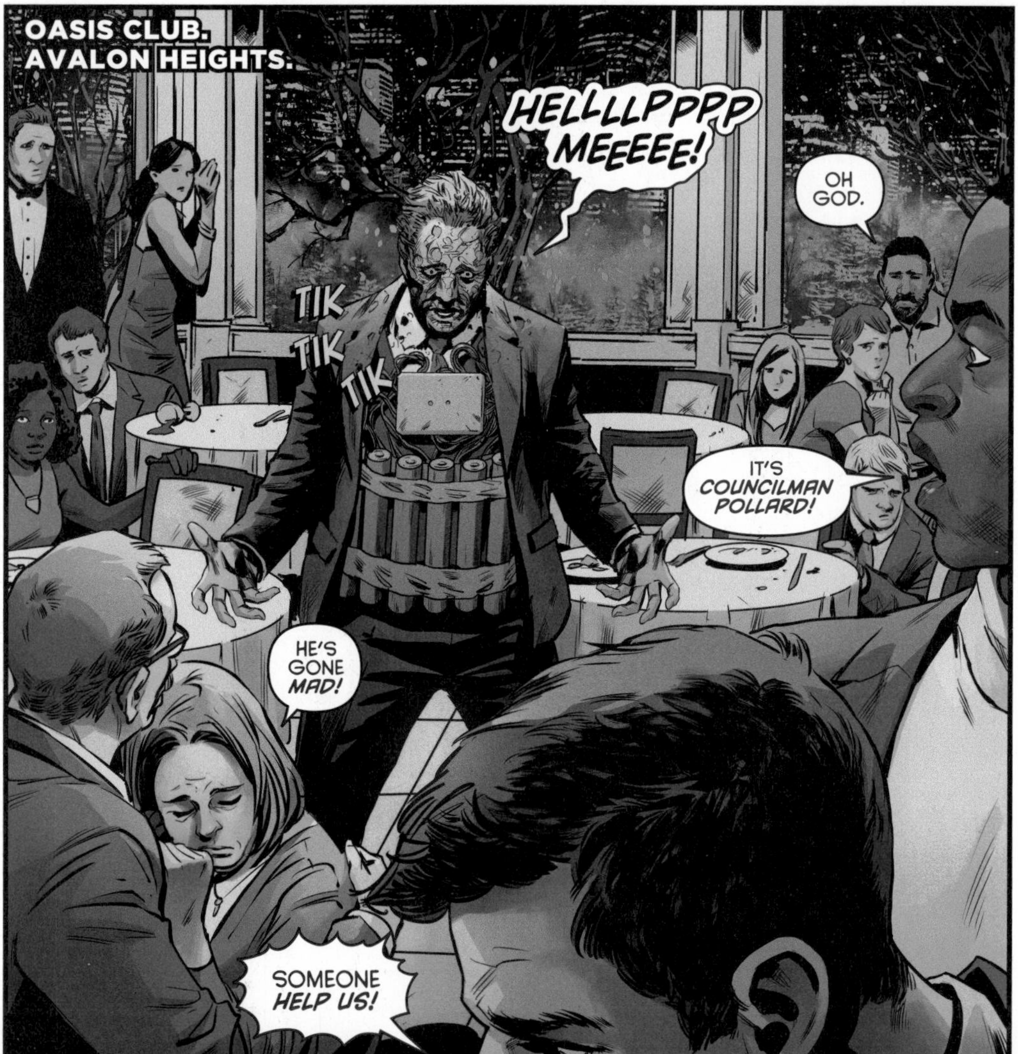
OASIS CLUB. AVALON HEIGHTS.
HELLLLPPPP MEEEEE!
OH GOD.
TIK TIK TIK
IT'S COUNCILMAN POLLARD!
HE'S GONE MAD!
SOMEONE HELP US!

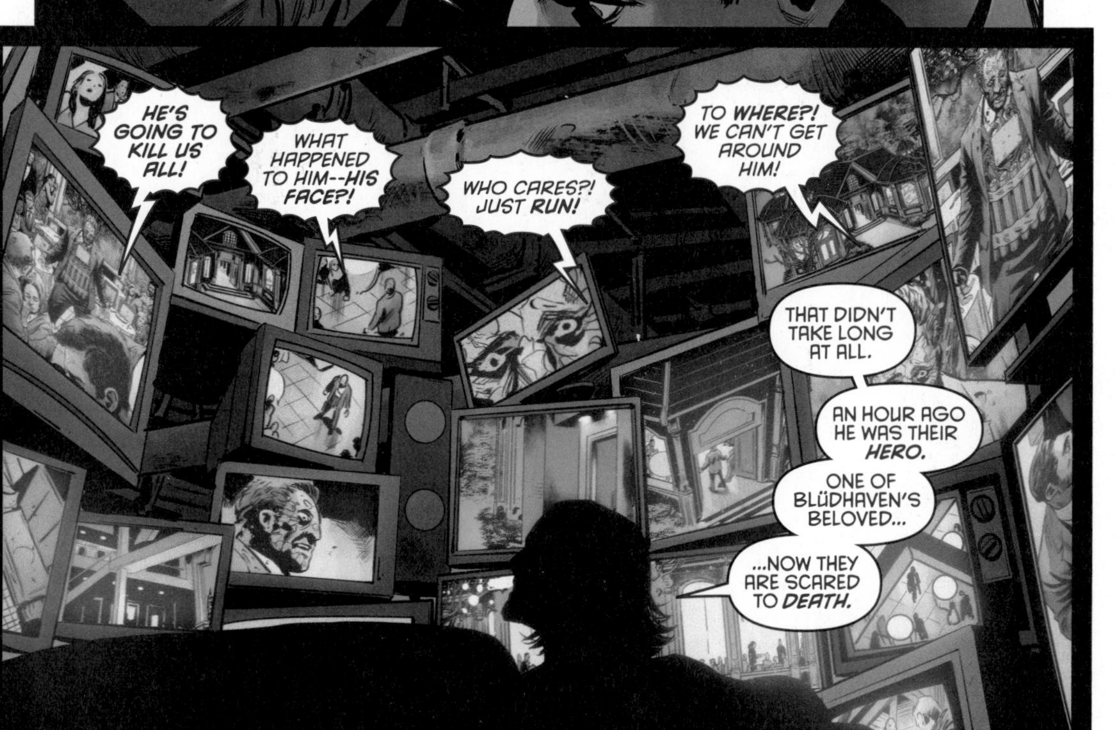
HE'S GOING TO KILL US ALL!
WHAT HAPPENED TO HIM--HIS FACE?!
WHO CARES?! JUST RUN!
TO WHERE?! WE CAN'T GET AROUND HIM!
THAT DIDN'T TAKE LONG AT ALL.
AN HOUR AGO HE WAS THEIR HERO.
ONE OF BLÜDHAVEN'S BELOVED...
...NOW THEY ARE SCARED TO DEATH.

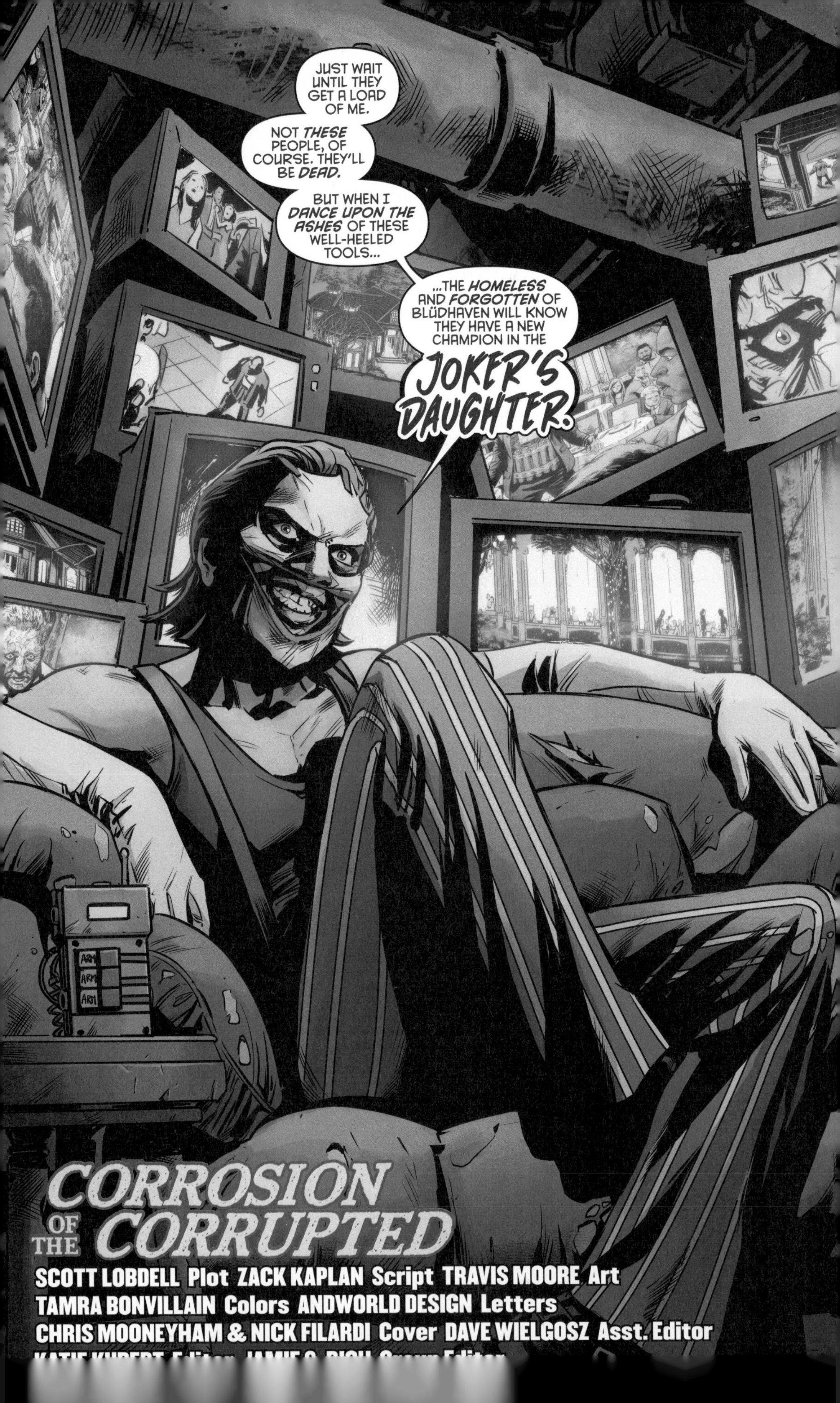
JUST WAIT UNTIL THEY GET A LOAD OF ME.
NOT *THESE* PEOPLE, OF COURSE. THEY'LL BE *DEAD.*
BUT WHEN I *DANCE UPON THE ASHES* OF THESE WELL-HEELED TOOLS...
...THE *HOMELESS* AND *FORGOTTEN* OF BLÜDHAVEN WILL KNOW THEY HAVE A NEW CHAMPION IN THE
JOKER'S DAUGHTER.
ARM
ARM
ARM
CORROSION OF THE CORRUPTED
SCOTT LOBDELL Plot ZACK KAPLAN Script TRAVIS MOORE Art
TAMRA BONVILLAIN Colors ANDWORLD DESIGN Letters
CHRIS MOONEYHAM & NICK FILARDI Cover DAVE WIELGOSZ Asst. Editor

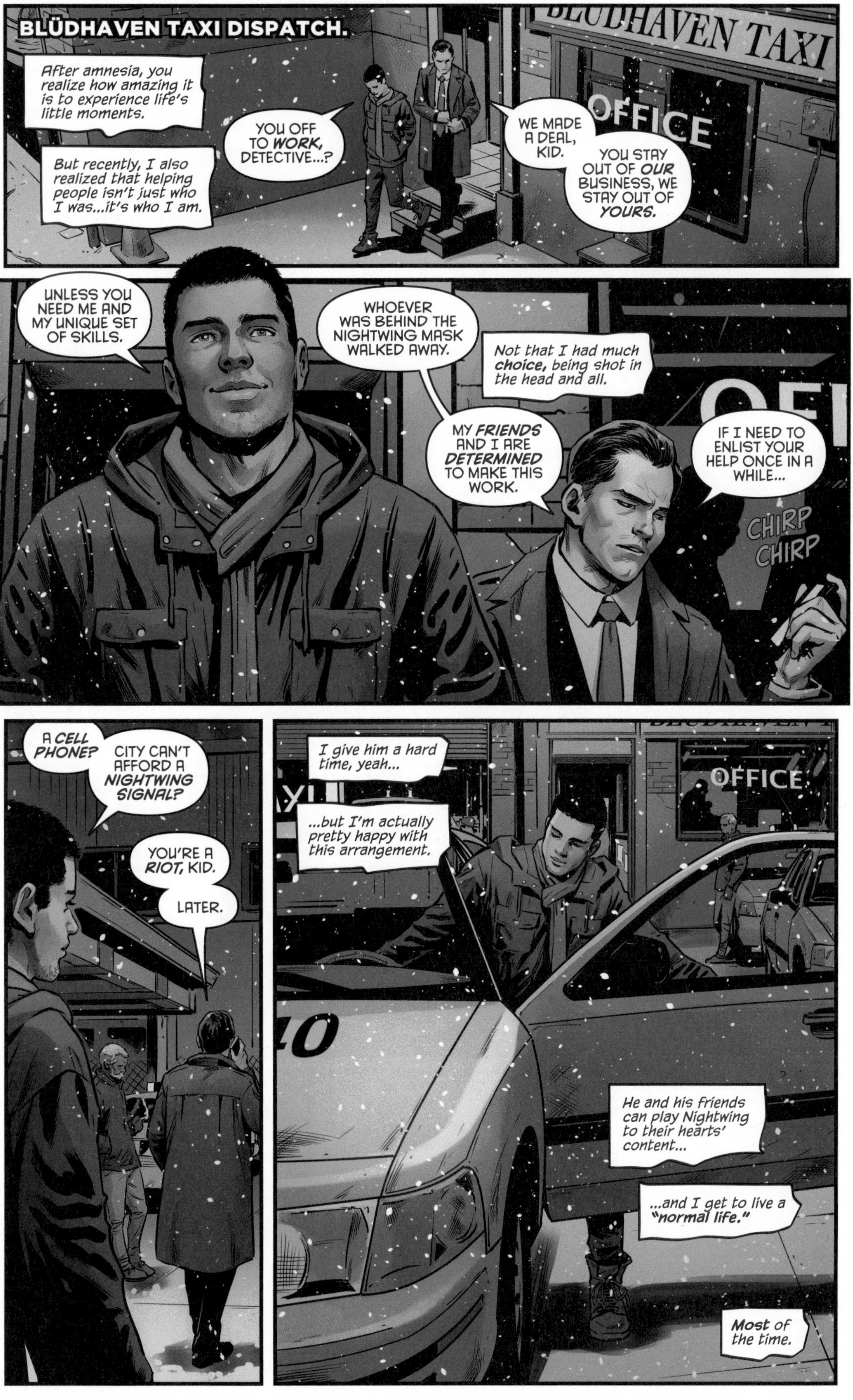
BLÜDHAVEN TAXI DISPATCH.
BLÜDHAVEN TAXI
After amnesia, you realize how amazing it is to experience life's little moments.
But recently, I also realized that helping people isn't just who I was...it's who I am.
YOU OFF TO WORK, DETECTIVE...?
OFFICE
WE MADE A DEAL, KID.
YOU STAY OUT OF OUR BUSINESS, WE STAY OUT OF YOURS.
UNLESS YOU NEED ME AND MY UNIQUE SET OF SKILLS.
WHOEVER WAS BEHIND THE NIGHTWING MASK WALKED AWAY.
Not that I had much choice, being shot in the head and all.
MY FRIENDS AND I ARE DETERMINED TO MAKE THIS WORK.
IF I NEED TO ENLIST YOUR HELP ONCE IN A WHILE...
CHIRP CHIRP
A CELL PHONE?
CITY CAN'T AFFORD A NIGHTWING SIGNAL?
YOU'RE A RIOT, KID.
LATER.
I give him a hard time, yeah...
...but I'm actually pretty happy with this arrangement.
OFFICE
He and his friends can play Nightwing to their hearts' content...
...and I get to live a "normal life."
Most of the time.

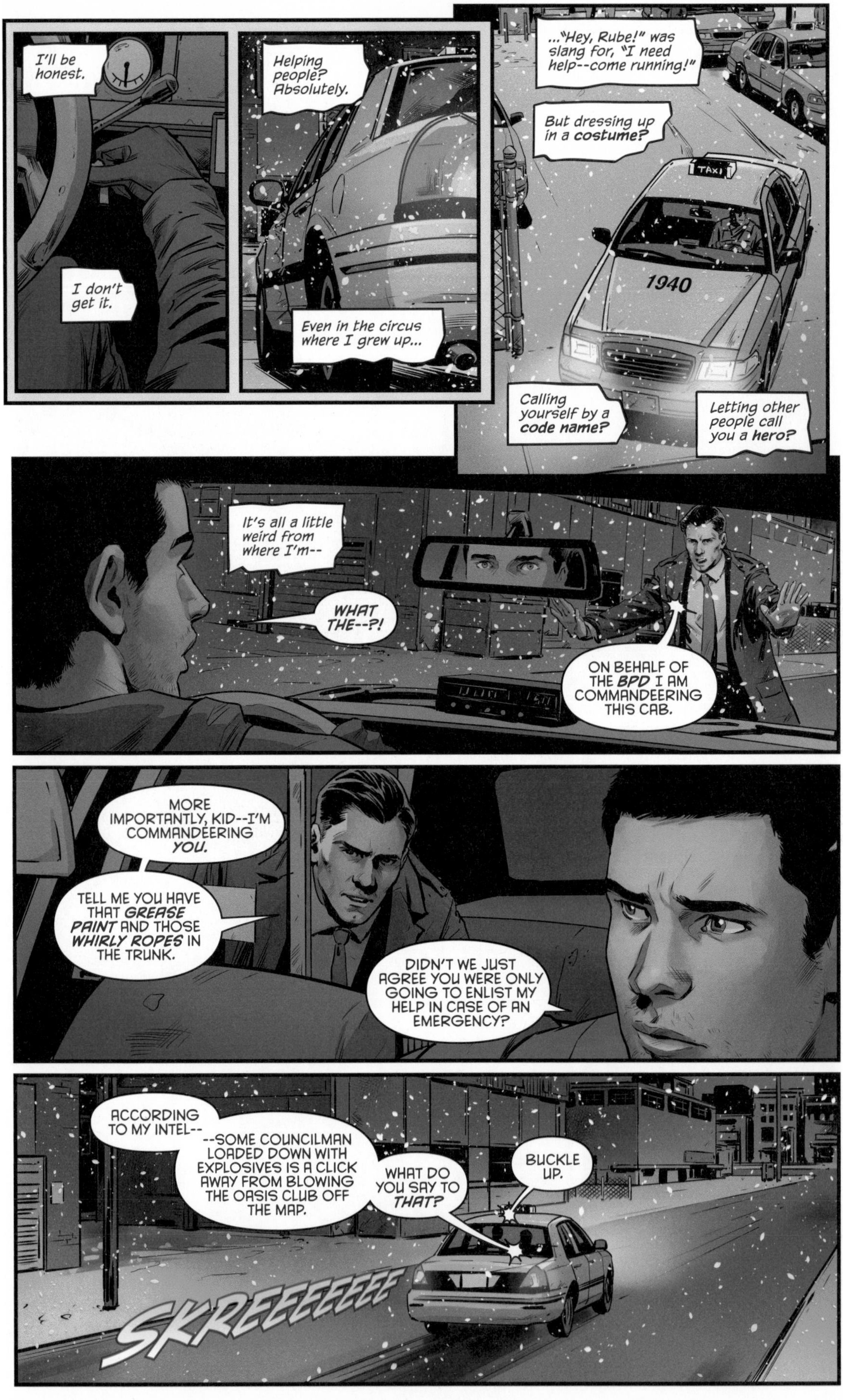

I'll be honest.
I don't get it.
Helping people? Absolutely.
Even in the circus where I grew up...
..."Hey, Rube!" was slang for, "I need help--come running!"
But dressing up in a costume?
TAXI
1940
Calling yourself by a code name?
Letting other people call you a hero?
It's all a little weird from where I'm--
WHAT THE--?!
ON BEHALF OF THE BPD I AM COMMANDEERING THIS CAB.
MORE IMPORTANTLY, KID--I'M COMMANDEERING YOU.
TELL ME YOU HAVE THAT GREASE PAINT AND THOSE WHIRLY ROPES IN THE TRUNK.
DIDN'T WE JUST AGREE YOU WERE ONLY GOING TO ENLIST MY HELP IN CASE OF AN EMERGENCY?
ACCORDING TO MY INTEL--
--SOME COUNCILMAN LOADED DOWN WITH EXPLOSIVES IS A CLICK AWAY FROM BLOWING THE OASIS CLUB OFF THE MAP.
WHAT DO YOU SAY TO THAT?
BUCKLE UP.
SKREEEEEEEE

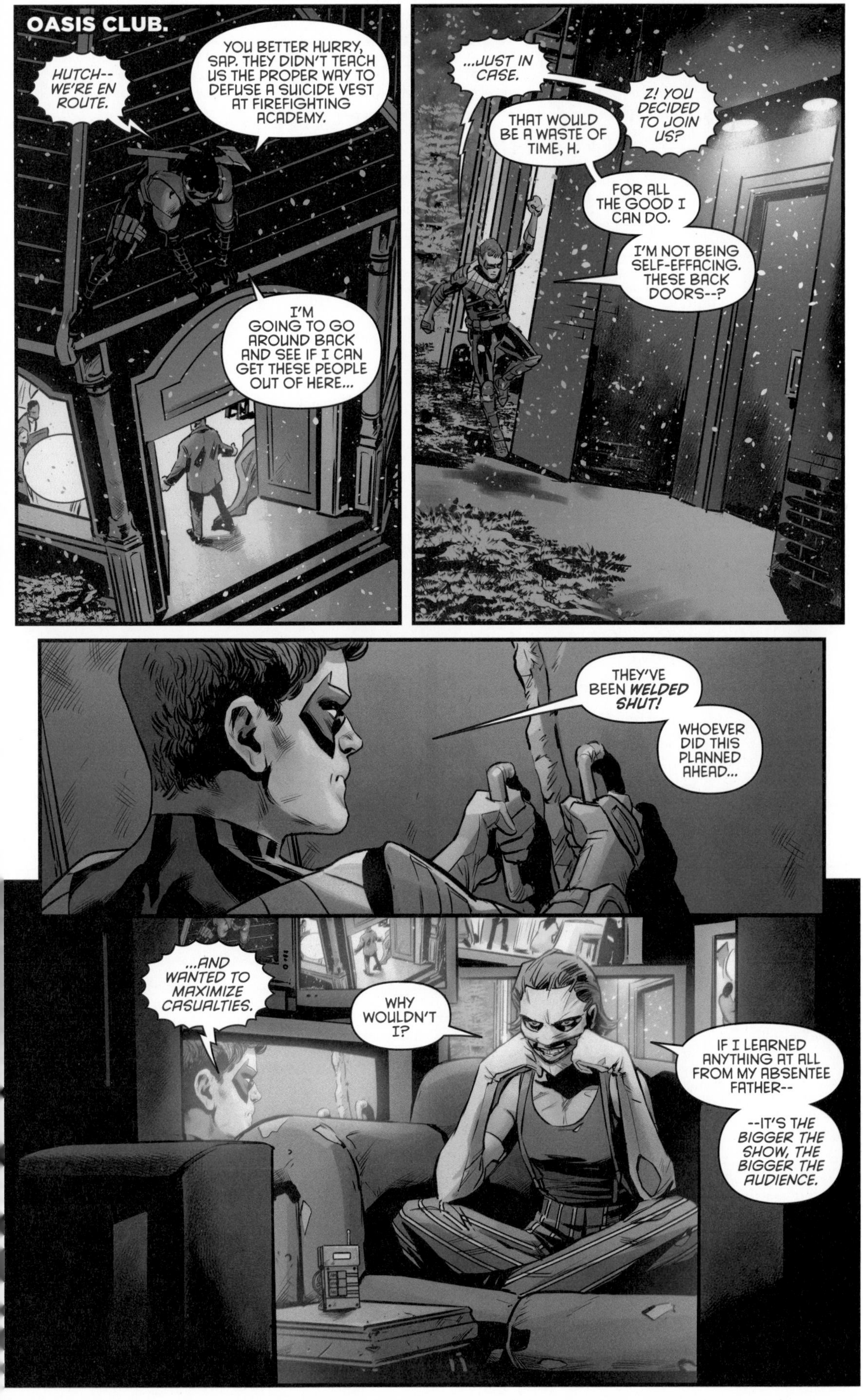
OASIS CLUB.
HUTCH-- WE'RE EN ROUTE.
YOU BETTER HURRY, SAP. THEY DIDN'T TEACH US THE PROPER WAY TO DEFUSE A SUICIDE VEST AT FIREFIGHTING ACADEMY.
I'M GOING TO GO AROUND BACK AND SEE IF I CAN GET THESE PEOPLE OUT OF HERE...
...JUST IN CASE.
Z! YOU DECIDED TO JOIN US?
THAT WOULD BE A WASTE OF TIME, H.
FOR ALL THE GOOD I CAN DO.
I'M NOT BEING SELF-EFFACING. THESE BACK DOORS--?
THEY'VE BEEN WELDED SHUT!
WHOEVER DID THIS PLANNED AHEAD...
...AND WANTED TO MAXIMIZE CASUALTIES.
WHY WOULDN'T I?
IF I LEARNED ANYTHING AT ALL FROM MY ABSENTEE FATHER--
--IT'S THE BIGGER THE SHOW, THE BIGGER THE AUDIENCE.

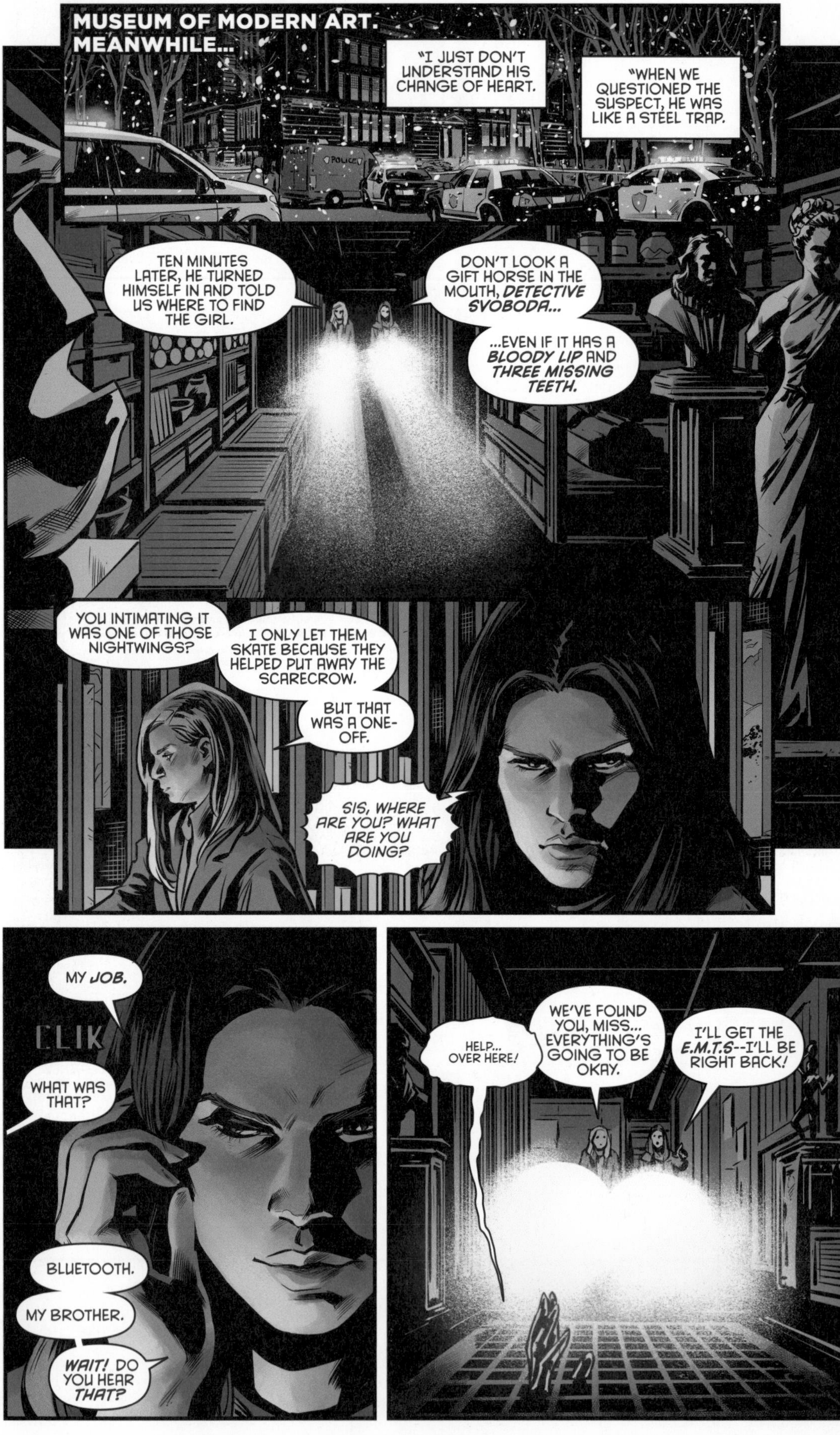
MUSEUM OF MODERN ART. MEANWHILE...
"I JUST DON'T UNDERSTAND HIS CHANGE OF HEART.
"WHEN WE QUESTIONED THE SUSPECT, HE WAS LIKE A STEEL TRAP.
POLICE
TEN MINUTES LATER, HE TURNED HIMSELF IN AND TOLD US WHERE TO FIND THE GIRL.
DON'T LOOK A GIFT HORSE IN THE MOUTH, *DETECTIVE SVOBODA...*
...EVEN IF IT HAS A *BLOODY LIP* AND *THREE MISSING TEETH.*
YOU INTIMATING IT WAS ONE OF THOSE NIGHTWINGS?
I ONLY LET THEM SKATE BECAUSE THEY HELPED PUT AWAY THE SCARECROW.
BUT THAT WAS A ONE-OFF.
SIS, WHERE ARE YOU? WHAT ARE YOU DOING?
MY *JOB.*
CLIK
WHAT WAS THAT?
BLUETOOTH.
MY BROTHER.
WAIT! DO YOU HEAR *THAT?*
HELP... OVER HERE!
WE'VE FOUND YOU, MISS... EVERYTHING'S GOING TO BE OKAY.
I'LL GET THE *E.M.T.S*--I'LL BE RIGHT BACK!

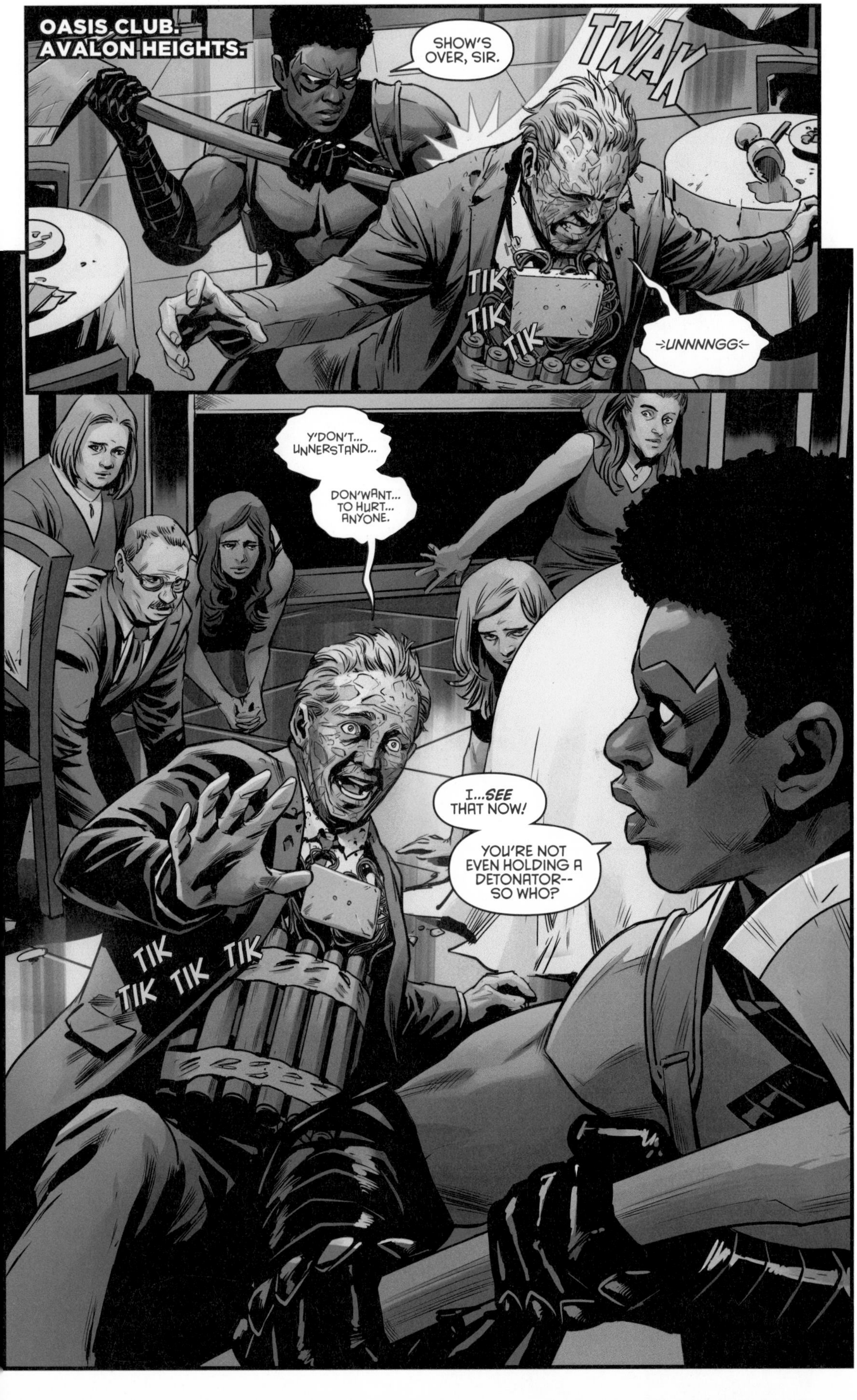
OASIS CLUB. AVALON HEIGHTS.
SHOW'S OVER, SIR.
TWAK
TIK TIK TIK
UNNNNGG
Y'DON'T... UNNERSTAND...
DON'WANT... TO HURT... ANYONE.
I...SEE THAT NOW!
YOU'RE NOT EVEN HOLDING A DETONATOR-- SO WHO?
TIK TIK TIK TIK

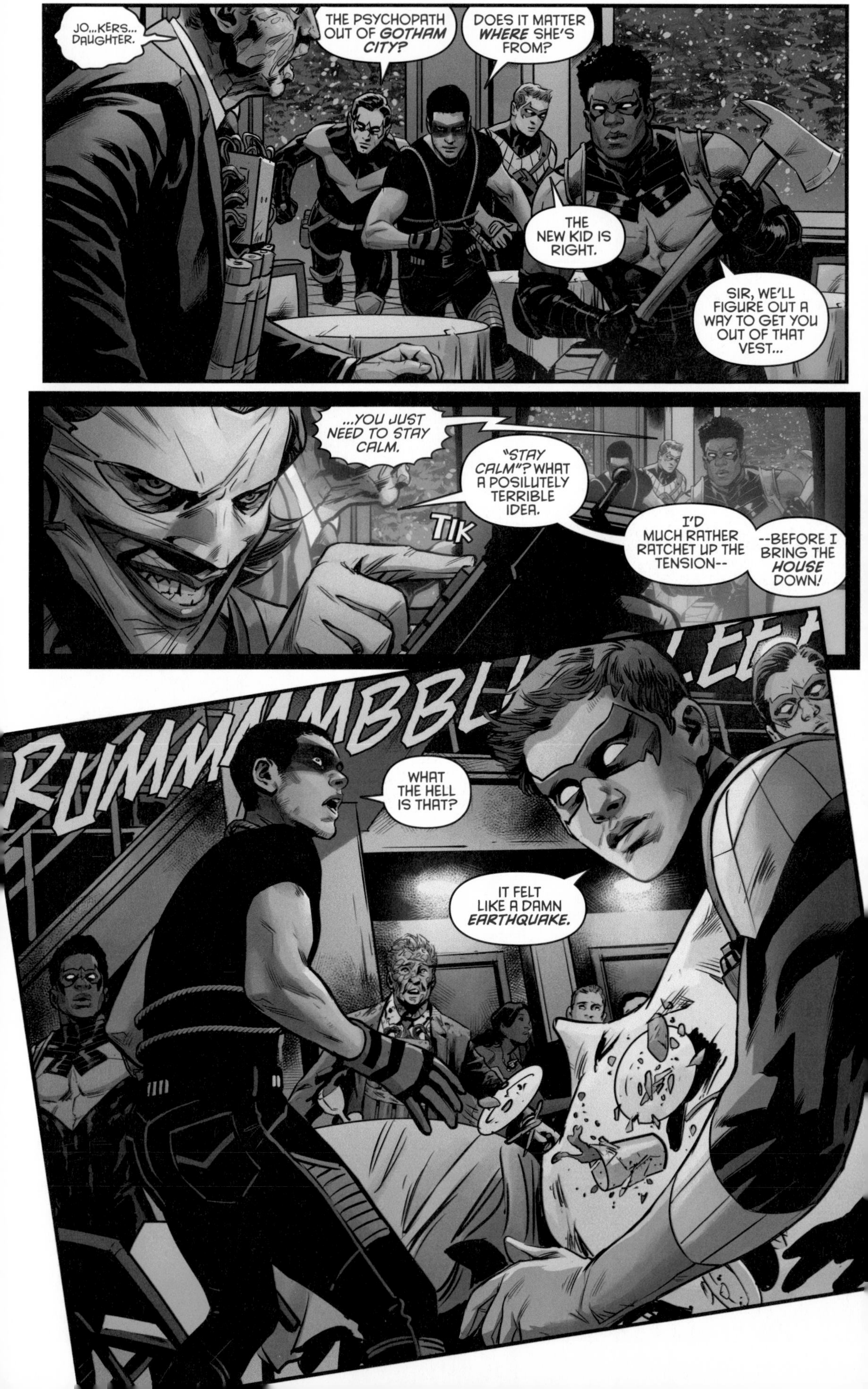

JO...KERS... DAUGHTER.
THE PSYCHOPATH OUT OF GOTHAM CITY?
DOES IT MATTER WHERE SHE'S FROM?
THE NEW KID IS RIGHT.
SIR, WE'LL FIGURE OUT A WAY TO GET YOU OUT OF THAT VEST...
...YOU JUST NEED TO STAY CALM.
"STAY CALM"? WHAT A POSILUTELY TERRIBLE IDEA.
TIK
I'D MUCH RATHER RATCHET UP THE TENSION--
--BEFORE I BRING THE HOUSE DOWN!
WHAT THE HELL IS THAT?
IT FELT LIKE A DAMN EARTHQUAKE.

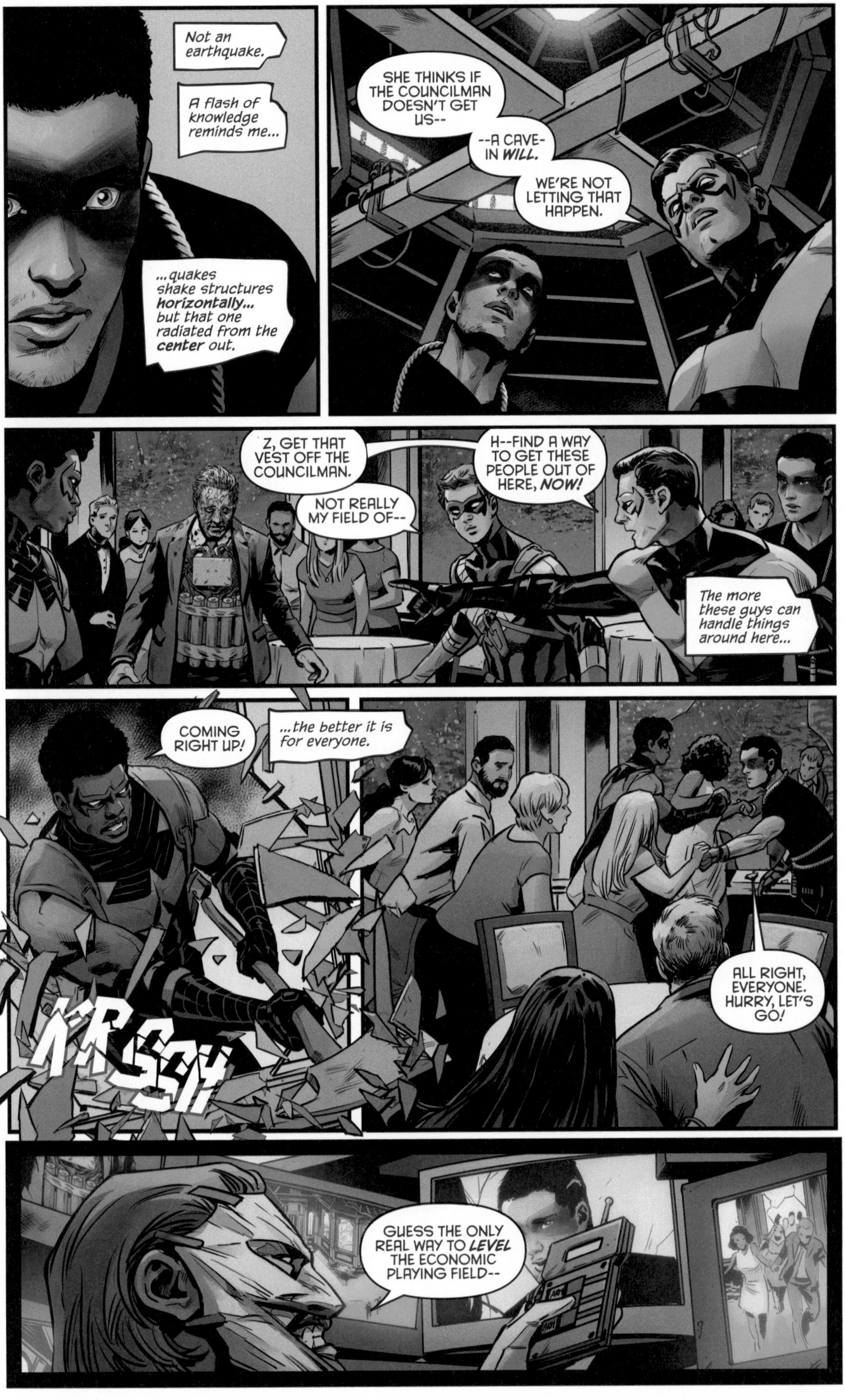
Not an earthquake.
A flash of knowledge reminds me...
...quakes shake structures **horizontally...** but that one radiated from the **center** out.
SHE THINKS IF THE COUNCILMAN DOESN'T GET US--
--A CAVE-IN **WILL.**
WE'RE NOT LETTING THAT HAPPEN.
Z, GET THAT VEST OFF THE COUNCILMAN.
H--FIND A WAY TO GET THESE PEOPLE OUT OF HERE, **NOW!**
NOT REALLY MY FIELD OF--
The more these guys can handle things around here...
COMING RIGHT UP!
...the better it is for everyone.
KRSSH
ALL RIGHT, EVERYONE. HURRY, LET'S GO!
GUESS THE ONLY REAL WAY TO **LEVEL** THE ECONOMIC PLAYING FIELD--

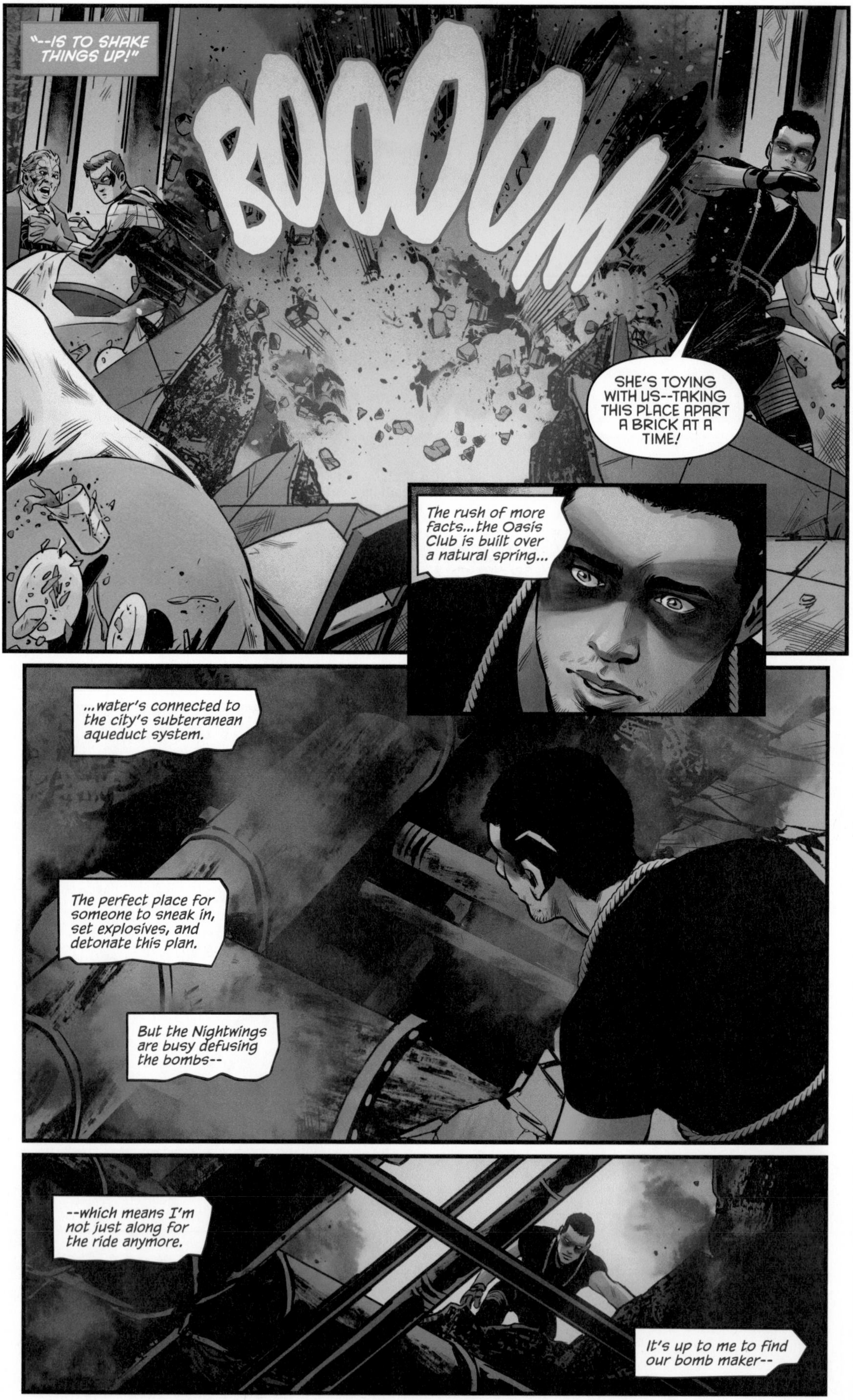
"--IS TO SHAKE THINGS UP!"
BOOOOM
SHE'S TOYING WITH US--TAKING THIS PLACE APART A BRICK AT A TIME!
The rush of more facts...the Oasis Club is built over a natural spring...
...water's connected to the city's subterranean aqueduct system.
The perfect place for someone to sneak in, set explosives, and detonate this plan.
But the Nightwings are busy defusing the bombs--
--which means I'm not just along for the ride anymore.
It's up to me to find our bomb maker--

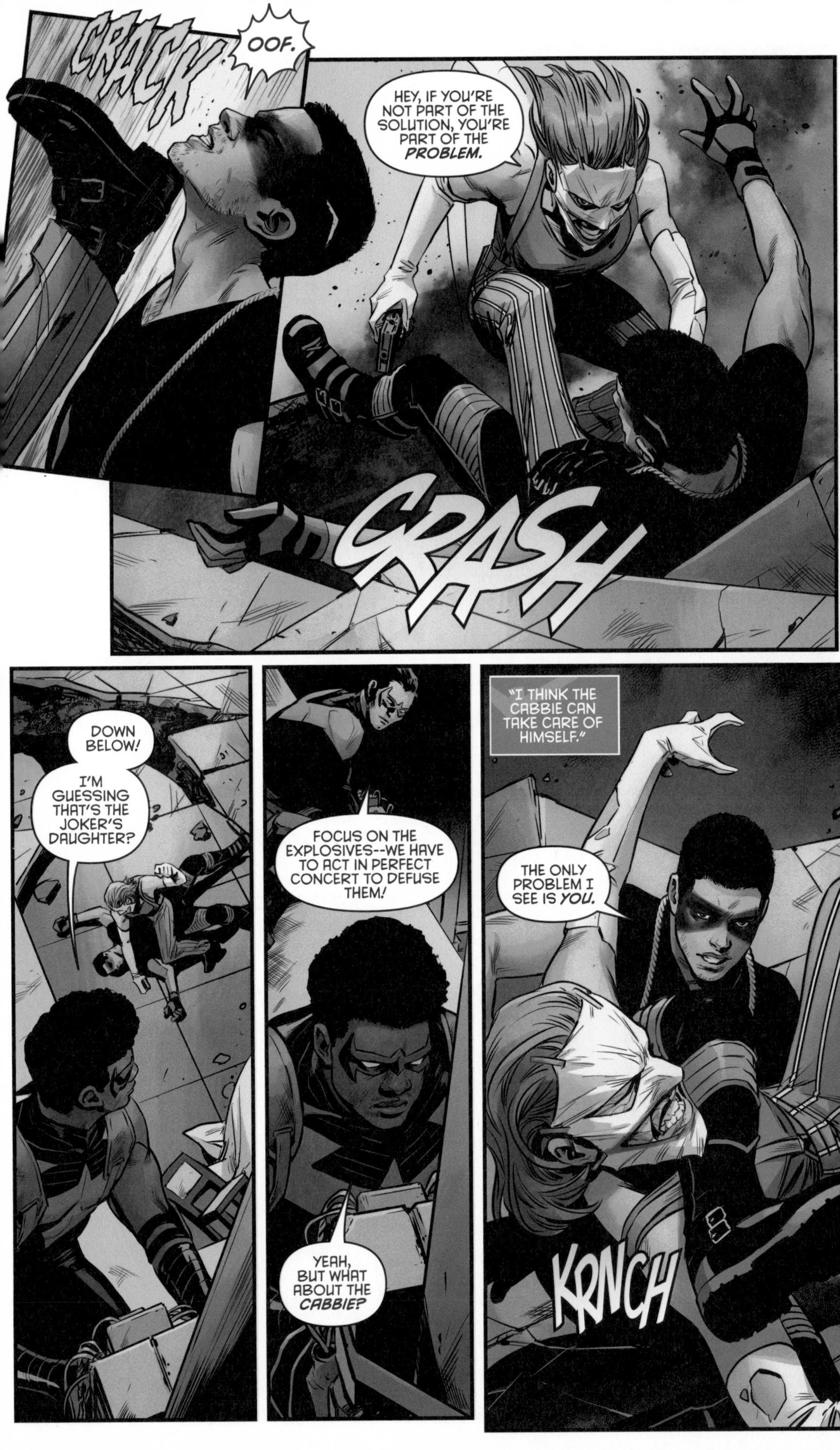
CRACK
OOF.
HEY, IF YOU'RE NOT PART OF THE SOLUTION, YOU'RE PART OF THE PROBLEM.
CRASH
DOWN BELOW!
I'M GUESSING THAT'S THE JOKER'S DAUGHTER?
FOCUS ON THE EXPLOSIVES--WE HAVE TO ACT IN PERFECT CONCERT TO DEFUSE THEM!
YEAH, BUT WHAT ABOUT THE CABBIE?
"I THINK THE CABBIE CAN TAKE CARE OF HIMSELF."
THE ONLY PROBLEM I SEE IS YOU.
KRNCH

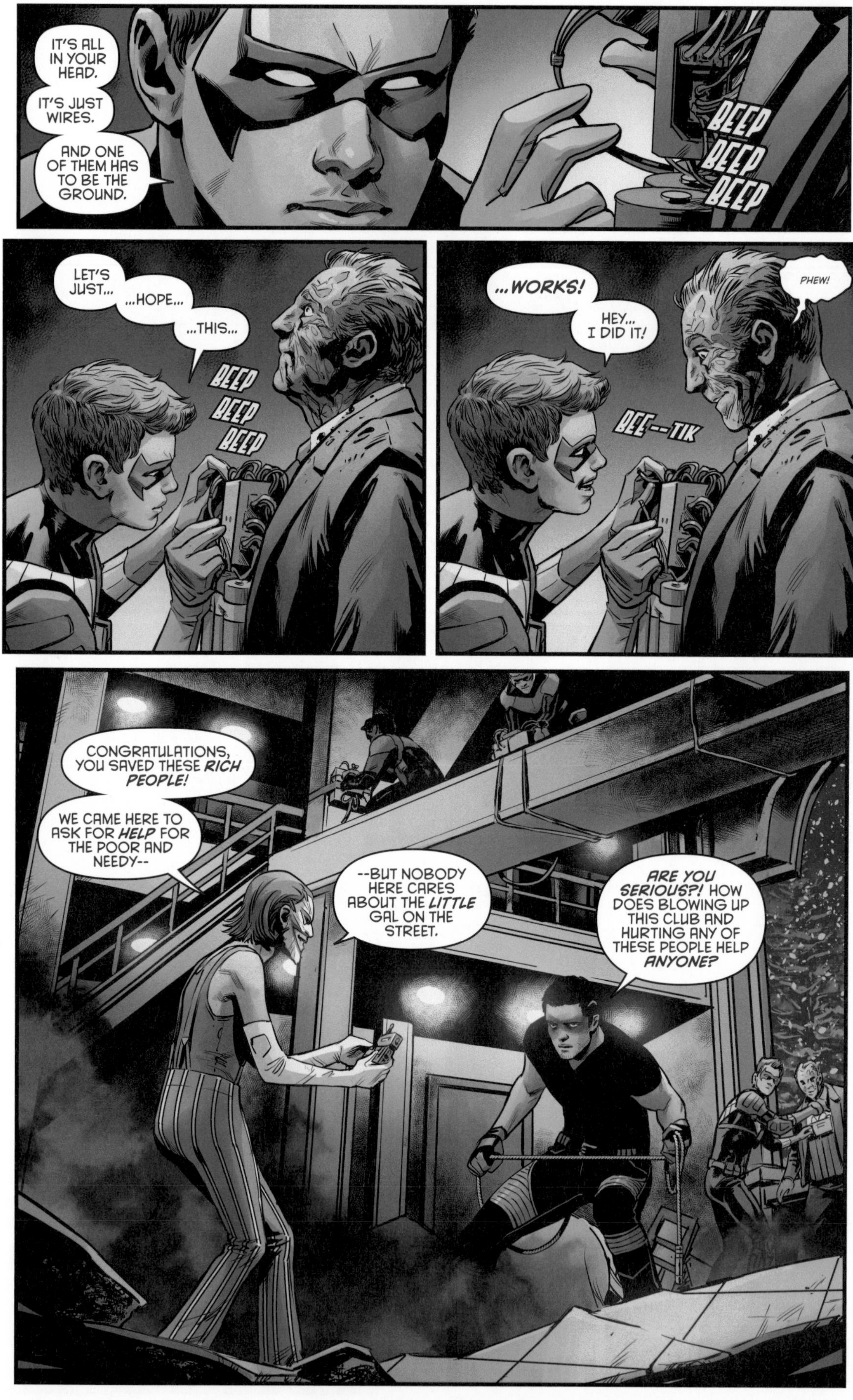
IT'S ALL IN YOUR HEAD.
IT'S JUST WIRES.
AND ONE OF THEM HAS TO BE THE GROUND.
BEEP BEEP BEEP
LET'S JUST...
...HOPE...
...THIS...
BEEP BEEP BEEP
...WORKS!
HEY... I DID IT!
PHEW!
BEE--TIK
CONGRATULATIONS, YOU SAVED THESE RICH PEOPLE!
WE CAME HERE TO ASK FOR HELP FOR THE POOR AND NEEDY--
--BUT NOBODY HERE CARES ABOUT THE LITTLE GAL ON THE STREET.
ARE YOU SERIOUS?! HOW DOES BLOWING UP THIS CLUB AND HURTING ANY OF THESE PEOPLE HELP ANYONE?

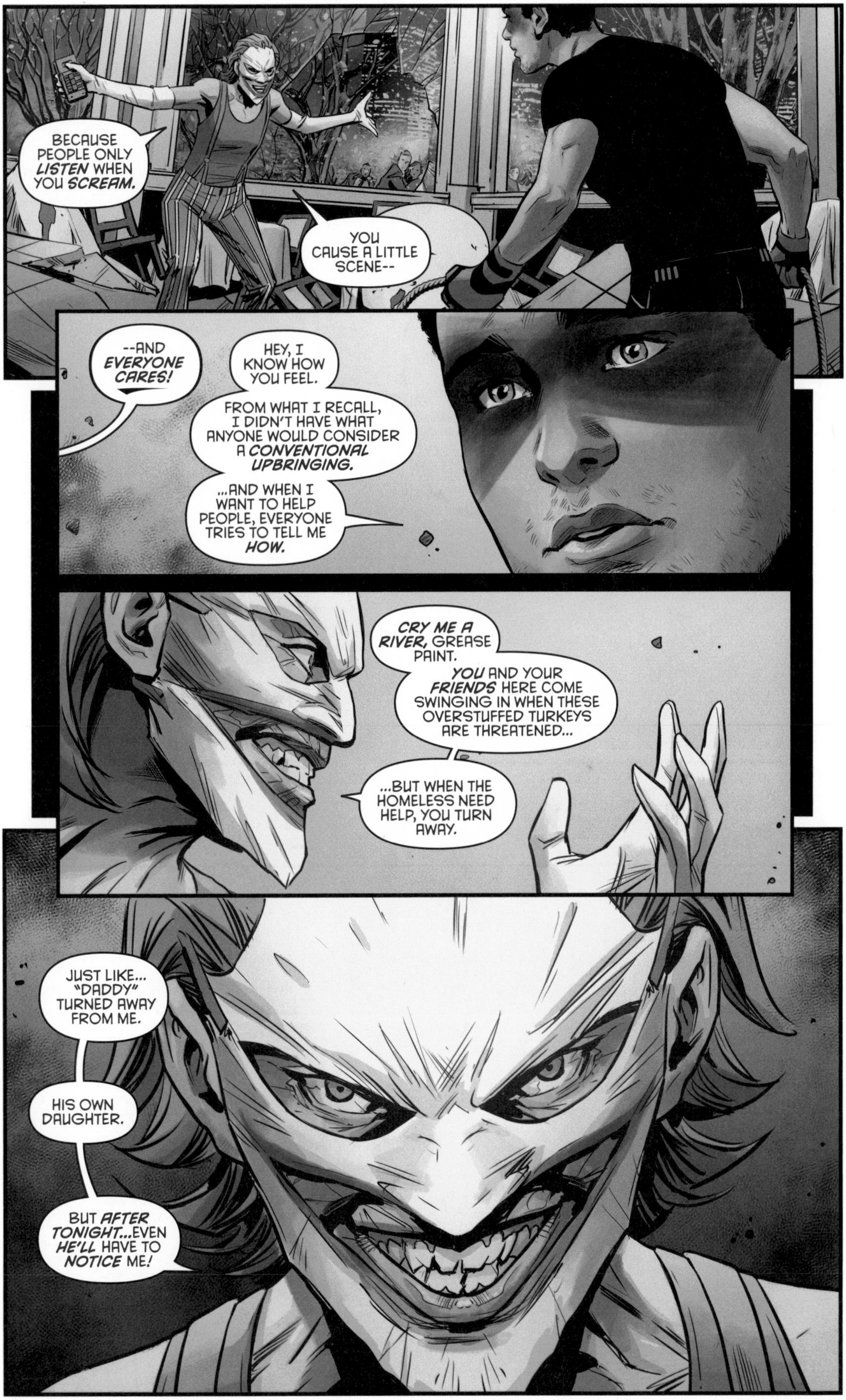
BECAUSE PEOPLE ONLY *LISTEN* WHEN YOU *SCREAM.*
YOU CAUSE A LITTLE SCENE--
--AND *EVERYONE CARES!*
HEY, I KNOW HOW YOU FEEL.
FROM WHAT I RECALL, I DIDN'T HAVE WHAT ANYONE WOULD CONSIDER A *CONVENTIONAL UPBRINGING.*
...AND WHEN I WANT TO HELP PEOPLE, EVERYONE TRIES TO TELL ME *HOW.*
CRY ME A RIVER, GREASE PAINT.
YOU AND YOUR *FRIENDS* HERE COME SWINGING IN WHEN THESE OVERSTUFFED TURKEYS ARE THREATENED...
...BUT WHEN THE HOMELESS NEED HELP, YOU TURN AWAY.
JUST LIKE... "DADDY" TURNED AWAY FROM ME.
HIS OWN DAUGHTER.
BUT *AFTER TONIGHT...*EVEN *HE'LL* HAVE TO *NOTICE* ME!

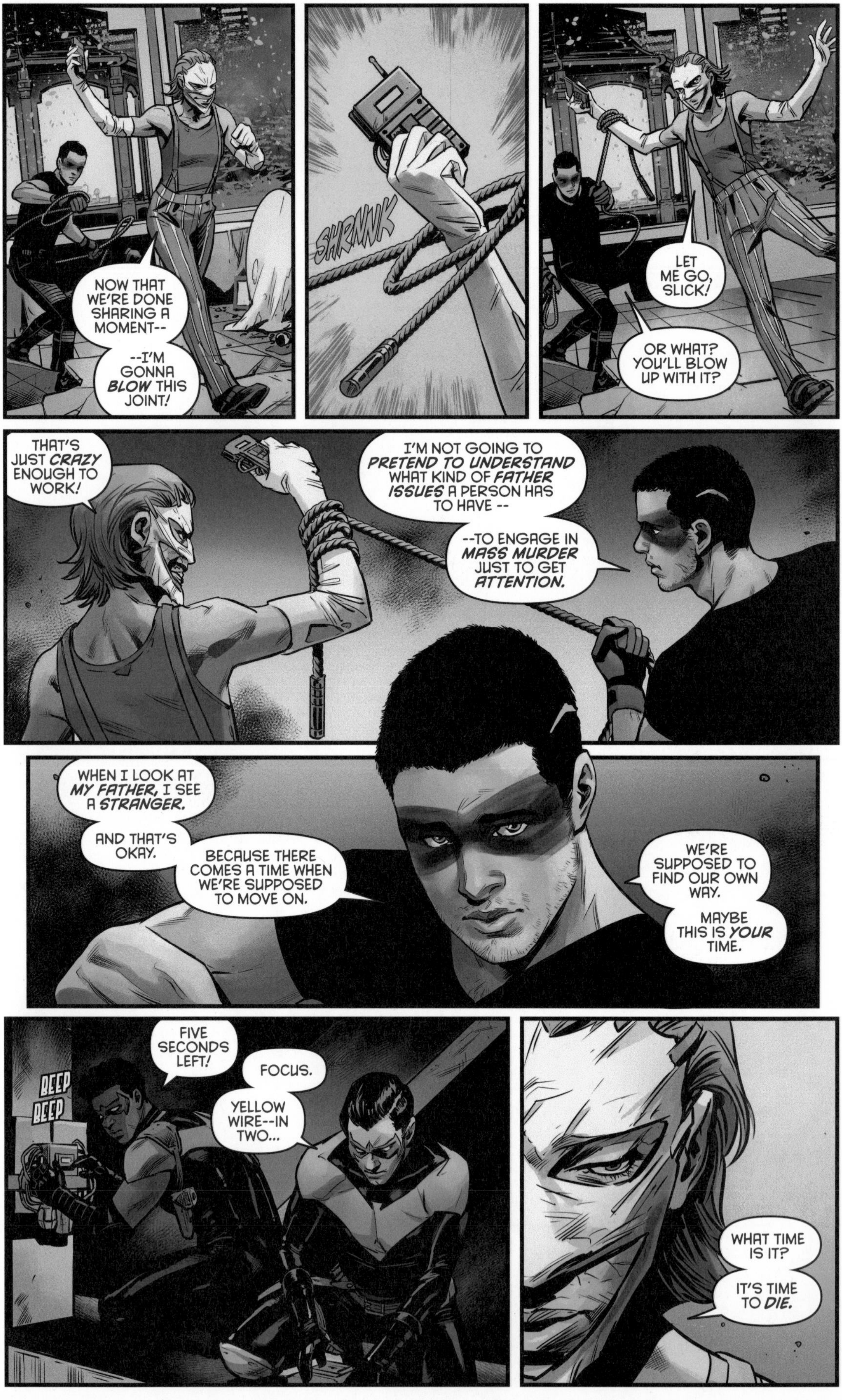
NOW THAT WE'RE DONE SHARING A MOMENT--
--I'M GONNA BLOW THIS JOINT!
SHRNNK
LET ME GO, SLICK!
OR WHAT? YOU'LL BLOW UP WITH IT?
THAT'S JUST CRAZY ENOUGH TO WORK!
I'M NOT GOING TO PRETEND TO UNDERSTAND WHAT KIND OF FATHER ISSUES A PERSON HAS TO HAVE --
--TO ENGAGE IN MASS MURDER JUST TO GET ATTENTION.
WHEN I LOOK AT MY FATHER, I SEE A STRANGER.
AND THAT'S OKAY.
BECAUSE THERE COMES A TIME WHEN WE'RE SUPPOSED TO MOVE ON.
WE'RE SUPPOSED TO FIND OUR OWN WAY.
MAYBE THIS IS YOUR TIME.
BEEP BEEP
FIVE SECONDS LEFT!
FOCUS.
YELLOW WIRE--IN TWO...
WHAT TIME IS IT?
IT'S TIME TO DIE.

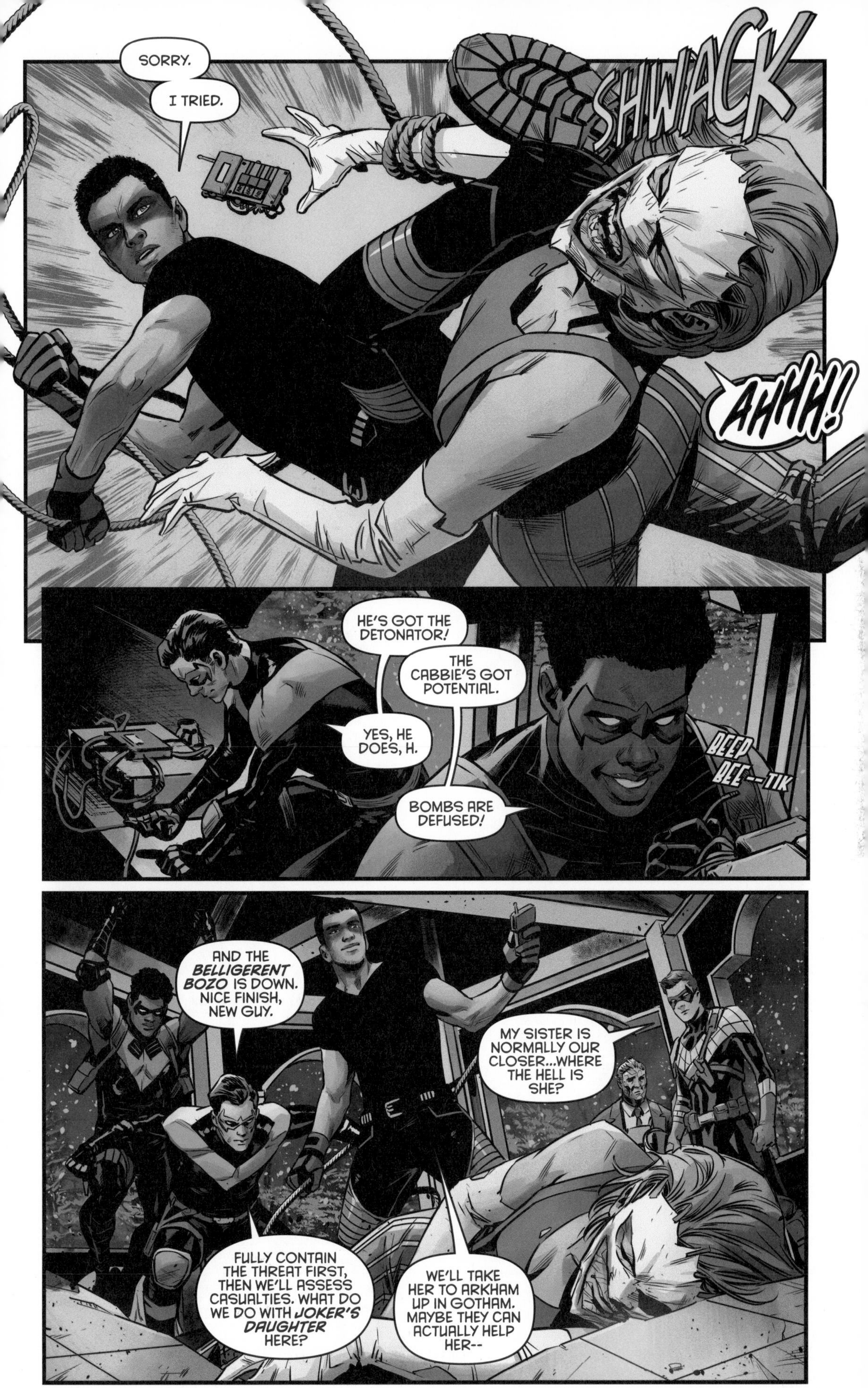
SORRY.
I TRIED.
SHWACK
AHHHH!
HE'S GOT THE DETONATOR!
THE CABBIE'S GOT POTENTIAL.
YES, HE DOES, H.
BOMBS ARE DEFUSED!
BEEP BEE--TIK
AND THE BELLIGERENT BOZO IS DOWN. NICE FINISH, NEW GUY.
MY SISTER IS NORMALLY OUR CLOSER...WHERE THE HELL IS SHE?
FULLY CONTAIN THE THREAT FIRST, THEN WE'LL ASSESS CASUALTIES. WHAT DO WE DO WITH JOKER'S DAUGHTER HERE?
WE'LL TAKE HER TO ARKHAM UP IN GOTHAM. MAYBE THEY CAN ACTUALLY HELP HER--

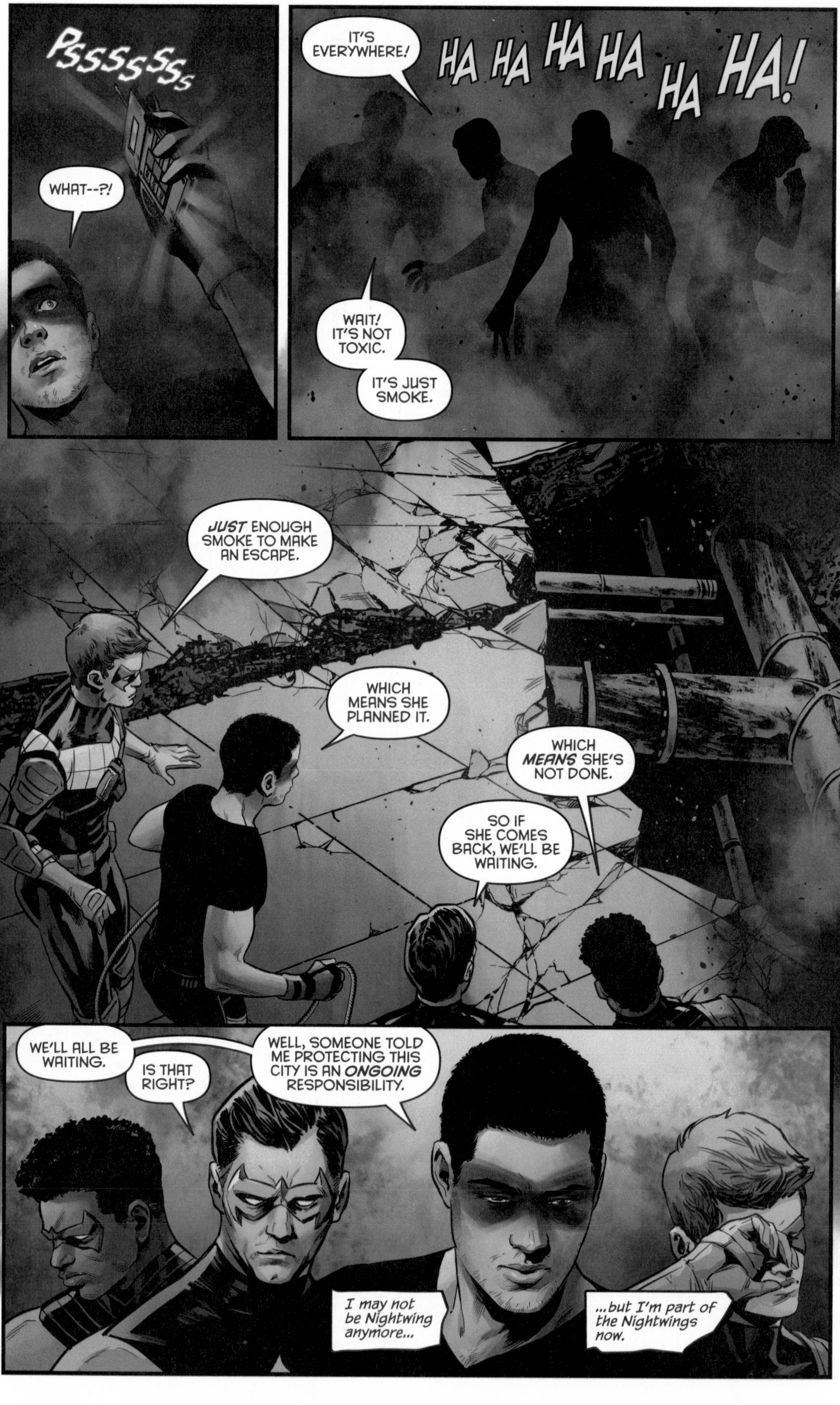
PSSSSSSS
WHAT--?!
IT'S EVERYWHERE!
HA HA HA HA HA HA!
WAIT! IT'S NOT TOXIC.
IT'S JUST SMOKE.
JUST ENOUGH SMOKE TO MAKE AN ESCAPE.
WHICH MEANS SHE PLANNED IT.
WHICH MEANS SHE'S NOT DONE.
SO IF SHE COMES BACK, WE'LL BE WAITING.
WE'LL ALL BE WAITING.
IS THAT RIGHT?
WELL, SOMEONE TOLD ME PROTECTING THIS CITY IS AN ONGOING RESPONSIBILITY.
I may not be Nightwing anymore...
...but I'm part of the Nightwings now.

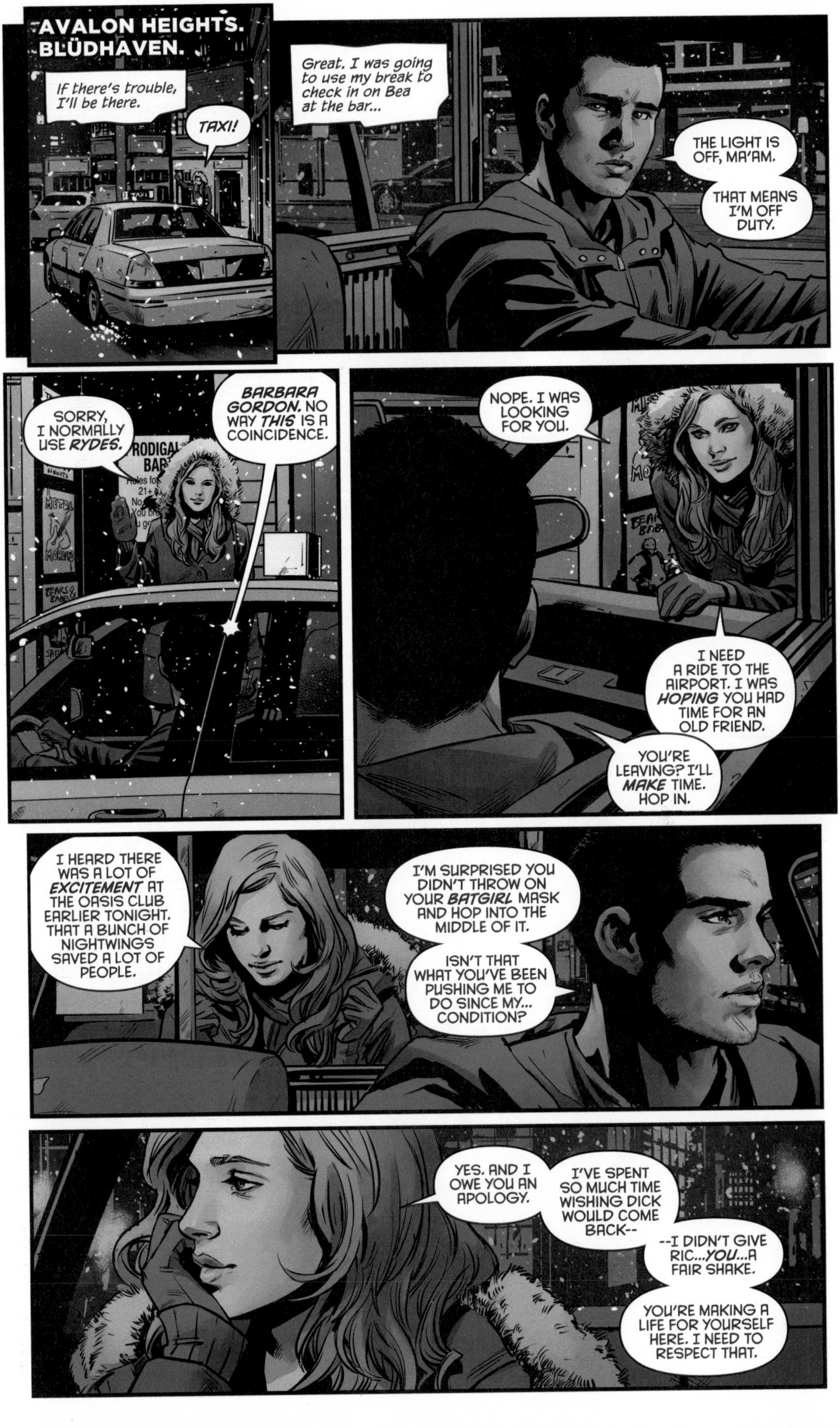
AVALON HEIGHTS. BLÜDHAVEN.
If there's trouble, I'll be there.
TAXI!
Great. I was going to use my break to check in on Bea at the bar...
THE LIGHT IS OFF, MA'AM.
THAT MEANS I'M OFF DUTY.
SORRY, I NORMALLY USE RYDES.
BARBARA GORDON. NO WAY THIS IS A COINCIDENCE.
NOPE. I WAS LOOKING FOR YOU.
I NEED A RIDE TO THE AIRPORT. I WAS HOPING YOU HAD TIME FOR AN OLD FRIEND.
YOU'RE LEAVING? I'LL MAKE TIME. HOP IN.
I HEARD THERE WAS A LOT OF EXCITEMENT AT THE OASIS CLUB EARLIER TONIGHT. THAT A BUNCH OF NIGHTWINGS SAVED A LOT OF PEOPLE.
I'M SURPRISED YOU DIDN'T THROW ON YOUR BATGIRL MASK AND HOP INTO THE MIDDLE OF IT.
ISN'T THAT WHAT YOU'VE BEEN PUSHING ME TO DO SINCE MY... CONDITION?
YES. AND I OWE YOU AN APOLOGY.
I'VE SPENT SO MUCH TIME WISHING DICK WOULD COME BACK--
--I DIDN'T GIVE RIC...YOU...A FAIR SHAKE.
YOU'RE MAKING A LIFE FOR YOURSELF HERE. I NEED TO RESPECT THAT.

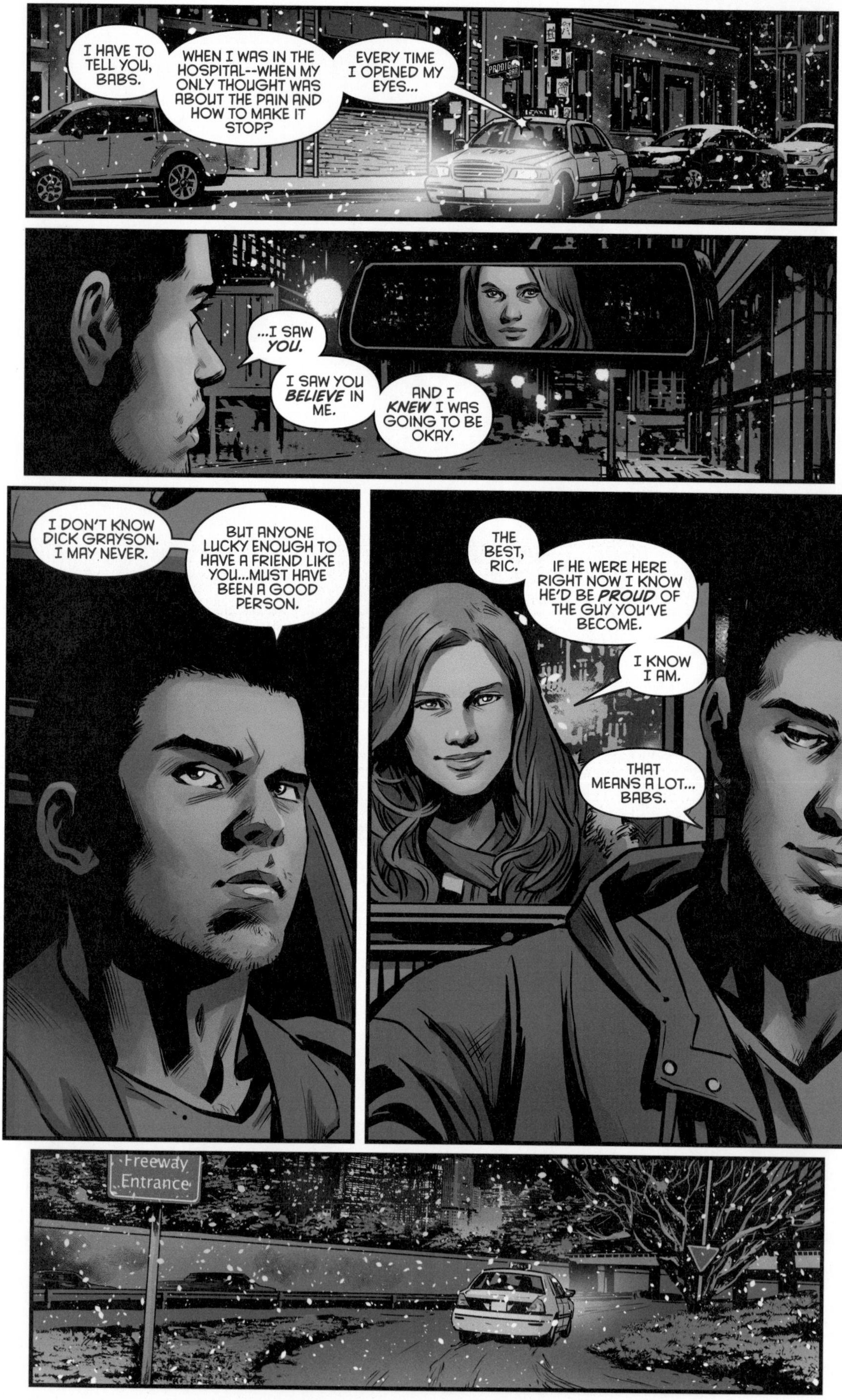
I HAVE TO TELL YOU, BABS.
WHEN I WAS IN THE HOSPITAL--WHEN MY ONLY THOUGHT WAS ABOUT THE PAIN AND HOW TO MAKE IT STOP?
EVERY TIME I OPENED MY EYES...
PRODIGAL BAR
TAXI
...I SAW *YOU.*
I SAW YOU *BELIEVE* IN ME.
AND I *KNEW* I WAS GOING TO BE OKAY.
I DON'T KNOW DICK GRAYSON. I MAY NEVER.
BUT ANYONE LUCKY ENOUGH TO HAVE A FRIEND LIKE YOU...MUST HAVE BEEN A GOOD PERSON.
THE BEST, RIC.
IF HE WERE HERE RIGHT NOW I KNOW HE'D BE *PROUD* OF THE GUY YOU'VE BECOME.
I KNOW I AM.
THAT MEANS A LOT... BABS.
Freeway Entrance

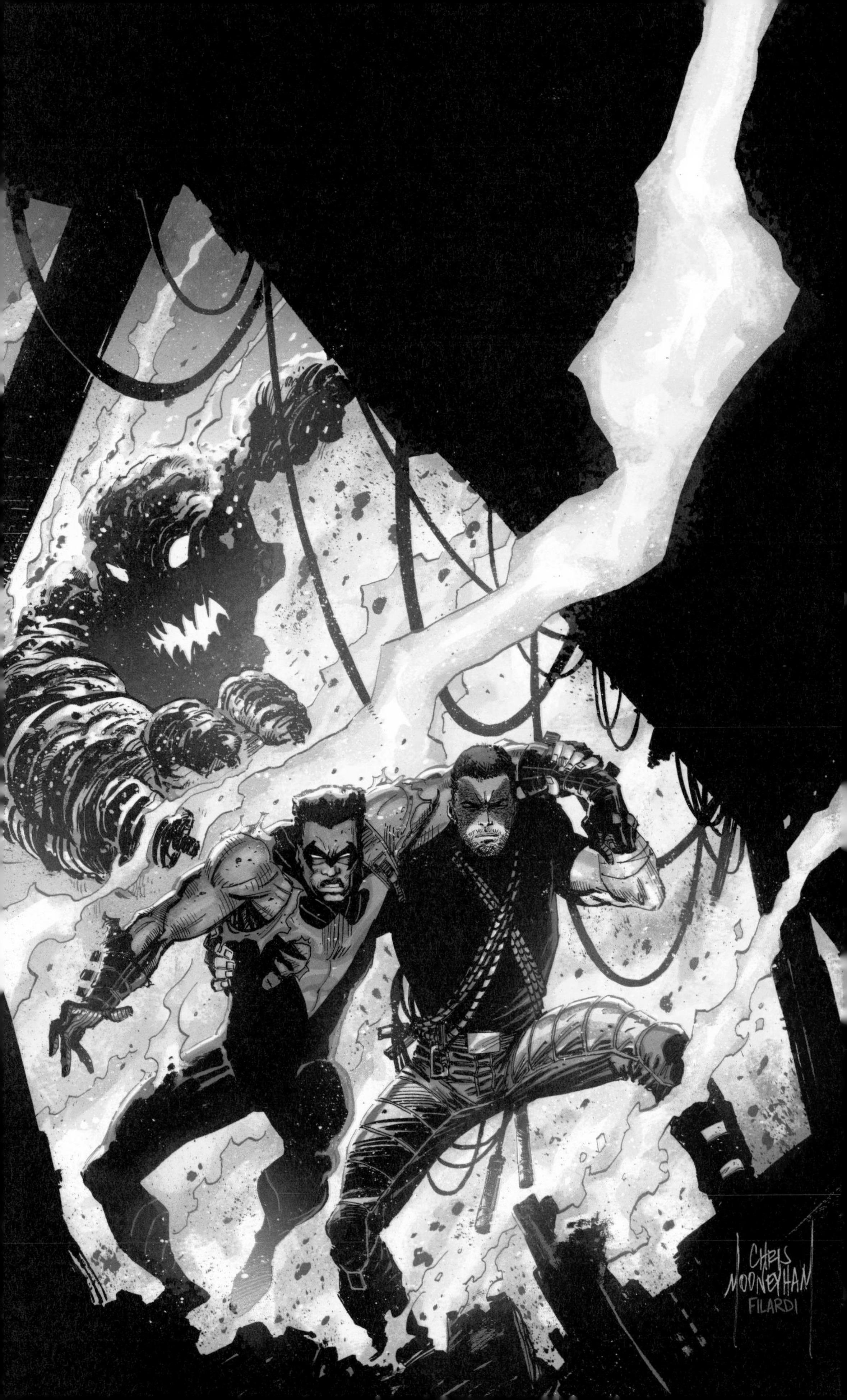
CHRIS
MOONEYHAN
FILARDI

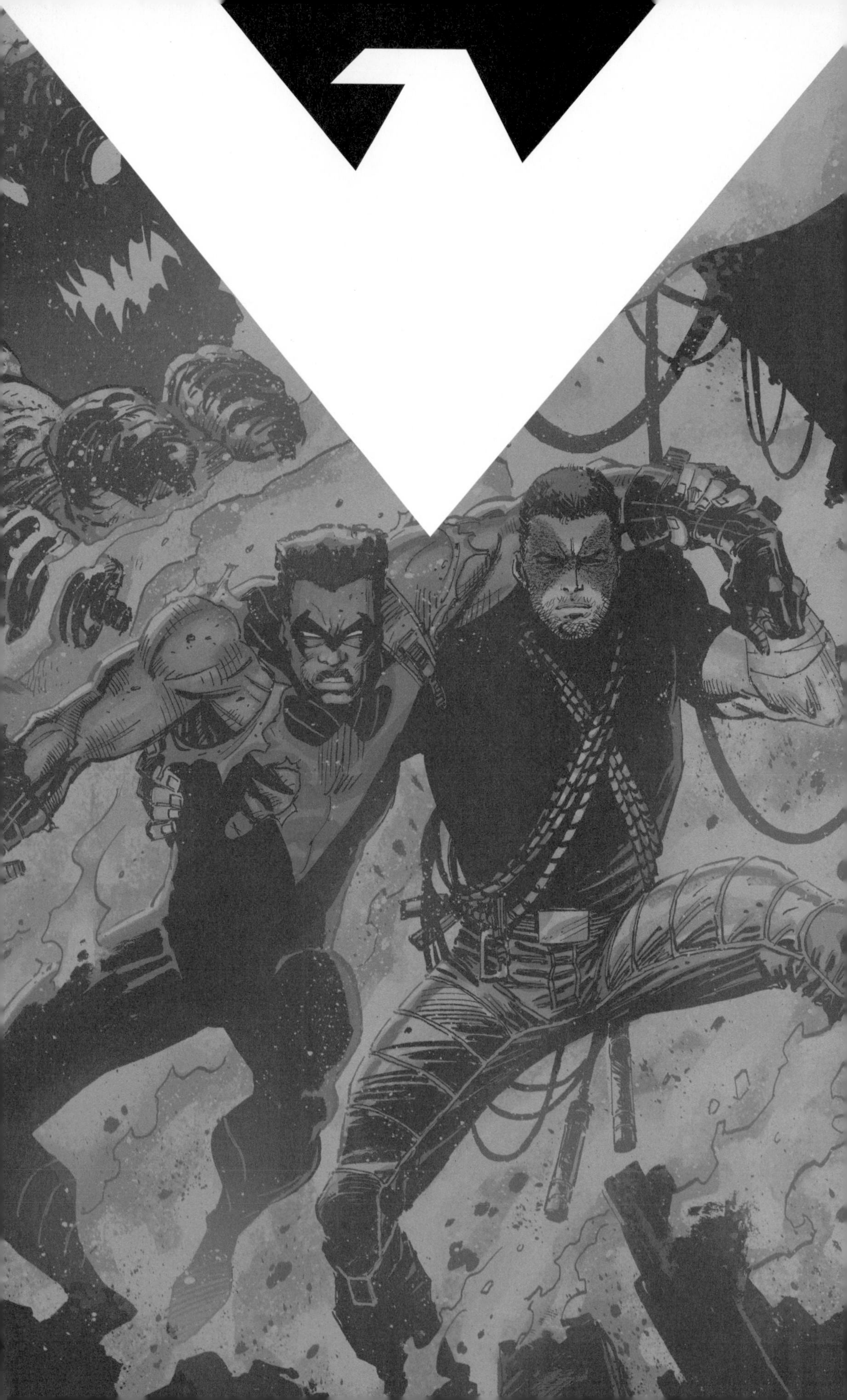

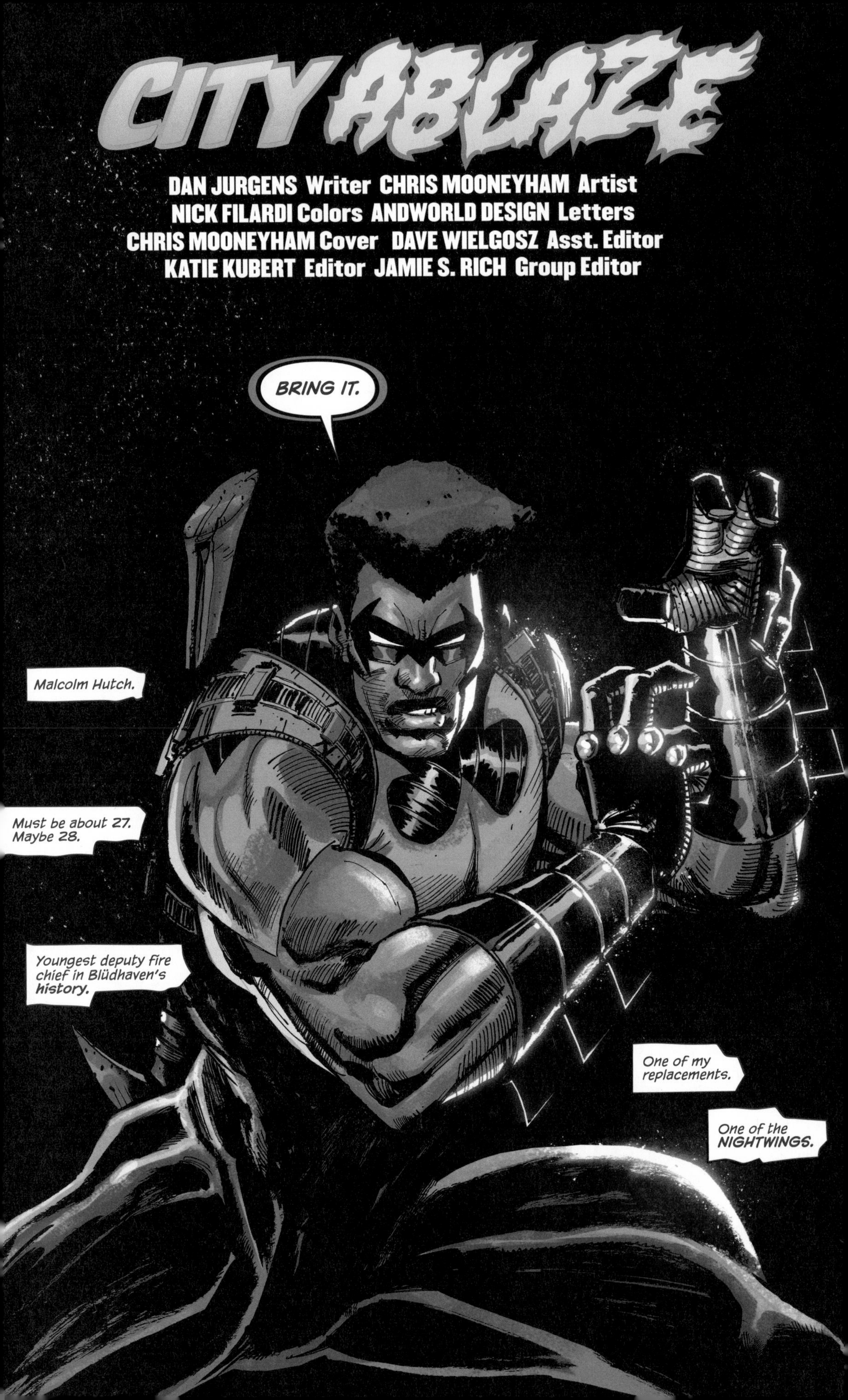
CITY ABLAZE
DAN JURGENS Writer CHRIS MOONEYHAM Artist
NICK FILARDI Colors ANDWORLD DESIGN Letters
CHRIS MOONEYHAM Cover DAVE WIELGOSZ Asst. Editor
KATIE KUBERT Editor JAMIE S. RICH Group Editor
BRING IT.
Malcolm Hutch.
Must be about 27. Maybe 28.
Youngest deputy fire chief in Blüdhaven's history.
One of my replacements.
One of the NIGHTWINGS.

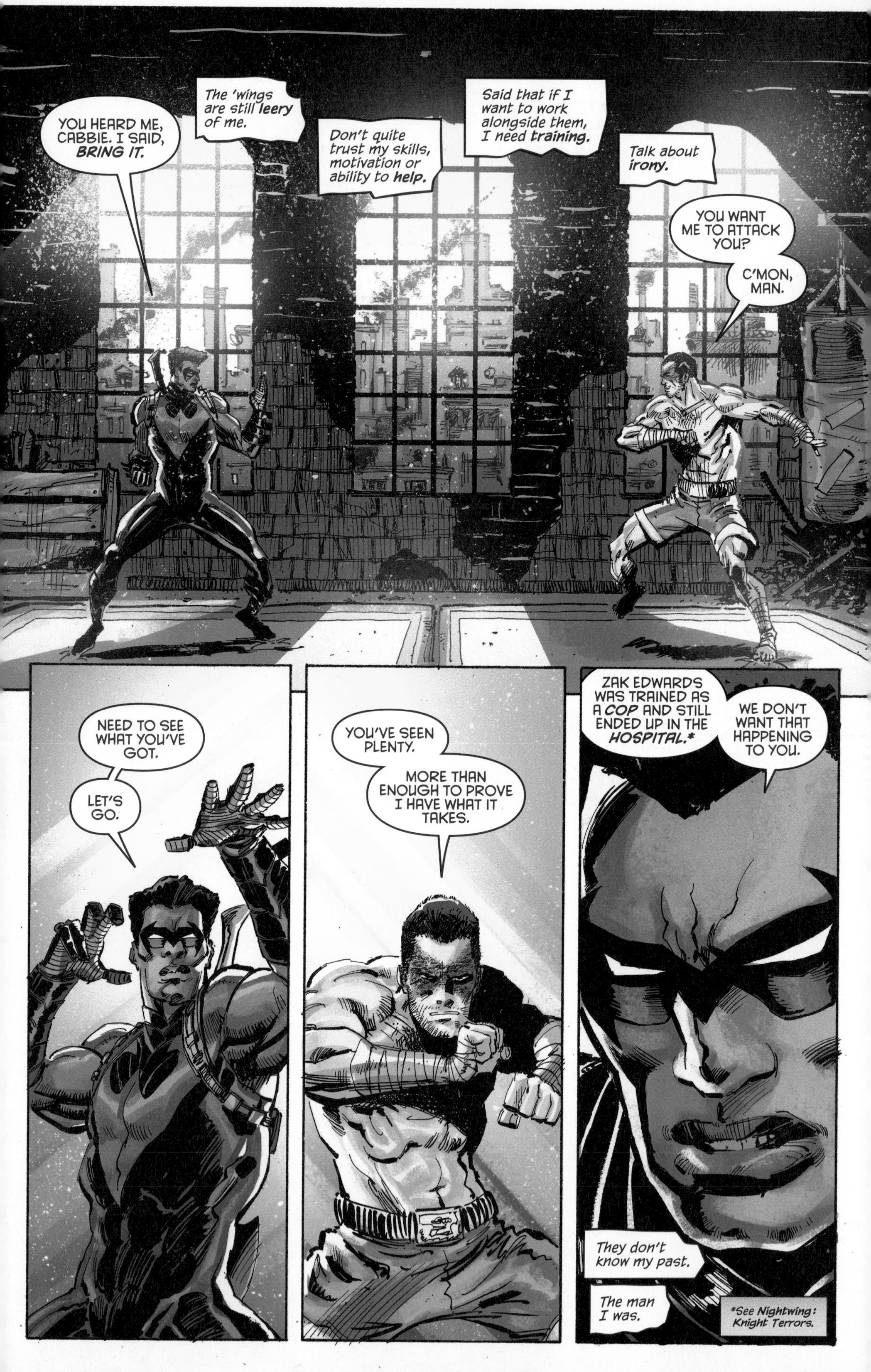

YOU HEARD ME, CABBIE. I SAID, BRING IT.
The 'wings are still leery of me.
Don't quite trust my skills, motivation or ability to help.
Said that if I want to work alongside them, I need training.
Talk about irony.
YOU WANT ME TO ATTACK YOU?
C'MON, MAN.
NEED TO SEE WHAT YOU'VE GOT.
LET'S GO.
YOU'VE SEEN PLENTY.
MORE THAN ENOUGH TO PROVE I HAVE WHAT IT TAKES.
ZAK EDWARDS WAS TRAINED AS A COP AND STILL ENDED UP IN THE HOSPITAL.*
WE DON'T WANT THAT HAPPENING TO YOU.
They don't know my past.
The man I was.
*See Nightwing: Knight Terrors.

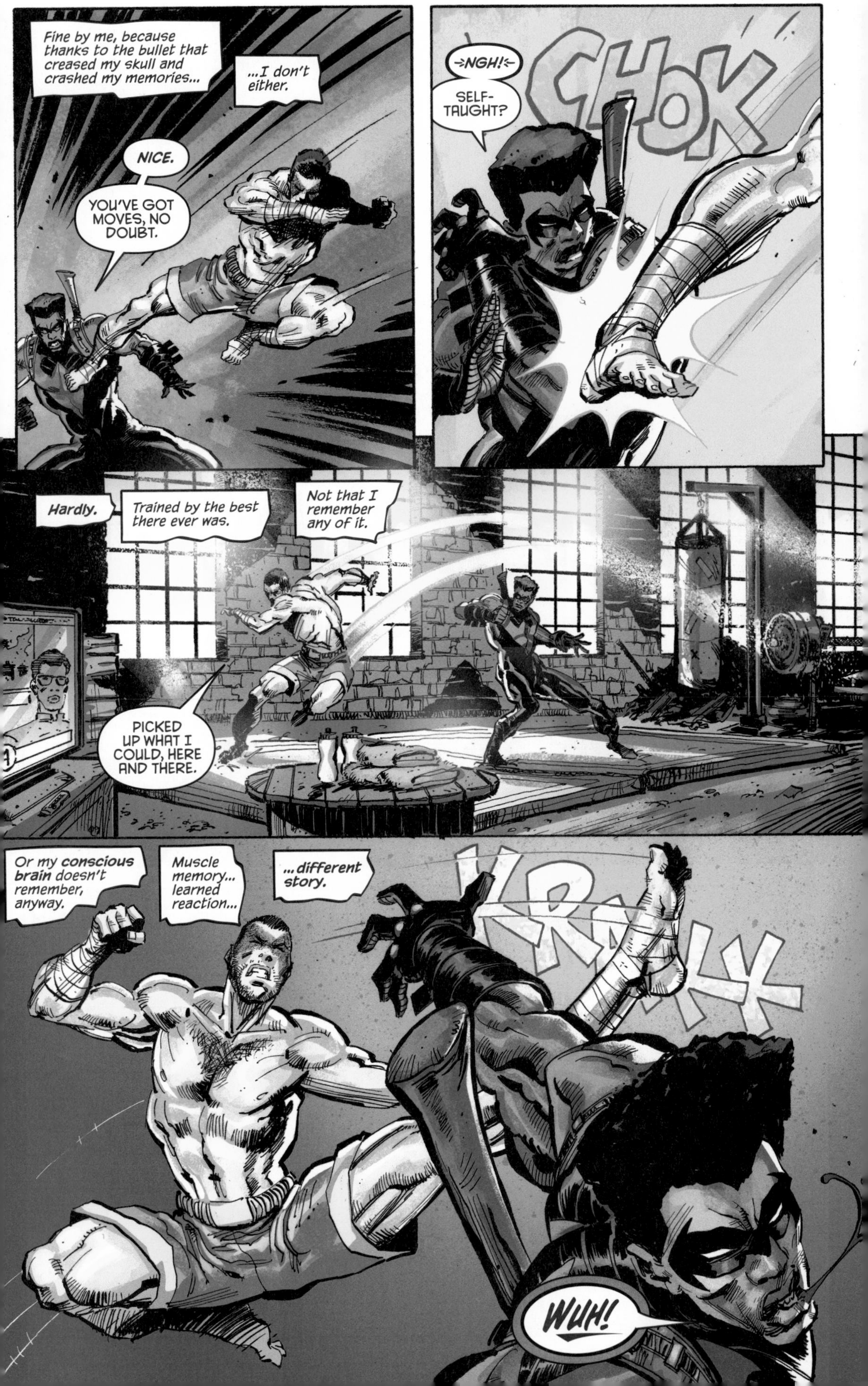
Fine by me, because thanks to the bullet that creased my skull and crashed my memories...
...I don't either.
NICE.
YOU'VE GOT MOVES, NO DOUBT.
-NGH!-
SELF-TAUGHT?
CHOK
Hardly.
Trained by the best there ever was.
Not that I remember any of it.
PICKED UP WHAT I COULD, HERE AND THERE.
Or my conscious brain doesn't remember, anyway.
Muscle memory... learned reaction...
...different story.
WUH!

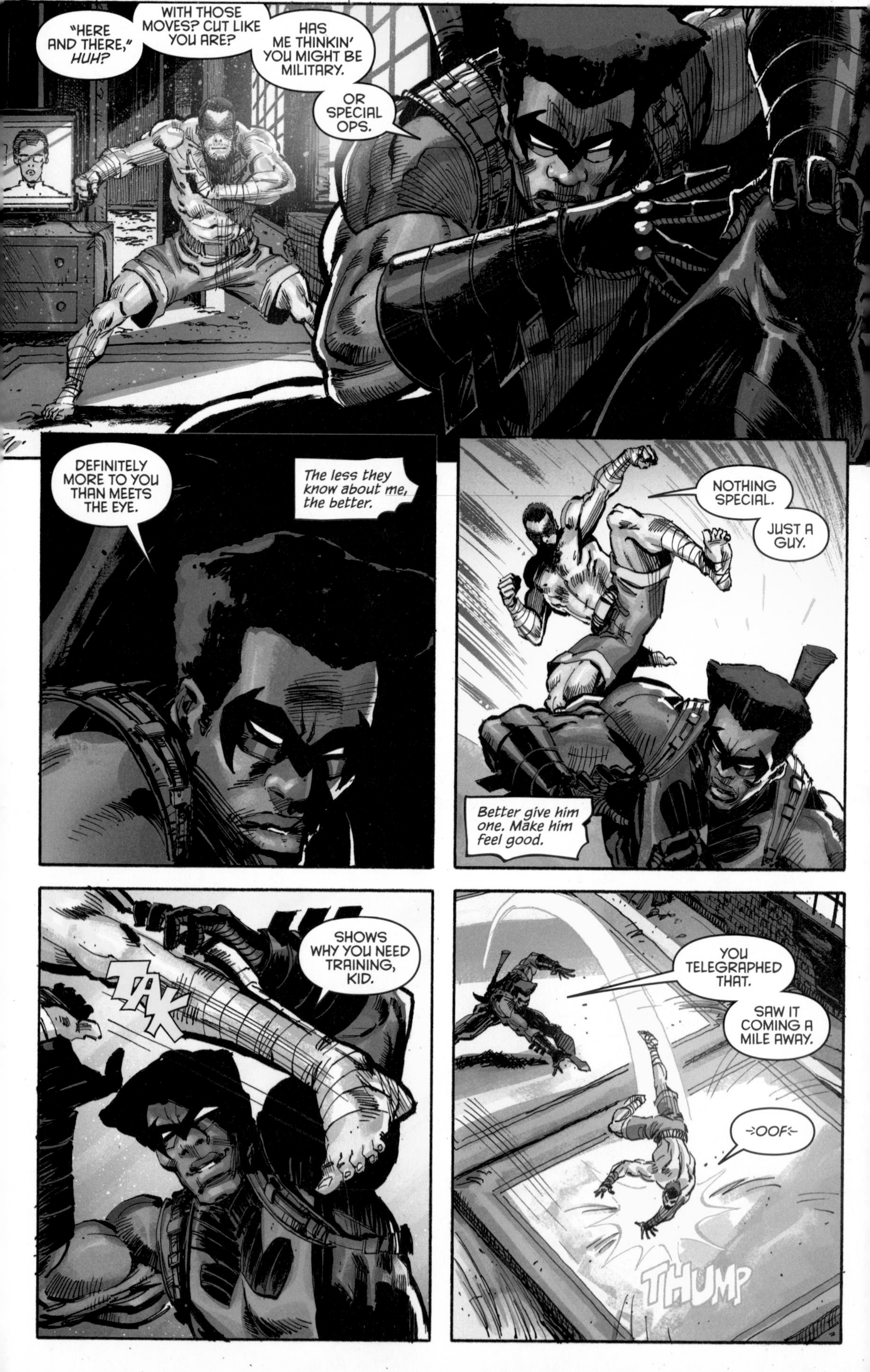

"HERE AND THERE," HUH?
WITH THOSE MOVES? CUT LIKE YOU ARE?
HAS ME THINKIN' YOU MIGHT BE MILITARY.
OR SPECIAL OPS.
DEFINITELY MORE TO YOU THAN MEETS THE EYE.
The less they know about me, the better.
NOTHING SPECIAL.
JUST A GUY.
Better give him one. Make him feel good.
TAK
SHOWS WHY YOU NEED TRAINING, KID.
YOU TELEGRAPHED THAT.
SAW IT COMING A MILE AWAY.
OOF
THUMP

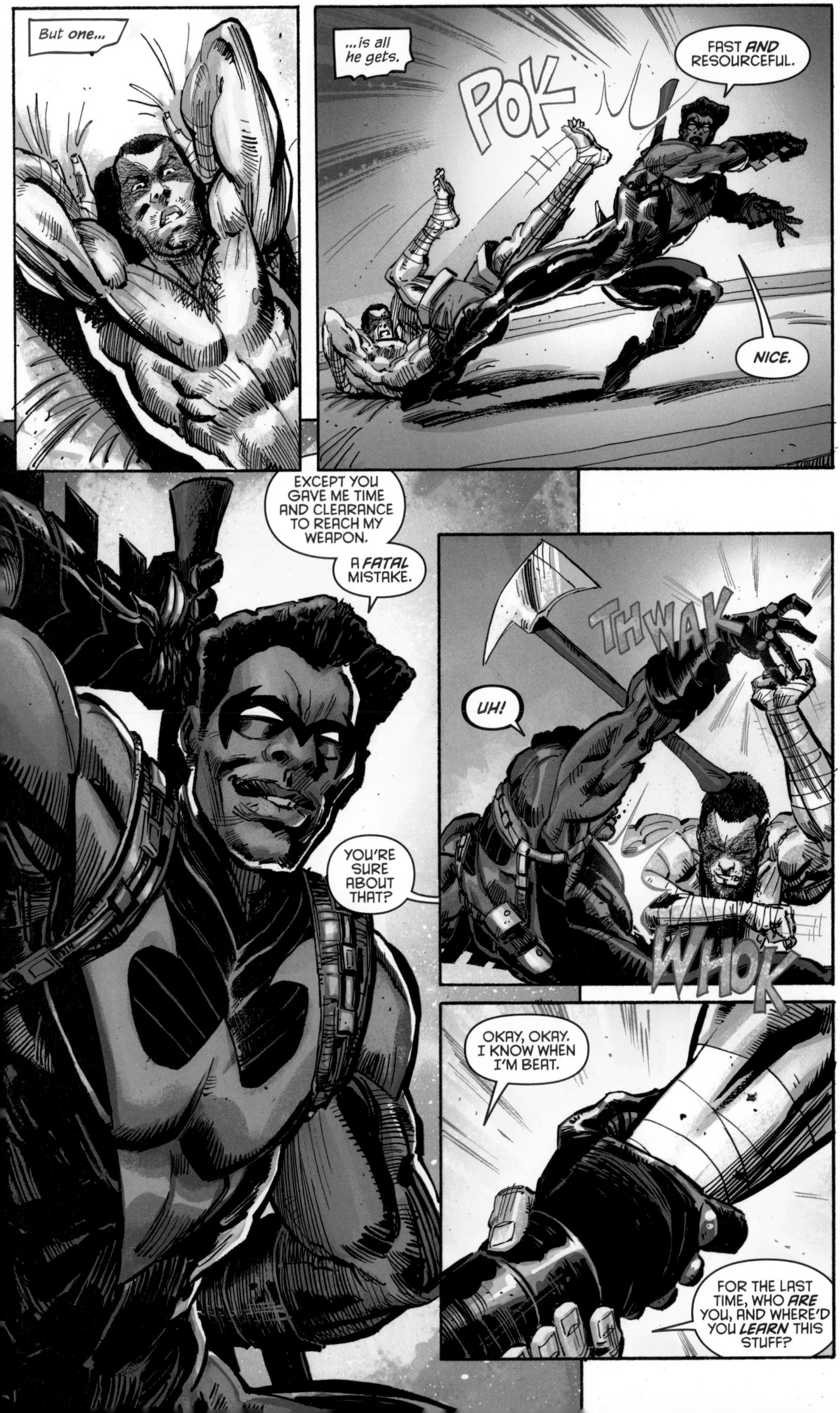
But one...
...is all he gets.
POK
FAST AND RESOURCEFUL.
NICE.
EXCEPT YOU GAVE ME TIME AND CLEARANCE TO REACH MY WEAPON.
A FATAL MISTAKE.
THWAK
UH!
YOU'RE SURE ABOUT THAT?
WHOK
OKAY, OKAY. I KNOW WHEN I'M BEAT.
FOR THE LAST TIME, WHO ARE YOU, AND WHERE'D YOU LEARN THIS STUFF?

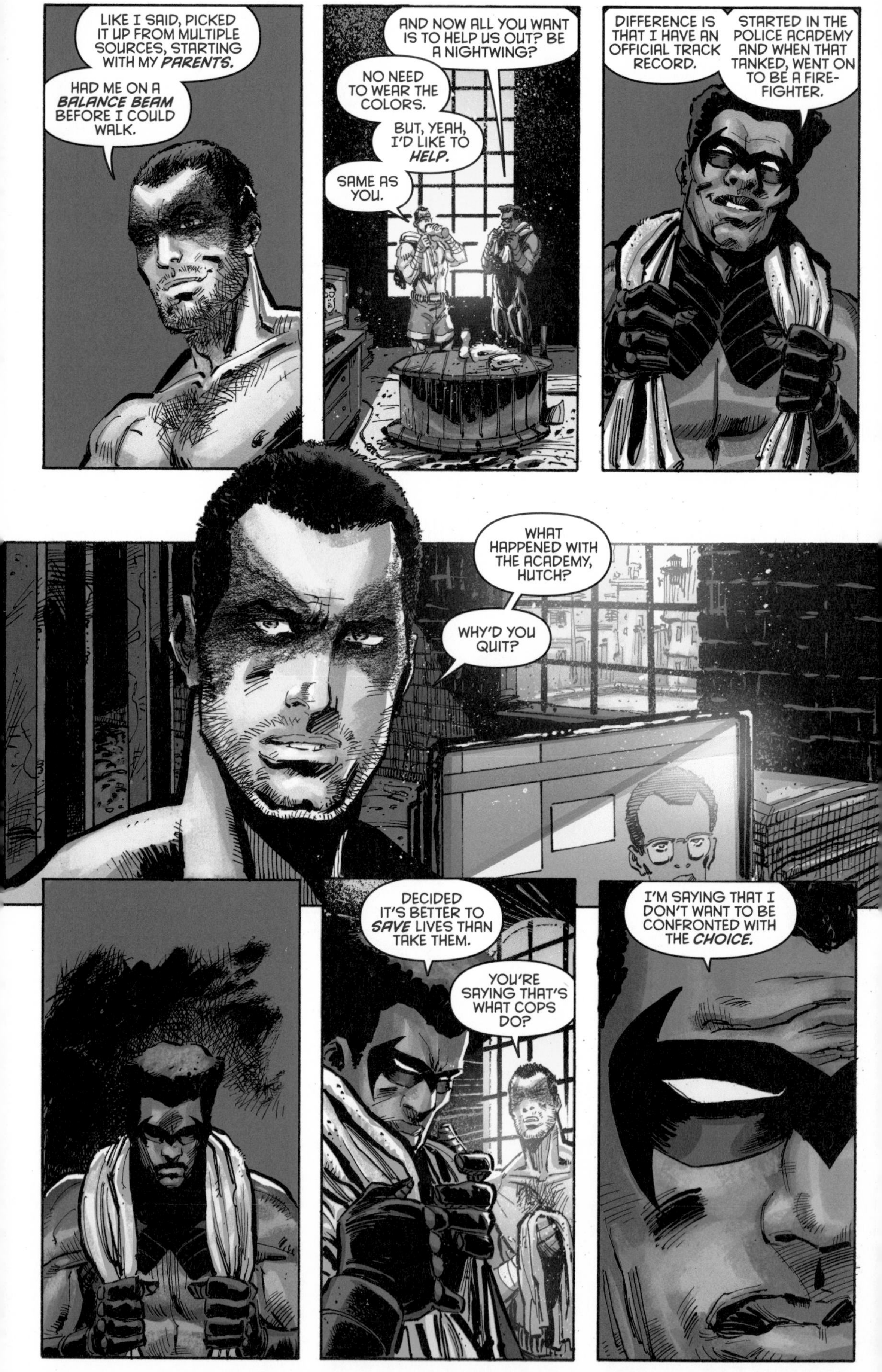

LIKE I SAID, PICKED IT UP FROM MULTIPLE SOURCES, STARTING WITH MY PARENTS.
HAD ME ON A BALANCE BEAM BEFORE I COULD WALK.
AND NOW ALL YOU WANT IS TO HELP US OUT? BE A NIGHTWING?
NO NEED TO WEAR THE COLORS.
BUT, YEAH, I'D LIKE TO HELP.
SAME AS YOU.
DIFFERENCE IS THAT I HAVE AN OFFICIAL TRACK RECORD.
STARTED IN THE POLICE ACADEMY AND WHEN THAT TANKED, WENT ON TO BE A FIRE-FIGHTER.
WHAT HAPPENED WITH THE ACADEMY, HUTCH?
WHY'D YOU QUIT?
DECIDED IT'S BETTER TO SAVE LIVES THAN TAKE THEM.
YOU'RE SAYING THAT'S WHAT COPS DO?
I'M SAYING THAT I DON'T WANT TO BE CONFRONTED WITH THE CHOICE.

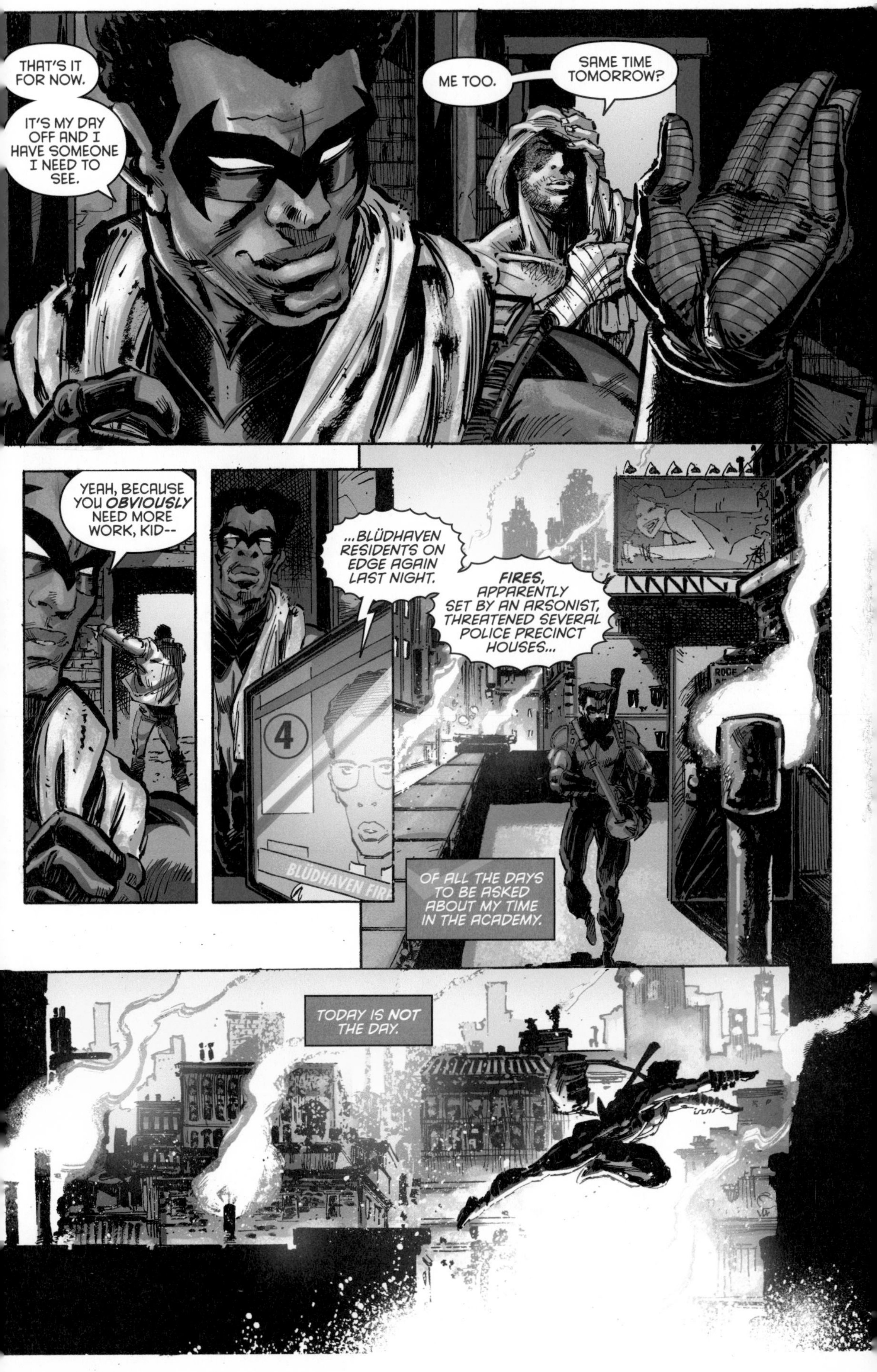
THAT'S IT FOR NOW.
IT'S MY DAY OFF AND I HAVE SOMEONE I NEED TO SEE.
ME TOO.
SAME TIME TOMORROW?
YEAH, BECAUSE YOU OBVIOUSLY NEED MORE WORK, KID--
...BLÜDHAVEN RESIDENTS ON EDGE AGAIN LAST NIGHT.
FIRES, APPARENTLY SET BY AN ARSONIST, THREATENED SEVERAL POLICE PRECINCT HOUSES...
4
BLÜDHAVEN FIR
OF ALL THE DAYS TO BE ASKED ABOUT MY TIME IN THE ACADEMY.
TODAY IS NOT THE DAY.

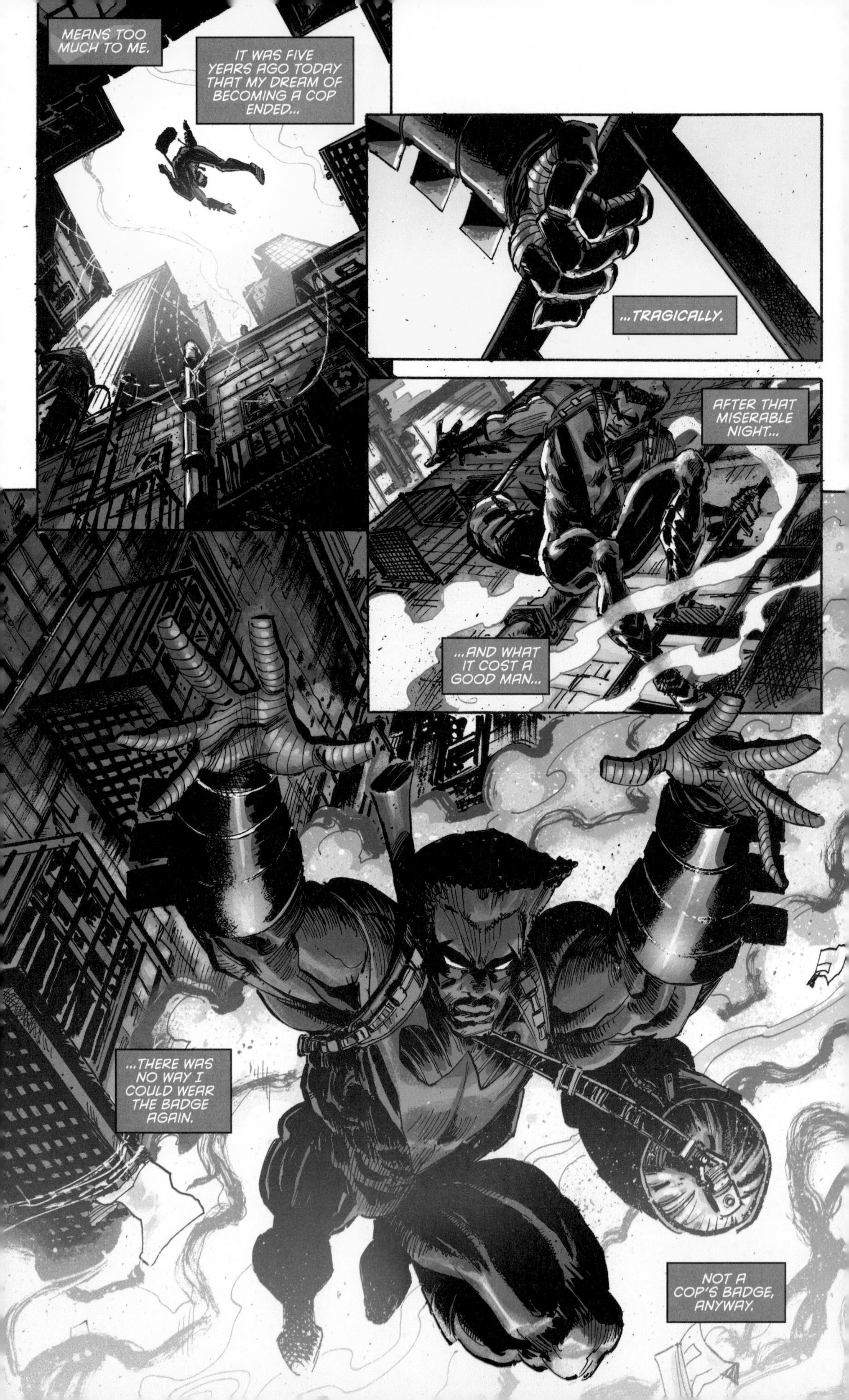
MEANS TOO MUCH TO ME.
IT WAS FIVE YEARS AGO TODAY THAT MY DREAM OF BECOMING A COP ENDED...
...TRAGICALLY.
AFTER THAT MISERABLE NIGHT...
...AND WHAT IT COST A GOOD MAN...
...THERE WAS NO WAY I COULD WEAR THE BADGE AGAIN.
NOT A COP'S BADGE, ANYWAY.

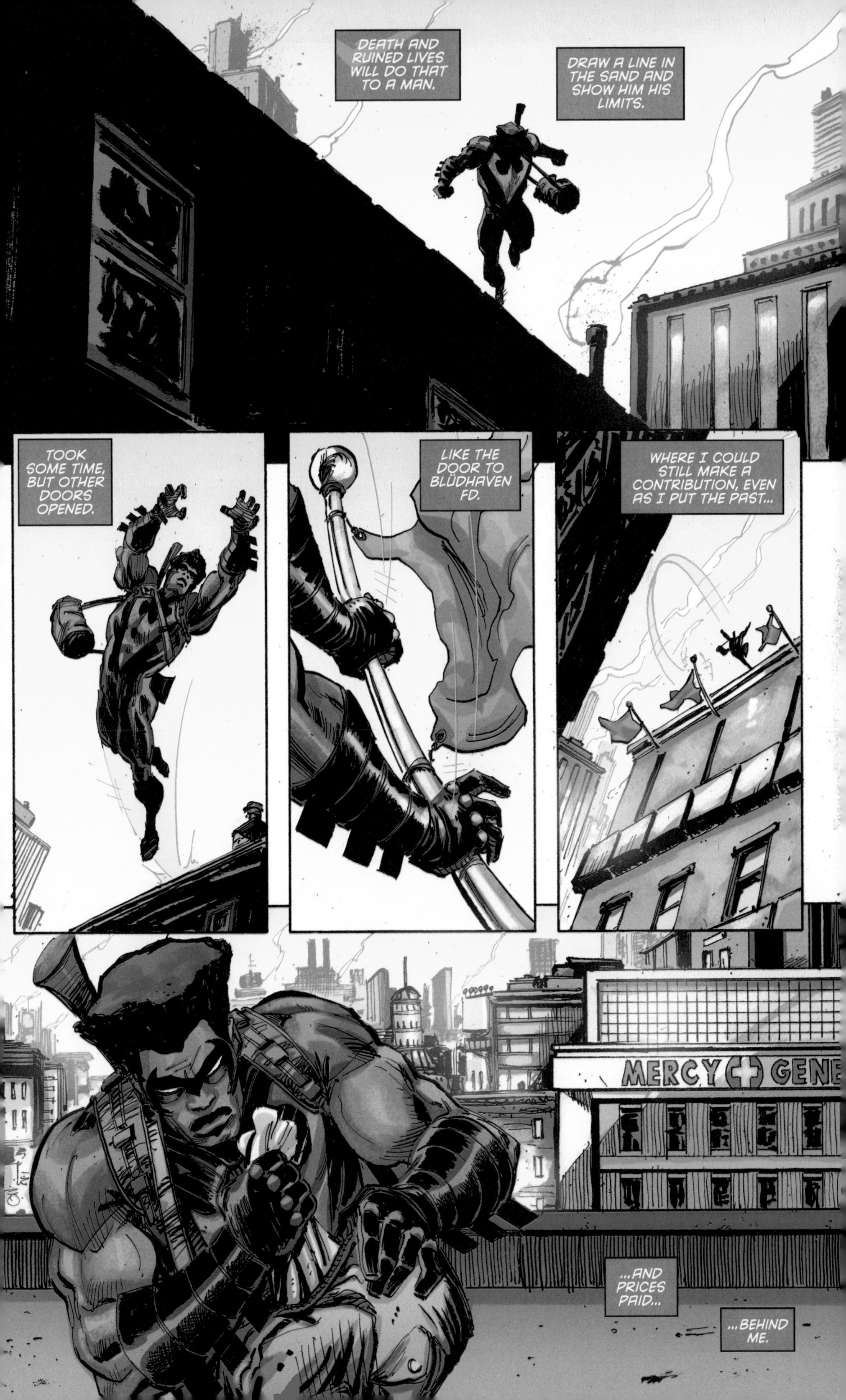
DEATH AND RUINED LIVES WILL DO THAT TO A MAN.
DRAW A LINE IN THE SAND AND SHOW HIM HIS LIMITS.
TOOK SOME TIME, BUT OTHER DOORS OPENED.
LIKE THE DOOR TO BLÜDHAVEN FD.
WHERE I COULD STILL MAKE A CONTRIBUTION, EVEN AS I PUT THE PAST...
MERCY GENE
...AND PRICES PAID...
...BEHIND ME.

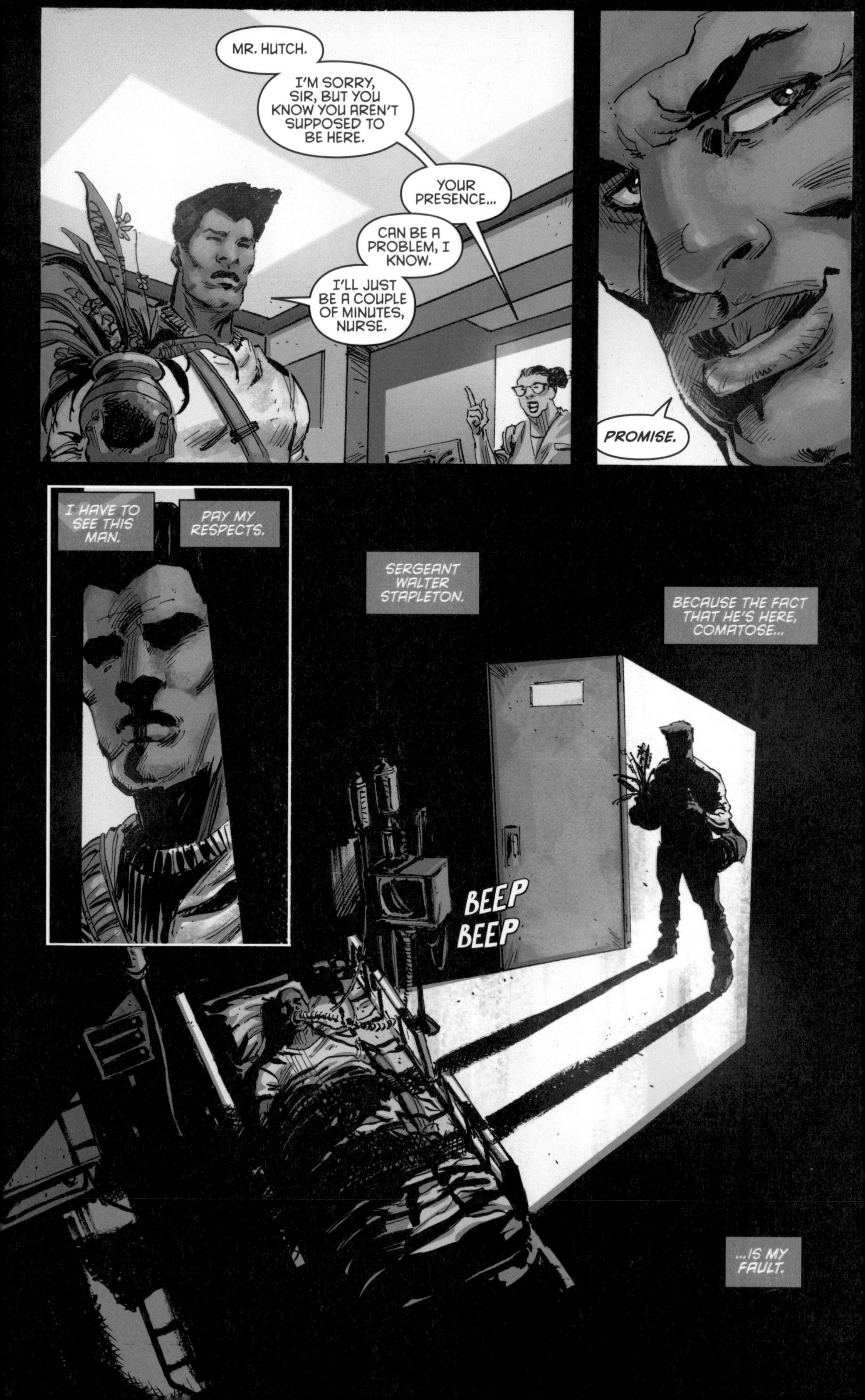
MR. HUTCH.
I'M SORRY, SIR, BUT YOU KNOW YOU AREN'T SUPPOSED TO BE HERE.
YOUR PRESENCE...
CAN BE A PROBLEM, I KNOW.
I'LL JUST BE A COUPLE OF MINUTES, NURSE.
PROMISE.
I HAVE TO SEE THIS MAN.
PAY MY RESPECTS.
SERGEANT WALTER STAPLETON.
BECAUSE THE FACT THAT HE'S HERE, COMATOSE...
BEEP BEEP
...IS MY FAULT.

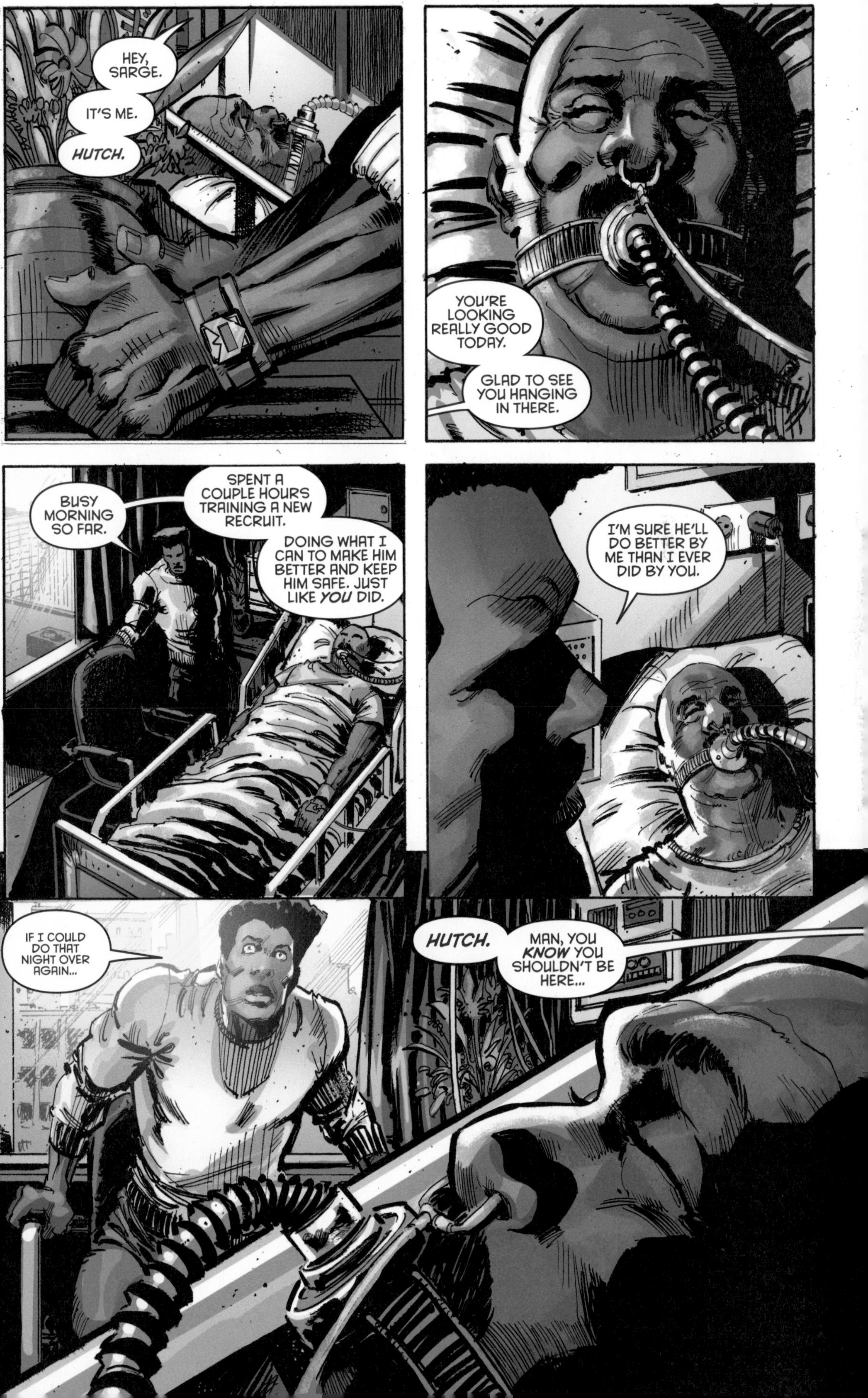
HEY, SARGE.
IT'S ME.
HUTCH.
YOU'RE LOOKING REALLY GOOD TODAY.
GLAD TO SEE YOU HANGING IN THERE.
BUSY MORNING SO FAR.
SPENT A COUPLE HOURS TRAINING A NEW RECRUIT.
DOING WHAT I CAN TO MAKE HIM BETTER AND KEEP HIM SAFE. JUST LIKE YOU DID.
I'M SURE HE'LL DO BETTER BY ME THAN I EVER DID BY YOU.
IF I COULD DO THAT NIGHT OVER AGAIN...
HUTCH.
MAN, YOU KNOW YOU SHOULDN'T BE HERE...

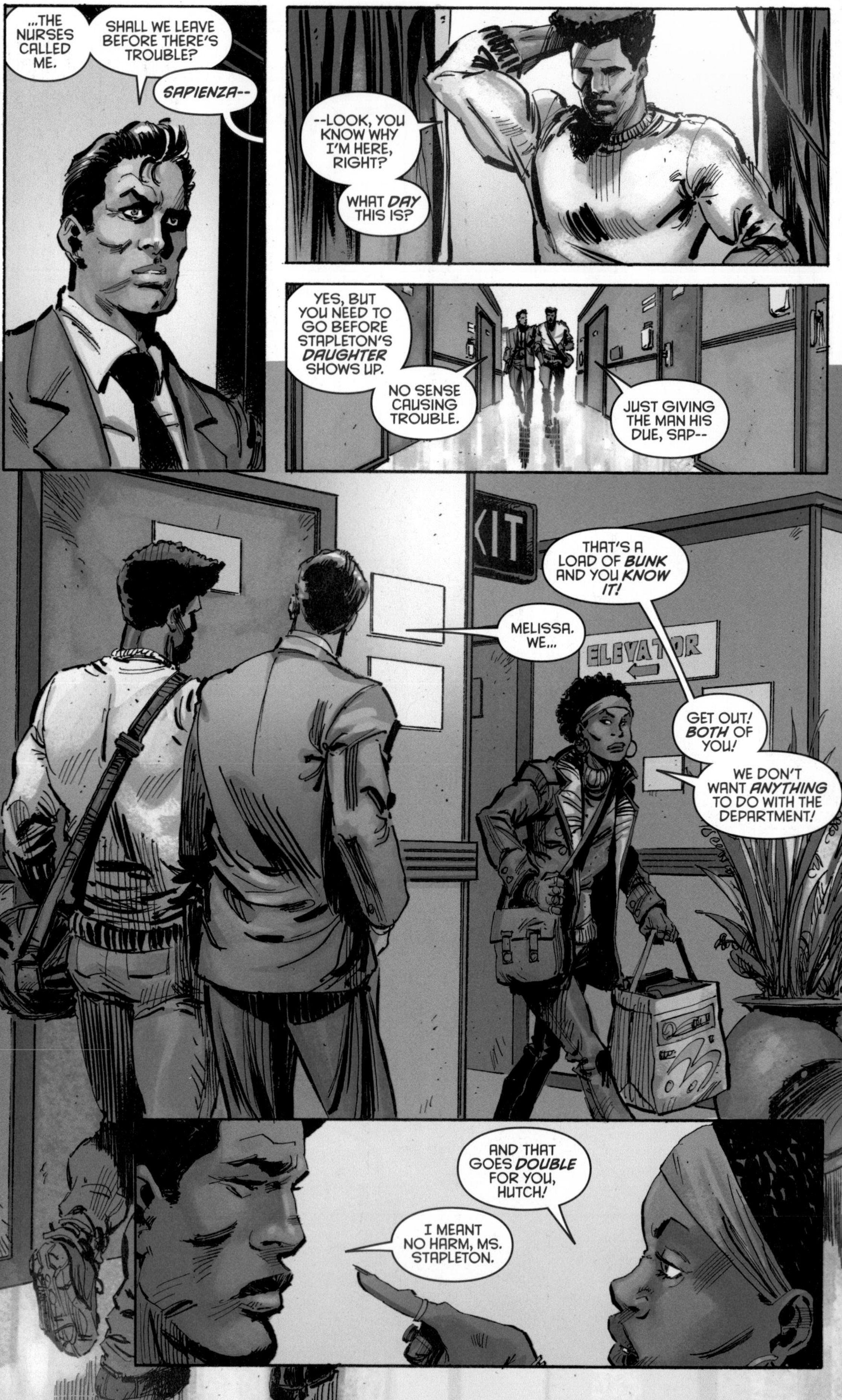
...THE NURSES CALLED ME.
SHALL WE LEAVE BEFORE THERE'S TROUBLE?
SAPIENZA--
--LOOK, YOU KNOW WHY I'M HERE, RIGHT?
WHAT DAY THIS IS?
YES, BUT YOU NEED TO GO BEFORE STAPLETON'S DAUGHTER SHOWS UP.
NO SENSE CAUSING TROUBLE.
JUST GIVING THE MAN HIS DUE, SAP--
XIT
THAT'S A LOAD OF BUNK AND YOU KNOW IT!
MELISSA. WE...
ELEVATOR
GET OUT! BOTH OF YOU!
WE DON'T WANT ANYTHING TO DO WITH THE DEPARTMENT!
AND THAT GOES DOUBLE FOR YOU, HUTCH!
I MEANT NO HARM, MS. STAPLETON.

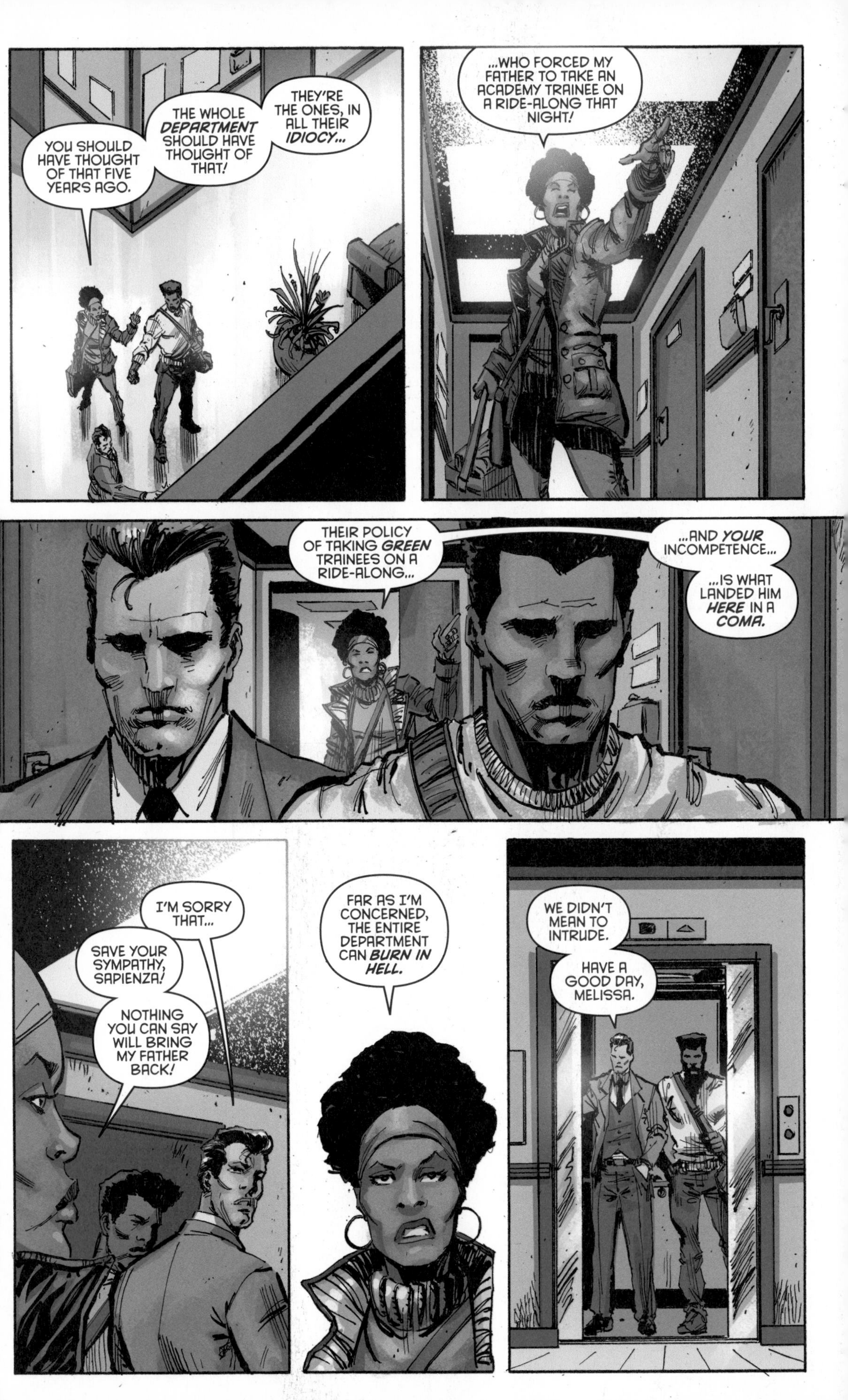

YOU SHOULD HAVE THOUGHT OF THAT FIVE YEARS AGO.
THE WHOLE DEPARTMENT SHOULD HAVE THOUGHT OF THAT!
THEY'RE THE ONES, IN ALL THEIR IDIOCY...
...WHO FORCED MY FATHER TO TAKE AN ACADEMY TRAINEE ON A RIDE-ALONG THAT NIGHT!
THEIR POLICY OF TAKING GREEN TRAINEES ON A RIDE-ALONG...
...AND YOUR INCOMPETENCE...
...IS WHAT LANDED HIM HERE IN A COMA.
I'M SORRY THAT...
SAVE YOUR SYMPATHY, SAPIENZA!
NOTHING YOU CAN SAY WILL BRING MY FATHER BACK!
FAR AS I'M CONCERNED, THE ENTIRE DEPARTMENT CAN BURN IN HELL.
WE DIDN'T MEAN TO INTRUDE.
HAVE A GOOD DAY, MELISSA.

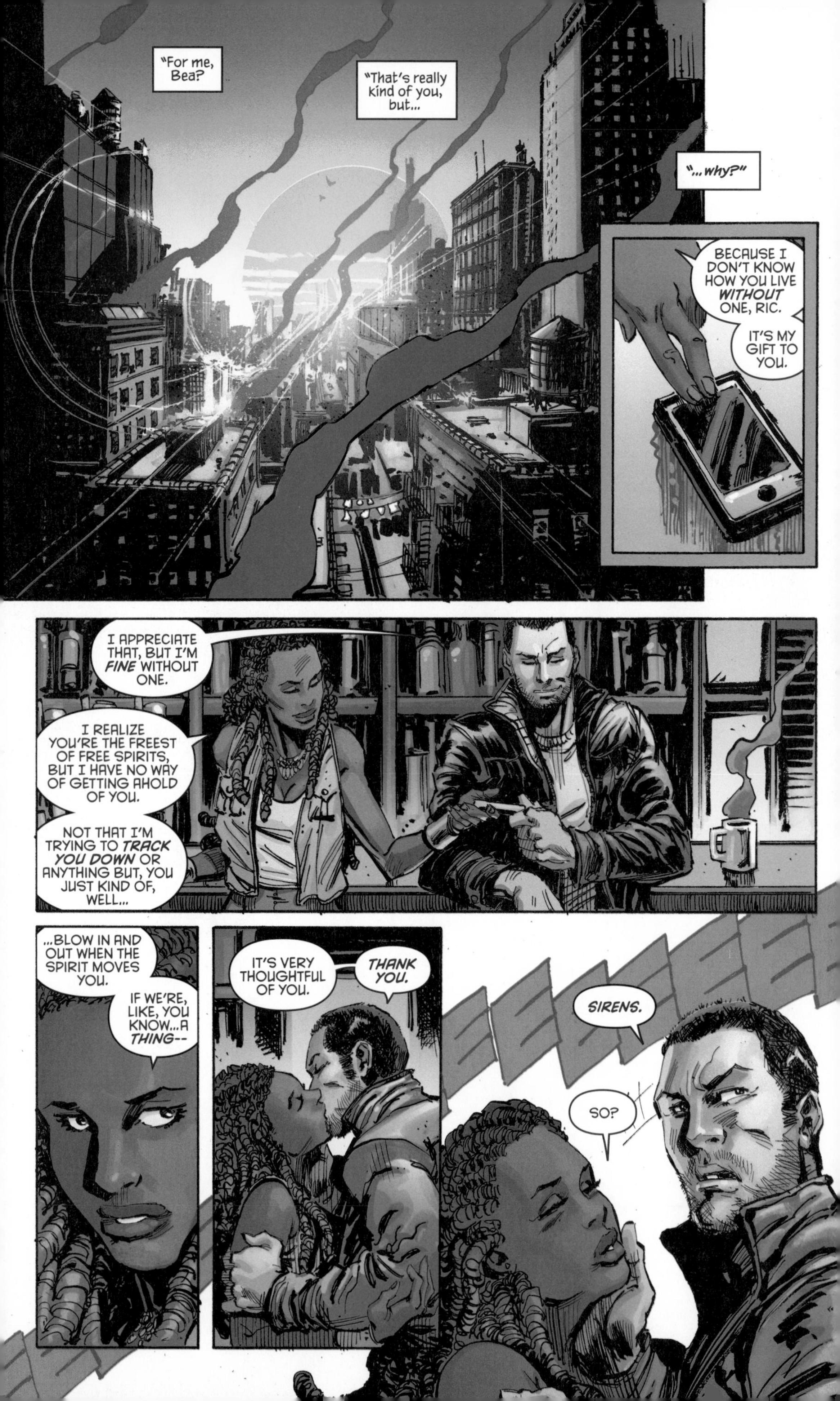

"For me, Bea?
"That's really kind of you, but...
"...why?"
BECAUSE I DON'T KNOW HOW YOU LIVE WITHOUT ONE, RIC.
IT'S MY GIFT TO YOU.
I APPRECIATE THAT, BUT I'M FINE WITHOUT ONE.
I REALIZE YOU'RE THE FREEST OF FREE SPIRITS, BUT I HAVE NO WAY OF GETTING AHOLD OF YOU.
NOT THAT I'M TRYING TO TRACK YOU DOWN OR ANYTHING BUT, YOU JUST KIND OF, WELL...
...BLOW IN AND OUT WHEN THE SPIRIT MOVES YOU.
IF WE'RE, LIKE, YOU KNOW...A THING--
IT'S VERY THOUGHTFUL OF YOU.
THANK YOU.
SIRENS.
SO?

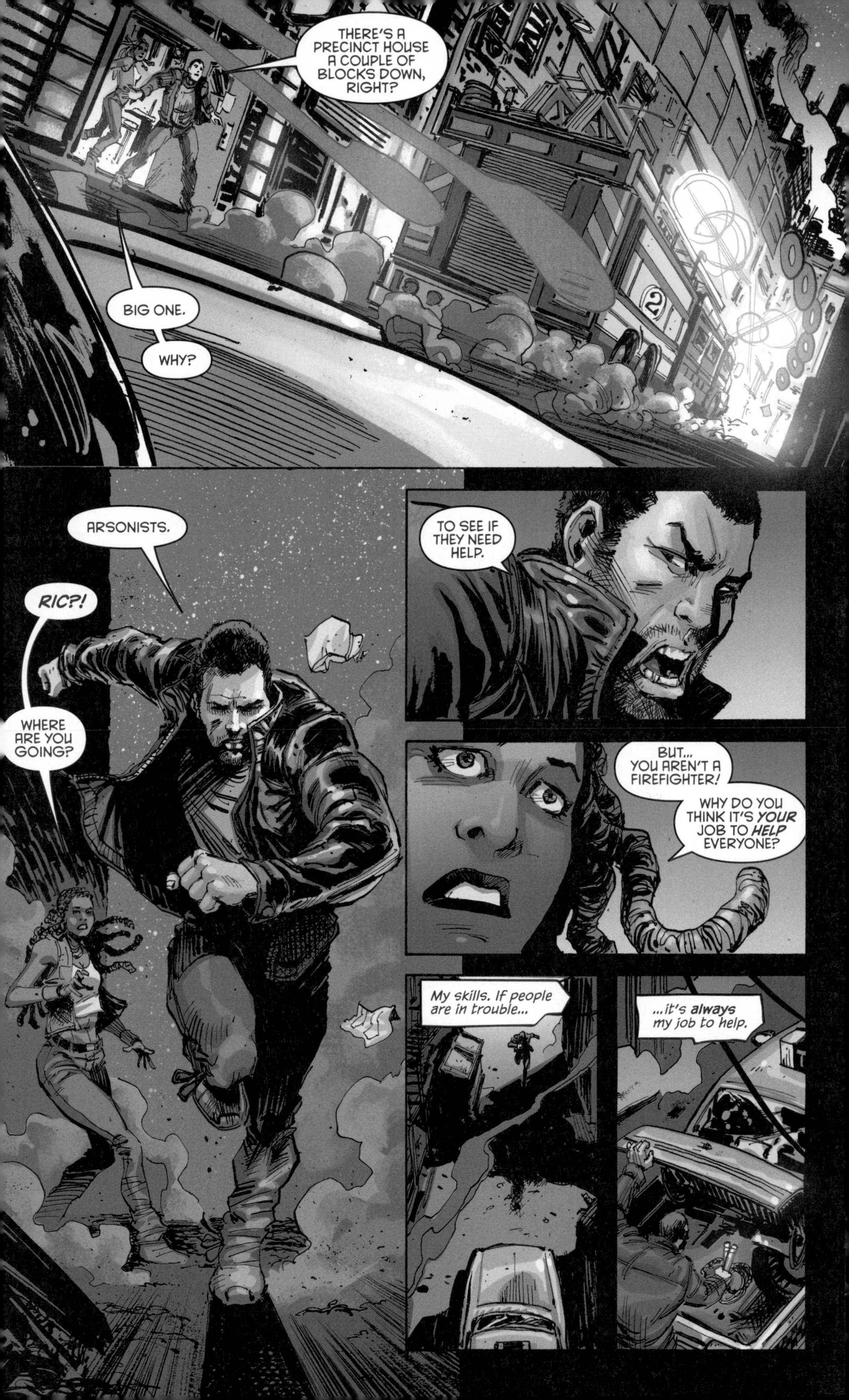
THERE'S A PRECINCT HOUSE A COUPLE OF BLOCKS DOWN, RIGHT?
BIG ONE.
WHY?
ARSONISTS.
RIC?!
WHERE ARE YOU GOING?
TO SEE IF THEY NEED HELP.
BUT... YOU AREN'T A FIREFIGHTER!
WHY DO YOU THINK IT'S *YOUR* JOB TO *HELP* EVERYONE?
My skills. If people are in trouble...
*...it's **always** my job to help.*
2

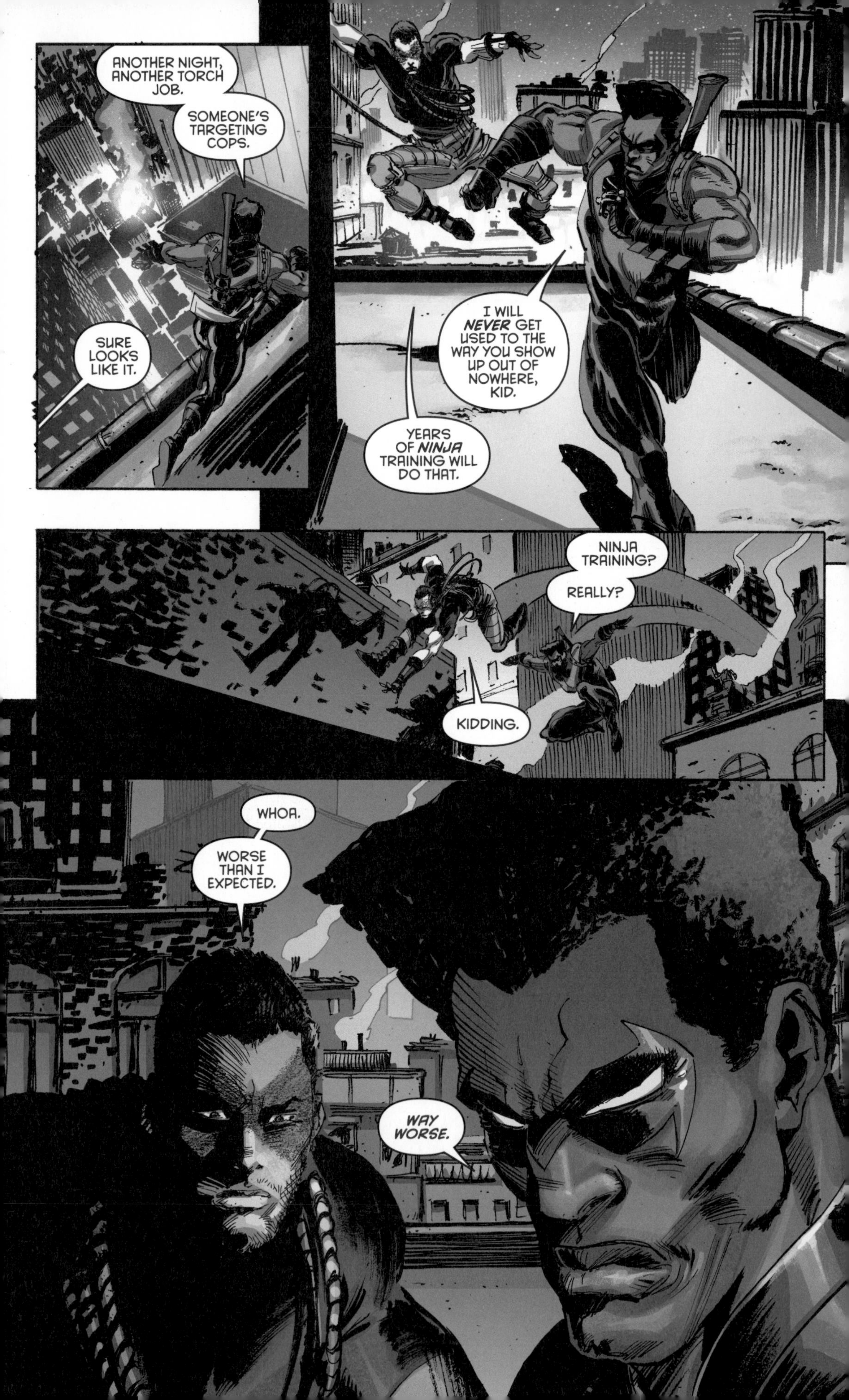

ANOTHER NIGHT, ANOTHER TORCH JOB.
SOMEONE'S TARGETING COPS.
SURE LOOKS LIKE IT.
I WILL *NEVER* GET USED TO THE WAY YOU SHOW UP OUT OF NOWHERE, KID.
YEARS OF *NINJA* TRAINING WILL DO THAT.
NINJA TRAINING?
REALLY?
KIDDING.
WHOA.
WORSE THAN I EXPECTED.
WAY WORSE.

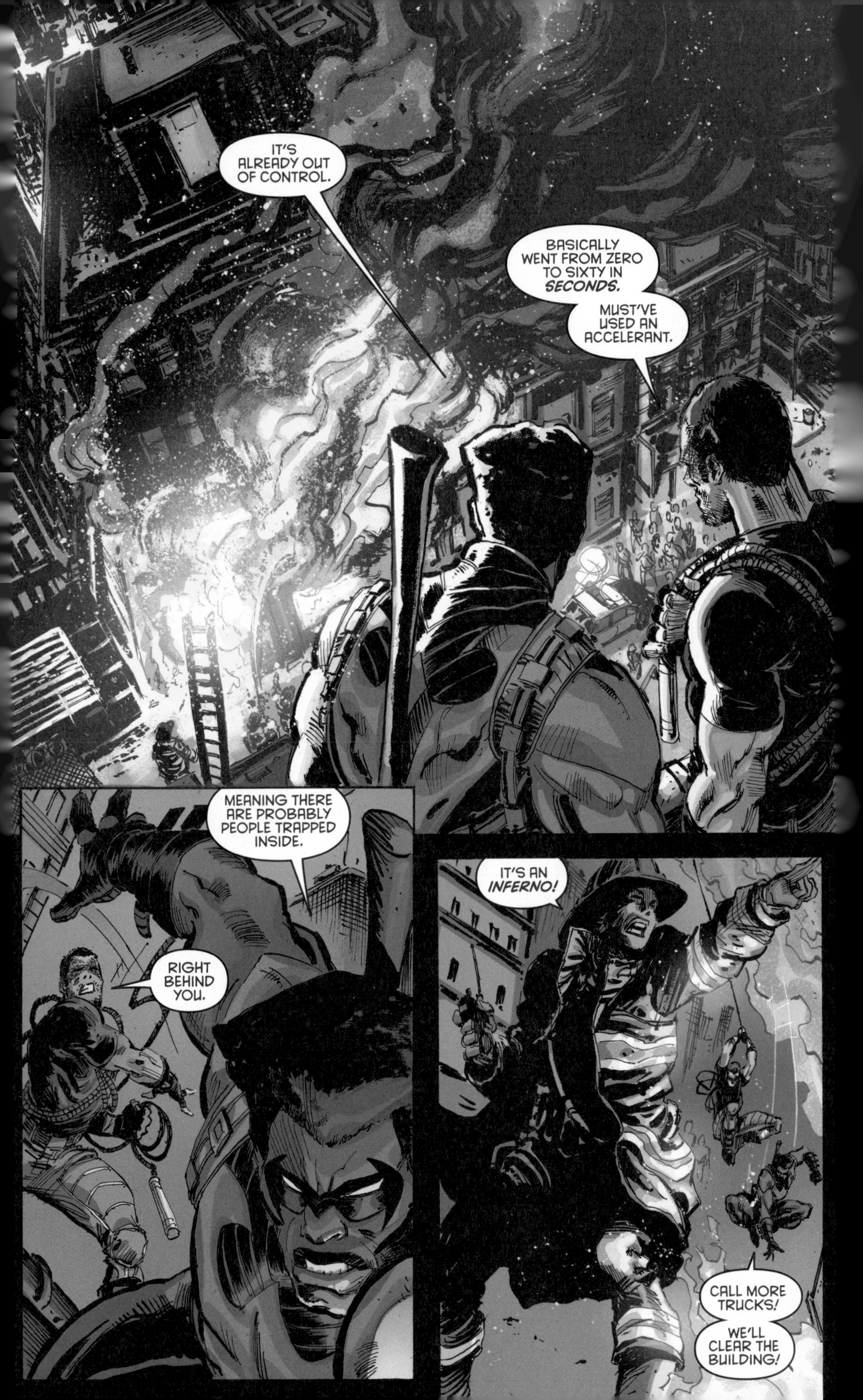
IT'S ALREADY OUT OF CONTROL.
BASICALLY WENT FROM ZERO TO SIXTY IN *SECONDS.*
MUST'VE USED AN ACCELERANT.
MEANING THERE ARE PROBABLY PEOPLE TRAPPED INSIDE.
RIGHT BEHIND YOU.
IT'S AN *INFERNO!*
CALL MORE TRUCKS!
WE'LL CLEAR THE BUILDING!

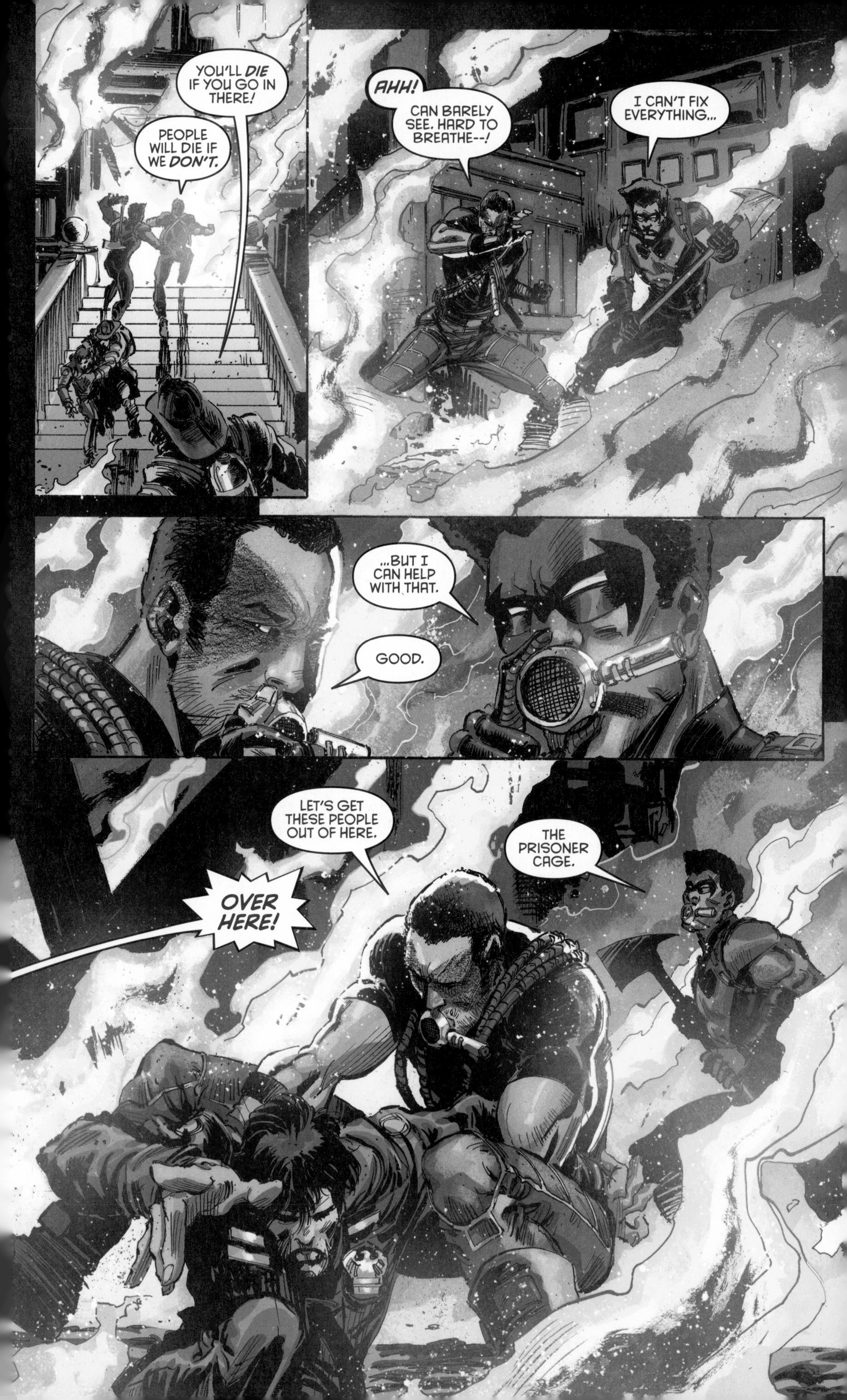
YOU'LL DIE IF YOU GO IN THERE!
PEOPLE WILL DIE IF WE DON'T.
AHH!
CAN BARELY SEE. HARD TO BREATHE--!
I CAN'T FIX EVERYTHING...
...BUT I CAN HELP WITH THAT.
GOOD.
LET'S GET THESE PEOPLE OUT OF HERE.
THE PRISONER CAGE.
OVER HERE!

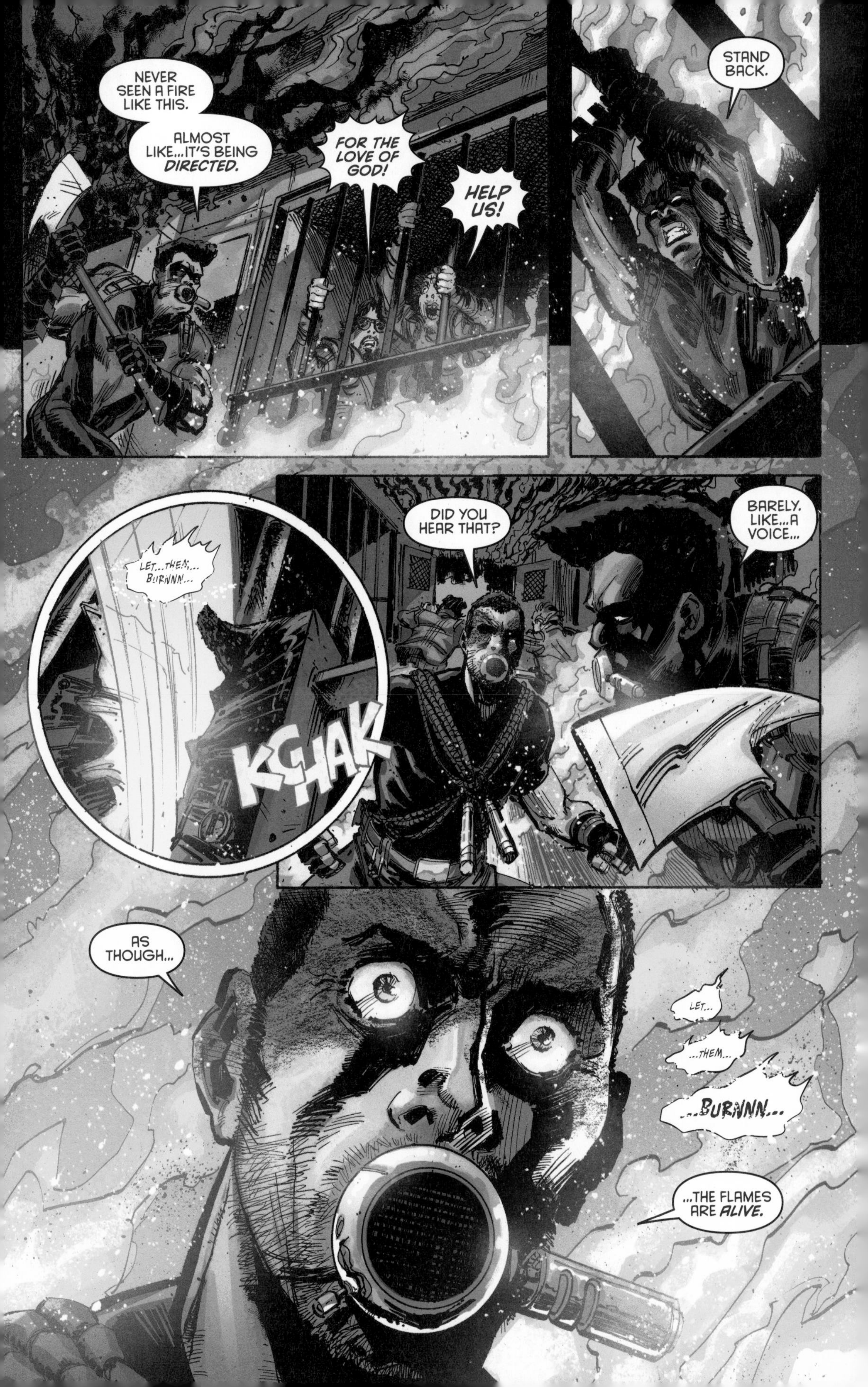
NEVER SEEN A FIRE LIKE THIS.
ALMOST LIKE...IT'S BEING *DIRECTED.*
FOR THE LOVE OF GOD!
HELP US!
STAND BACK.
LET...THEM... BURNNN...
KCHAK
DID YOU HEAR THAT?
BARELY. LIKE...A VOICE...
AS THOUGH...
LET...
...THEM...
...BURNNN...
...THE FLAMES ARE *ALIVE.*

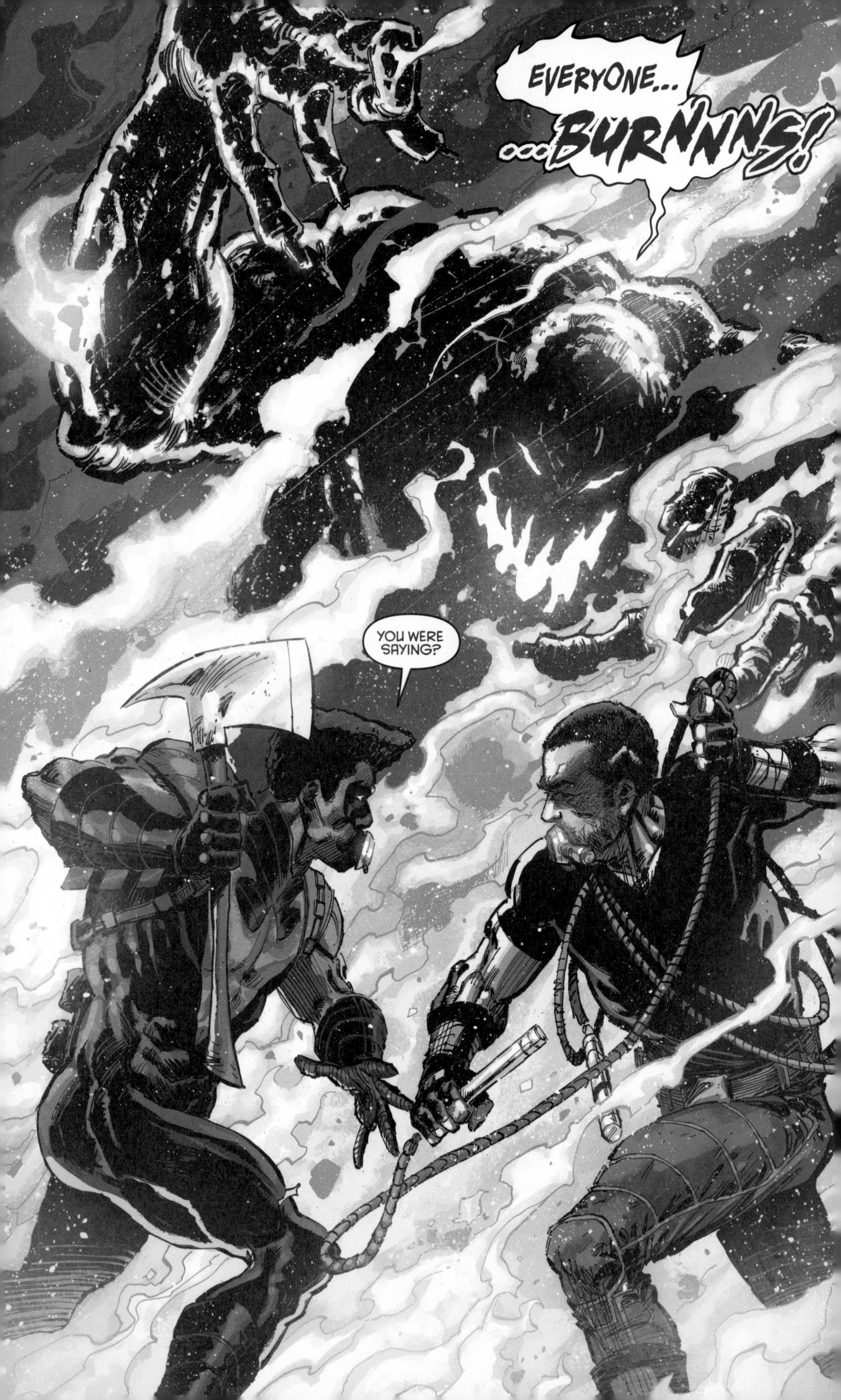
EVERYONE...
...BURNNNS!
YOU WERE SAYING?

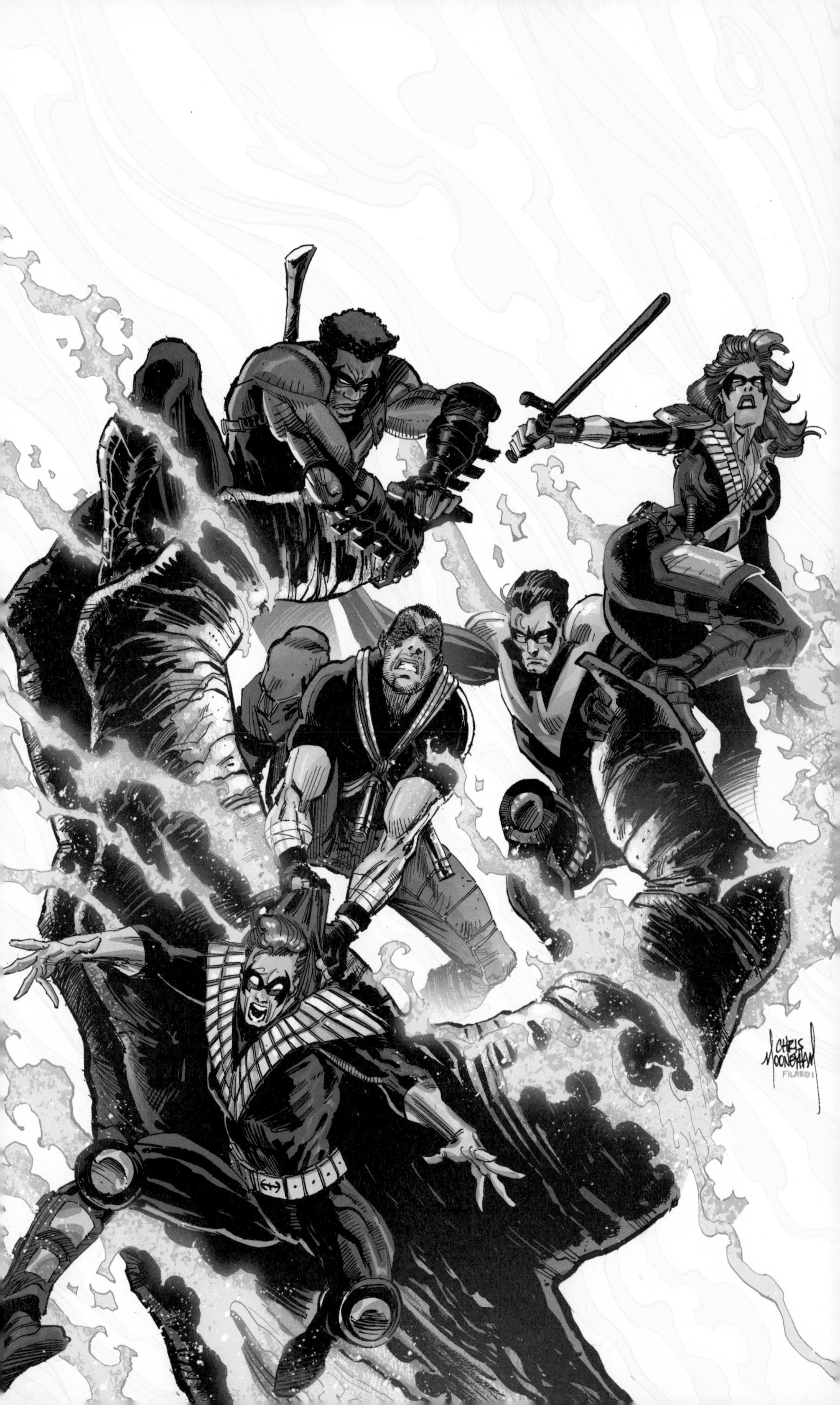
CHRIS MOONEYHAM
FILARDI

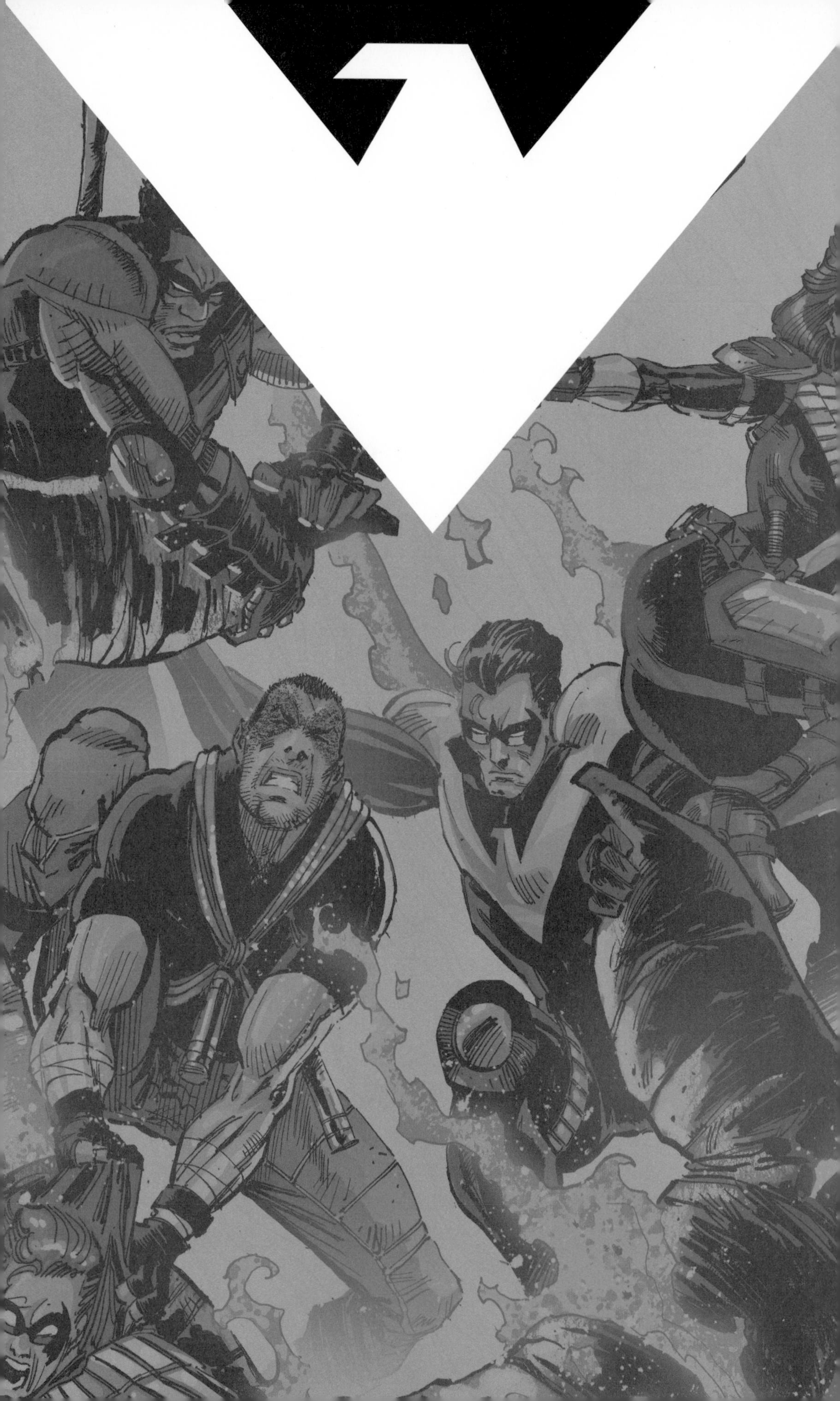

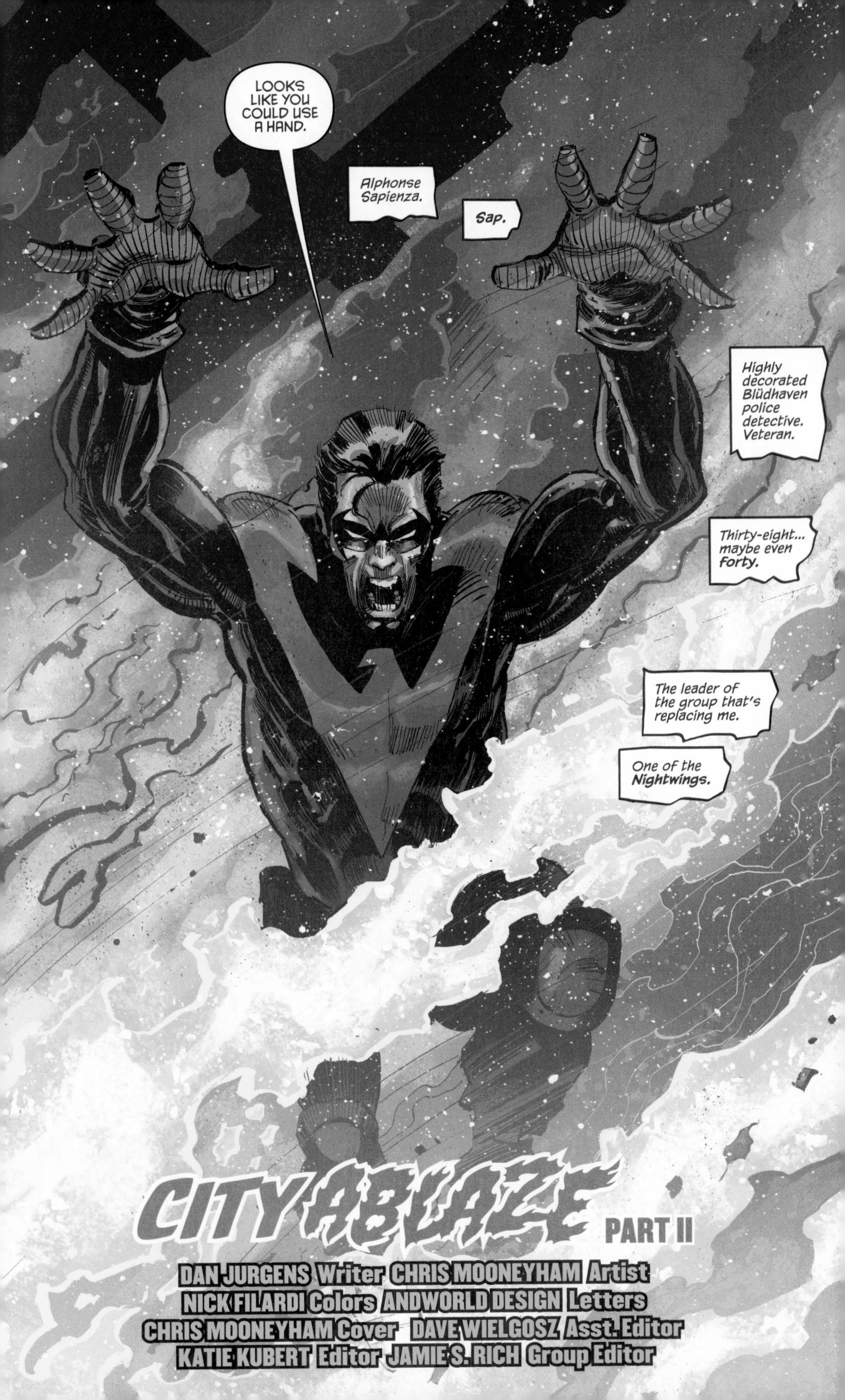
LOOKS LIKE YOU COULD USE A HAND.
Alphonse Sapienza.
Sap.
Highly decorated Blüdhaven police detective. Veteran.
Thirty-eight... maybe even Forty.
The leader of the group that's replacing me.
One of the Nightwings.
CITY ABLAZE PART II
DAN JURGENS Writer CHRIS MOONEYHAM Artist
NICK FILARDI Colors ANDWORLD DESIGN Letters
CHRIS MOONEYHAM Cover DAVE WIELGOSZ Asst. Editor
KATIE KUBERT Editor JAMIE S. RICH Group Editor

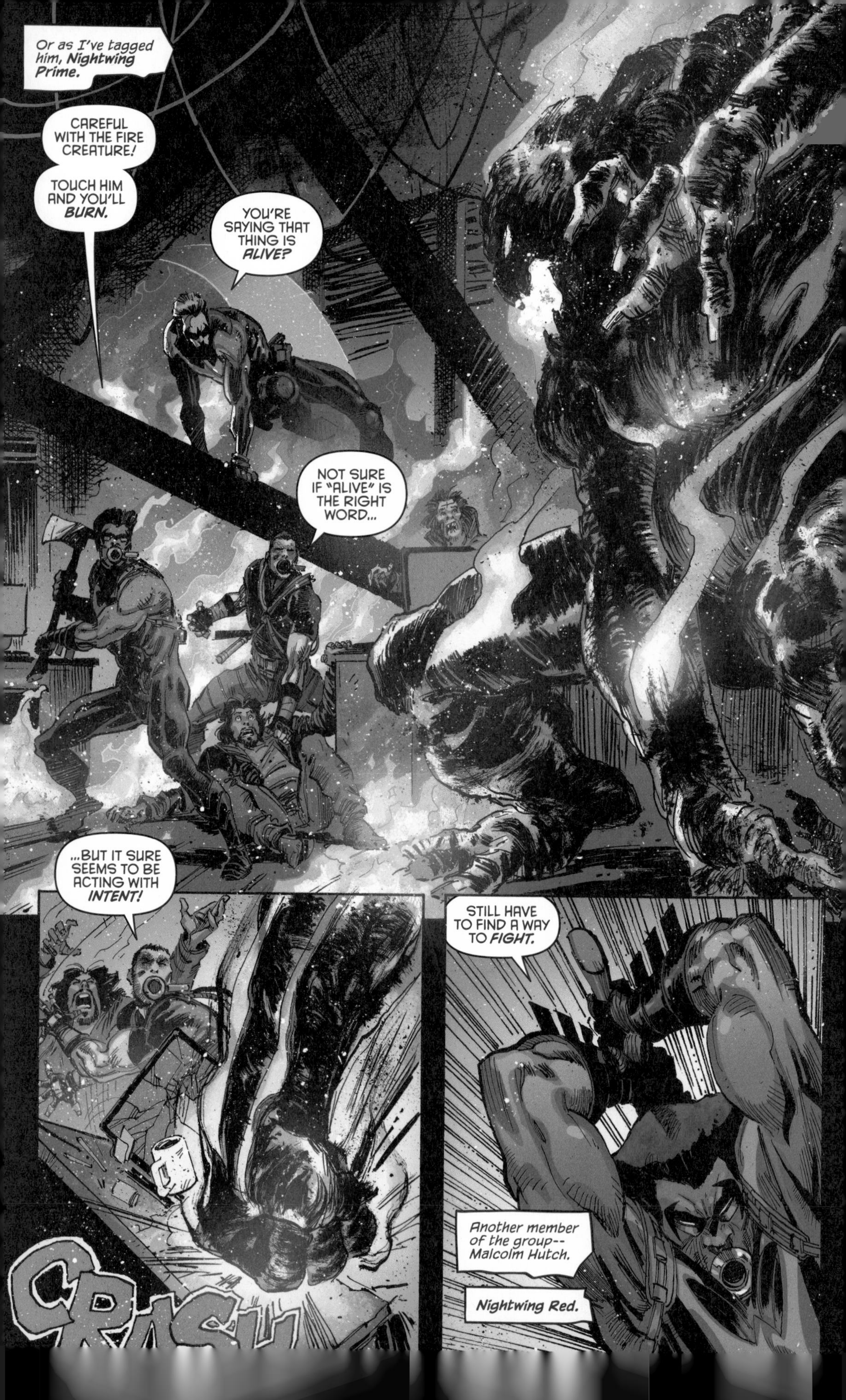
Or as I've tagged him, Nightwing Prime.
CAREFUL WITH THE FIRE CREATURE!
TOUCH HIM AND YOU'LL BURN.
YOU'RE SAYING THAT THING IS ALIVE?
NOT SURE IF "ALIVE" IS THE RIGHT WORD...
...BUT IT SURE SEEMS TO BE ACTING WITH INTENT!
CRASH
STILL HAVE TO FIND A WAY TO FIGHT.
Another member of the group-- Malcolm Hutch.
Nightwing Red.

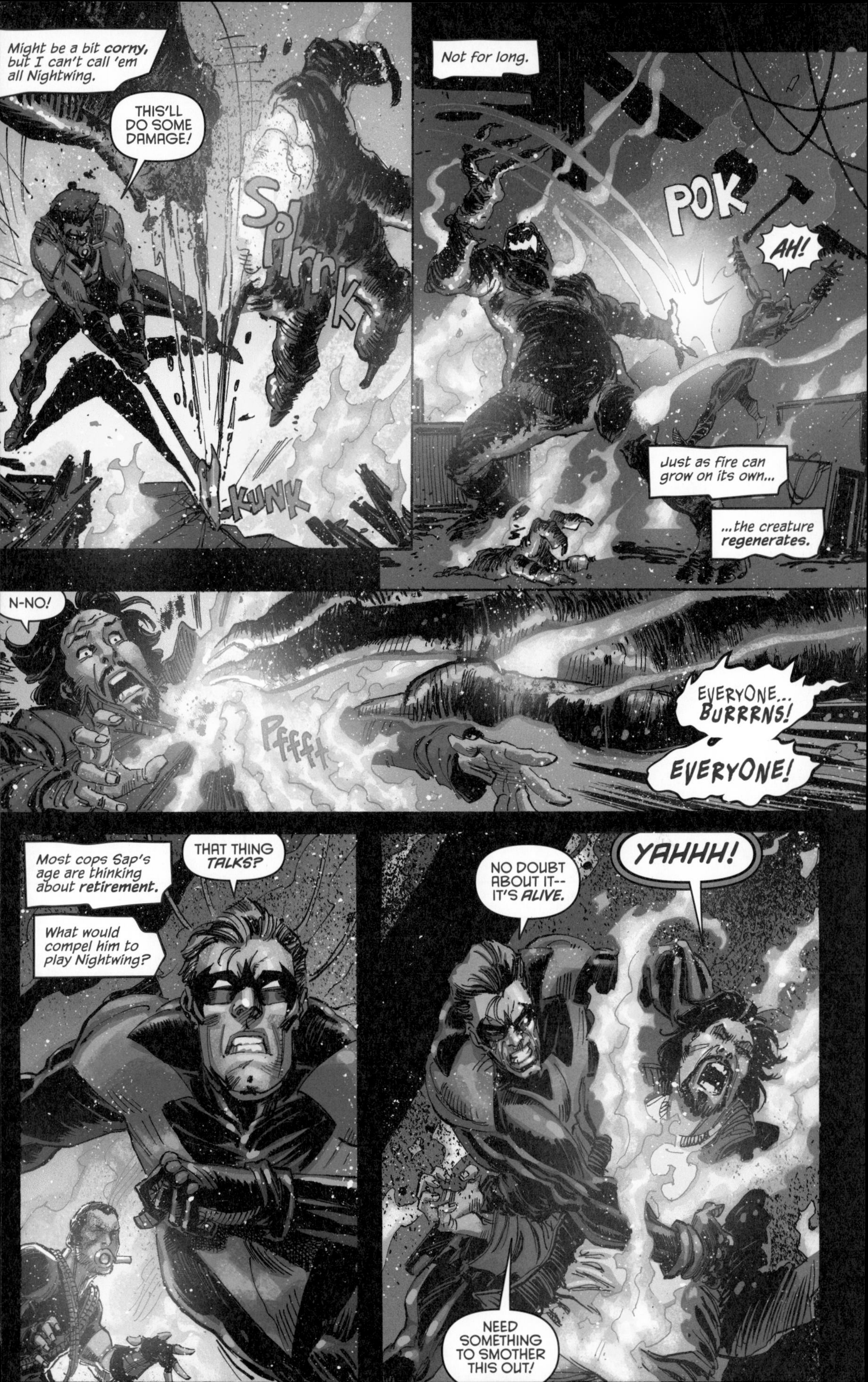
Might be a bit corny, but I can't call 'em all Nightwing.
THIS'LL DO SOME DAMAGE!
Splrrk
KUNK
Not for long.
POK
AH!
Just as fire can grow on its own...
...the creature regenerates.
N-NO!
Pffft
EVERYONE... BURRRNS!
EVERYONE!
Most cops Sap's age are thinking about retirement.
THAT THING TALKS?
What would compel him to play Nightwing?
NO DOUBT ABOUT IT-- IT'S ALIVE.
YAHHH!
NEED SOMETHING TO SMOTHER THIS OUT!

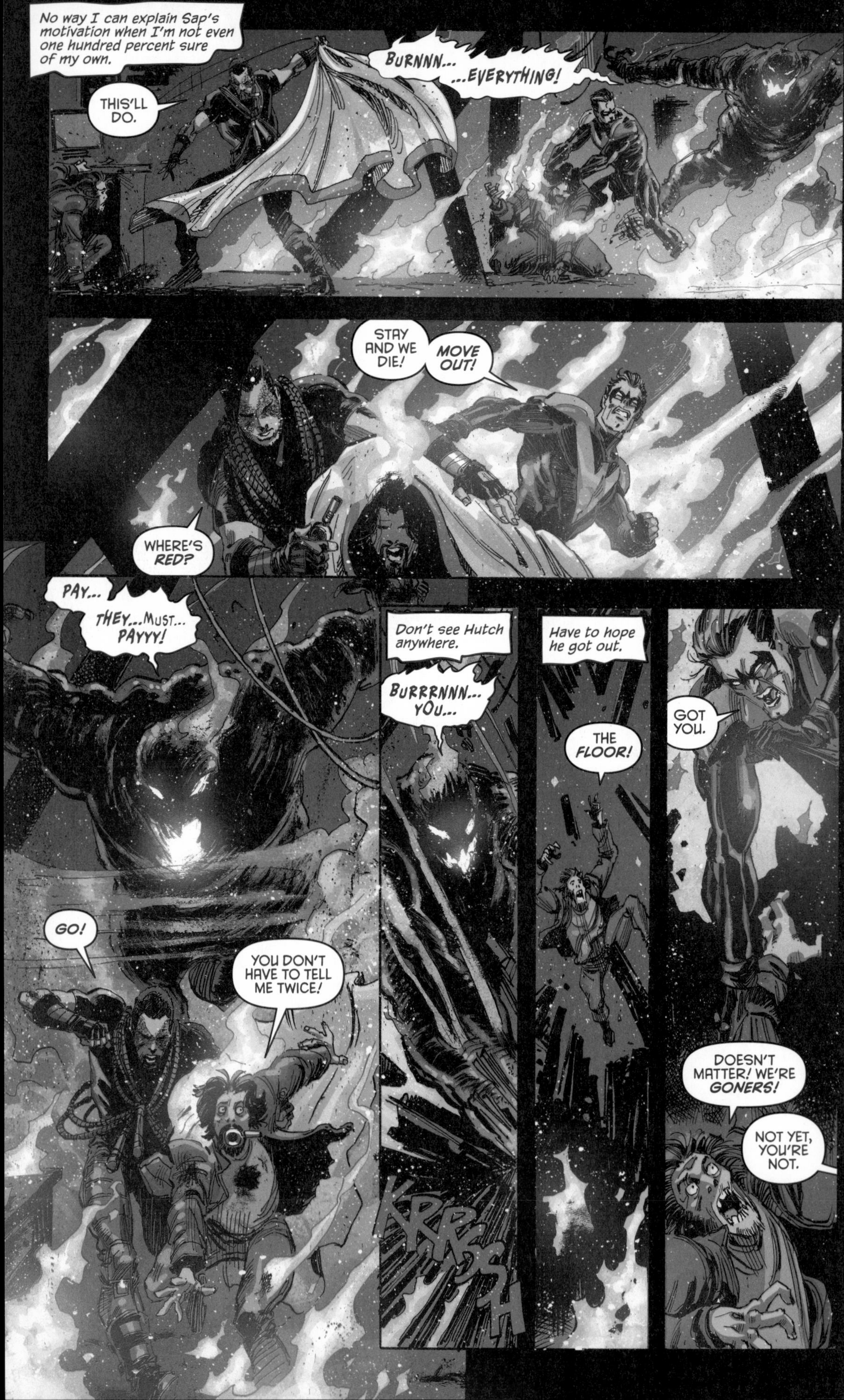

No way I can explain Sap's motivation when I'm not even one hundred percent sure of my own.
THIS'LL DO.
BURNNN... ...EVERYTHING!
STAY AND WE DIE!
MOVE OUT!
WHERE'S RED?
PAY...
THEY...MUST... PAYYY!
GO!
YOU DON'T HAVE TO TELL ME TWICE!
Don't see Hutch anywhere.
BURRRNNN... YOU...
KRRRSSH
Have to hope he got out.
THE FLOOR!
GOT YOU.
DOESN'T MATTER! WE'RE GONERS!
NOT YET, YOU'RE NOT.

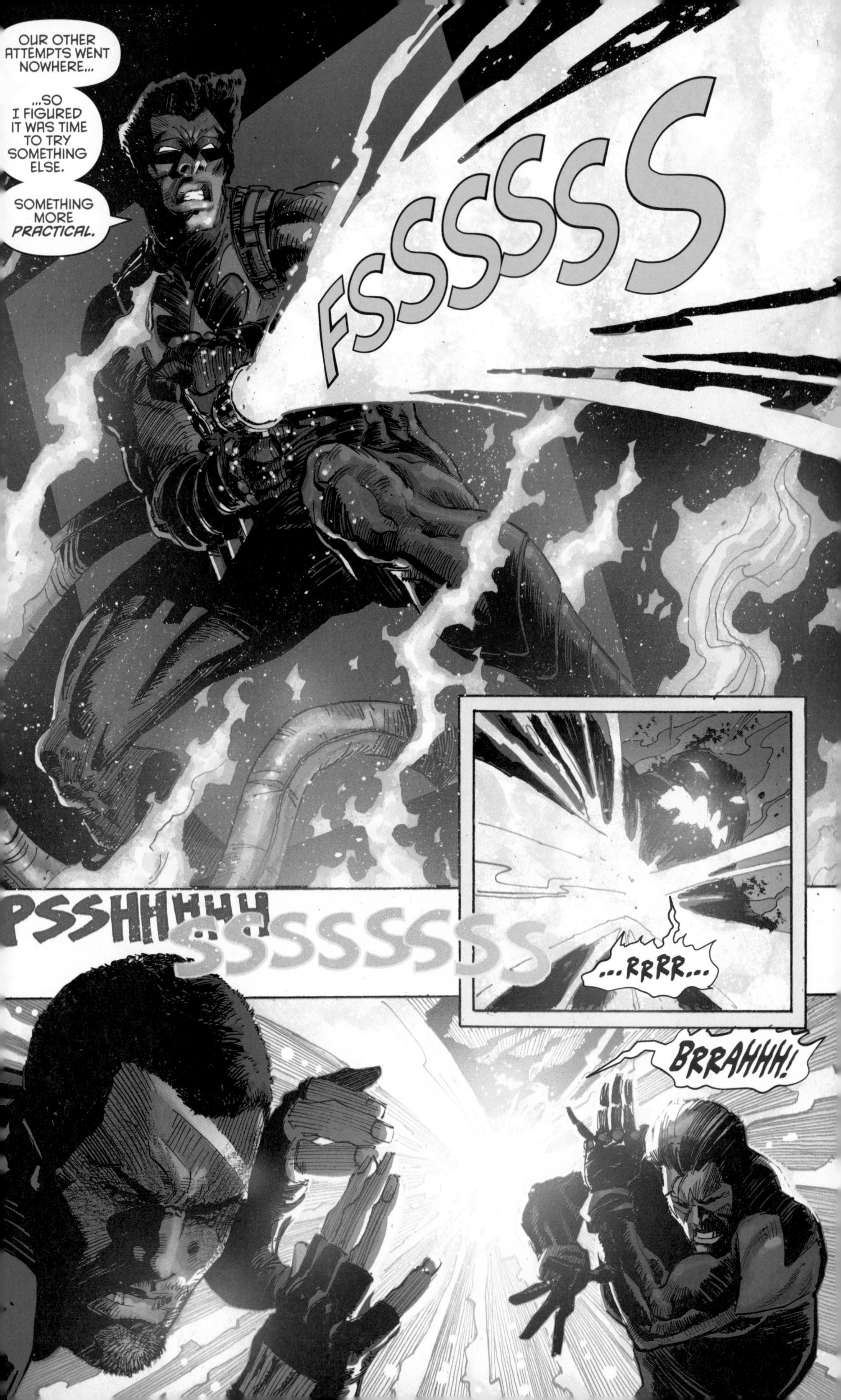
OUR OTHER ATTEMPTS WENT NOWHERE...
...SO I FIGURED IT WAS TIME TO TRY SOMETHING ELSE.
SOMETHING MORE *PRACTICAL.*
FSSSSSS
PSSHHHHH
SSSSSSSS
...RRRR...
BRRAHHH!

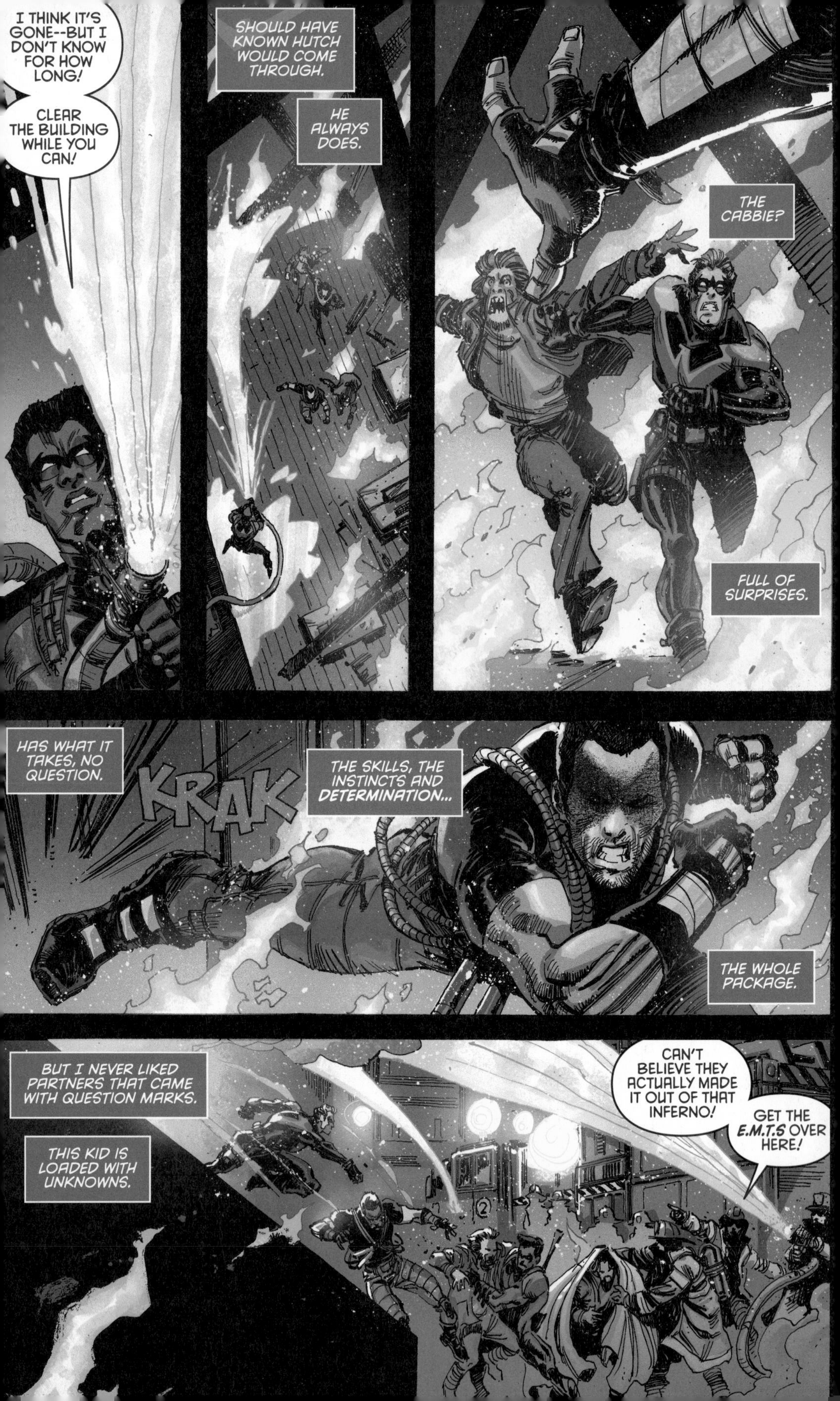
I THINK IT'S GONE--BUT I DON'T KNOW FOR HOW LONG!
CLEAR THE BUILDING WHILE YOU CAN!
SHOULD HAVE KNOWN HUTCH WOULD COME THROUGH.
HE ALWAYS DOES.
THE CABBIE?
FULL OF SURPRISES.
HAS WHAT IT TAKES, NO QUESTION.
KRAK
THE SKILLS, THE INSTINCTS AND DETERMINATION...
THE WHOLE PACKAGE.
BUT I NEVER LIKED PARTNERS THAT CAME WITH QUESTION MARKS.
THIS KID IS LOADED WITH UNKNOWNS.
CAN'T BELIEVE THEY ACTUALLY MADE IT OUT OF THAT INFERNO!
GET THE E.M.T.S OVER HERE!

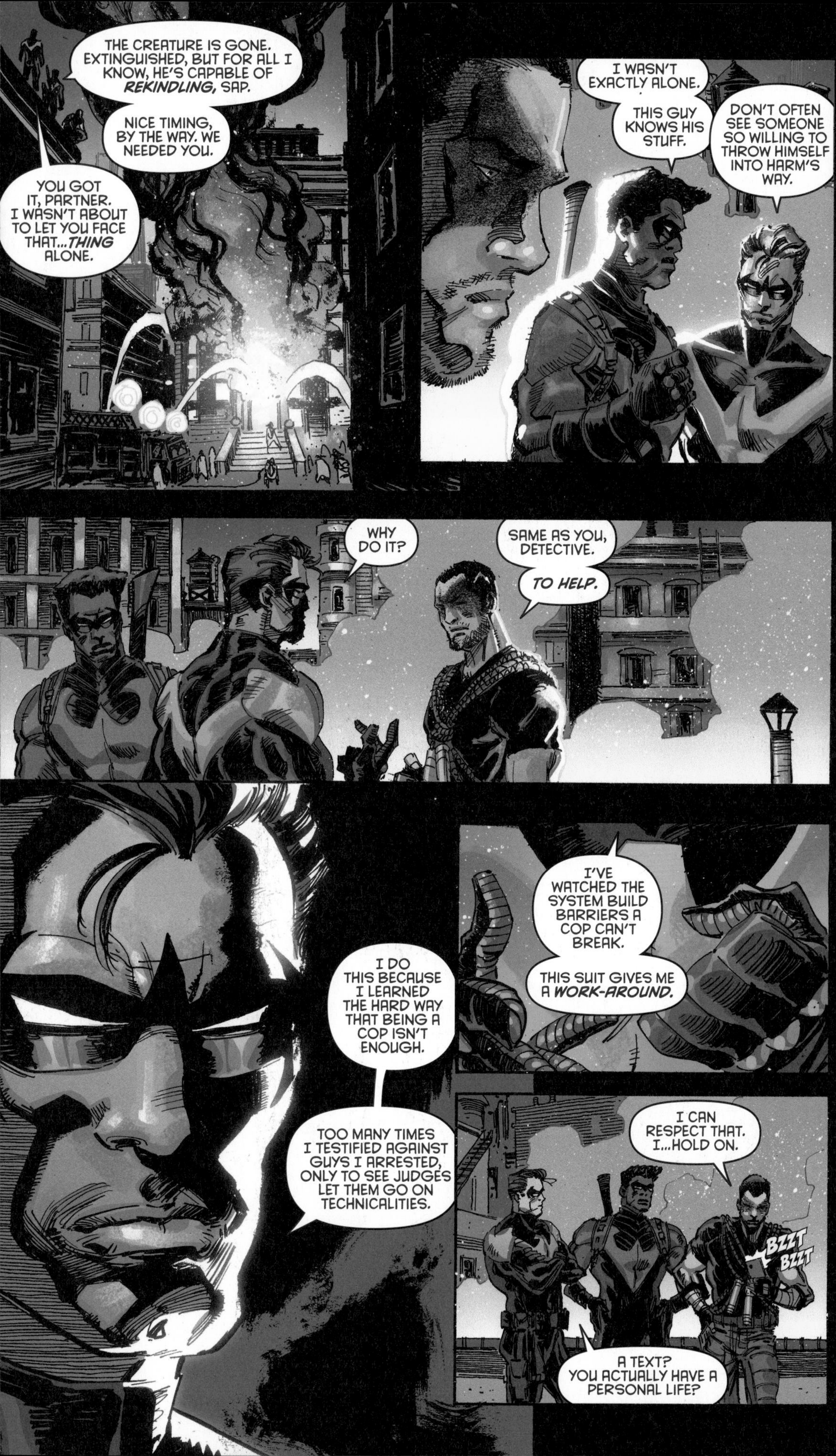
THE CREATURE IS GONE. EXTINGUISHED, BUT FOR ALL I KNOW, HE'S CAPABLE OF *REKINDLING*, SAP.
NICE TIMING, BY THE WAY. WE NEEDED YOU.
YOU GOT IT, PARTNER. I WASN'T ABOUT TO LET YOU FACE THAT...*THING* ALONE.
I WASN'T EXACTLY ALONE.
THIS GUY KNOWS HIS STUFF.
DON'T OFTEN SEE SOMEONE SO WILLING TO THROW HIMSELF INTO HARM'S WAY.
WHY DO IT?
SAME AS YOU, DETECTIVE.
TO HELP.
I DO THIS BECAUSE I LEARNED THE HARD WAY THAT BEING A COP ISN'T ENOUGH.
TOO MANY TIMES I TESTIFIED AGAINST GUYS I ARRESTED, ONLY TO SEE JUDGES LET THEM GO ON TECHNICALITIES.
I'VE WATCHED THE SYSTEM BUILD BARRIERS A COP CAN'T BREAK.
THIS SUIT GIVES ME A *WORK-AROUND.*
I CAN RESPECT THAT. I...HOLD ON.
BZZT BZZT
A TEXT? YOU ACTUALLY HAVE A PERSONAL LIFE?

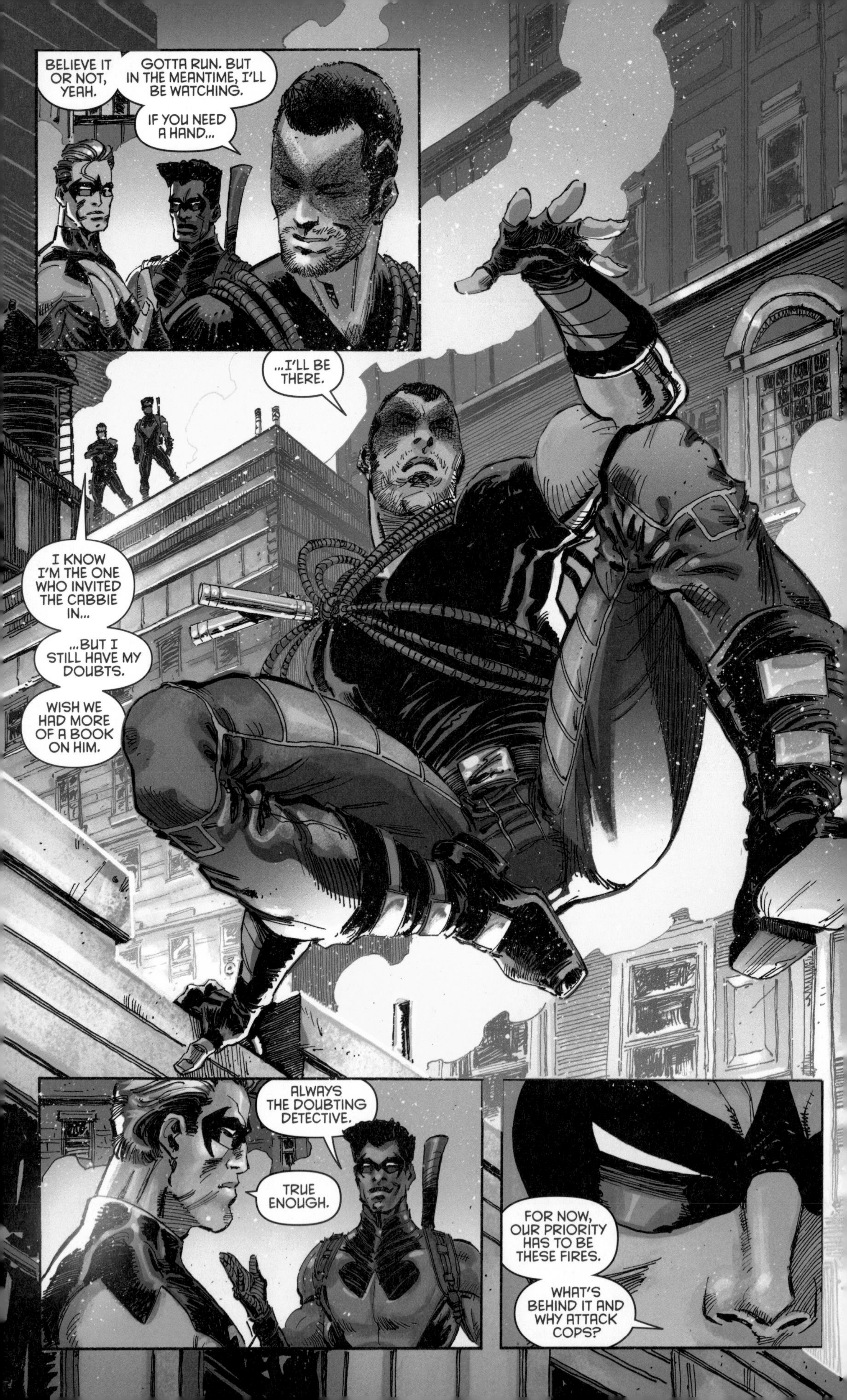
BELIEVE IT OR NOT, YEAH.
GOTTA RUN. BUT IN THE MEANTIME, I'LL BE WATCHING.
IF YOU NEED A HAND...
...I'LL BE THERE.
I KNOW I'M THE ONE WHO INVITED THE CABBIE IN...
...BUT I STILL HAVE MY DOUBTS.
WISH WE HAD MORE OF A BOOK ON HIM.
ALWAYS THE DOUBTING DETECTIVE.
TRUE ENOUGH.
FOR NOW, OUR PRIORITY HAS TO BE THESE FIRES.
WHAT'S BEHIND IT AND WHY ATTACK COPS?

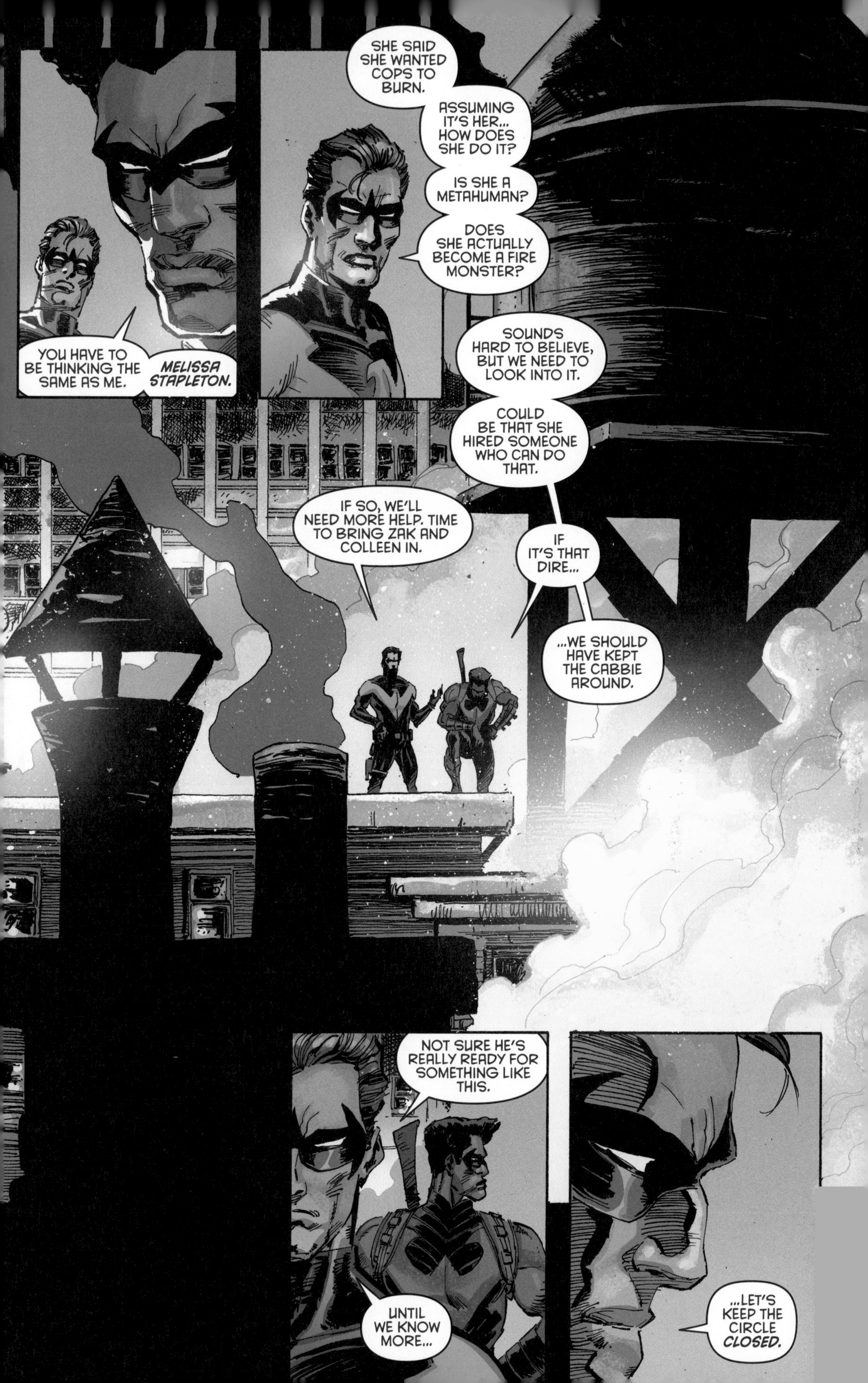
YOU HAVE TO BE THINKING THE SAME AS ME.
MELISSA STAPLETON.
SHE SAID SHE WANTED COPS TO BURN.
ASSUMING IT'S HER... HOW DOES SHE DO IT?
IS SHE A METAHUMAN?
DOES SHE ACTUALLY BECOME A FIRE MONSTER?
SOUNDS HARD TO BELIEVE, BUT WE NEED TO LOOK INTO IT.
COULD BE THAT SHE HIRED SOMEONE WHO CAN DO THAT.
IF SO, WE'LL NEED MORE HELP. TIME TO BRING ZAK AND COLLEEN IN.
IF IT'S THAT DIRE...
...WE SHOULD HAVE KEPT THE CABBIE AROUND.
NOT SURE HE'S REALLY READY FOR SOMETHING LIKE THIS.
UNTIL WE KNOW MORE...
...LET'S KEEP THE CIRCLE CLOSED.

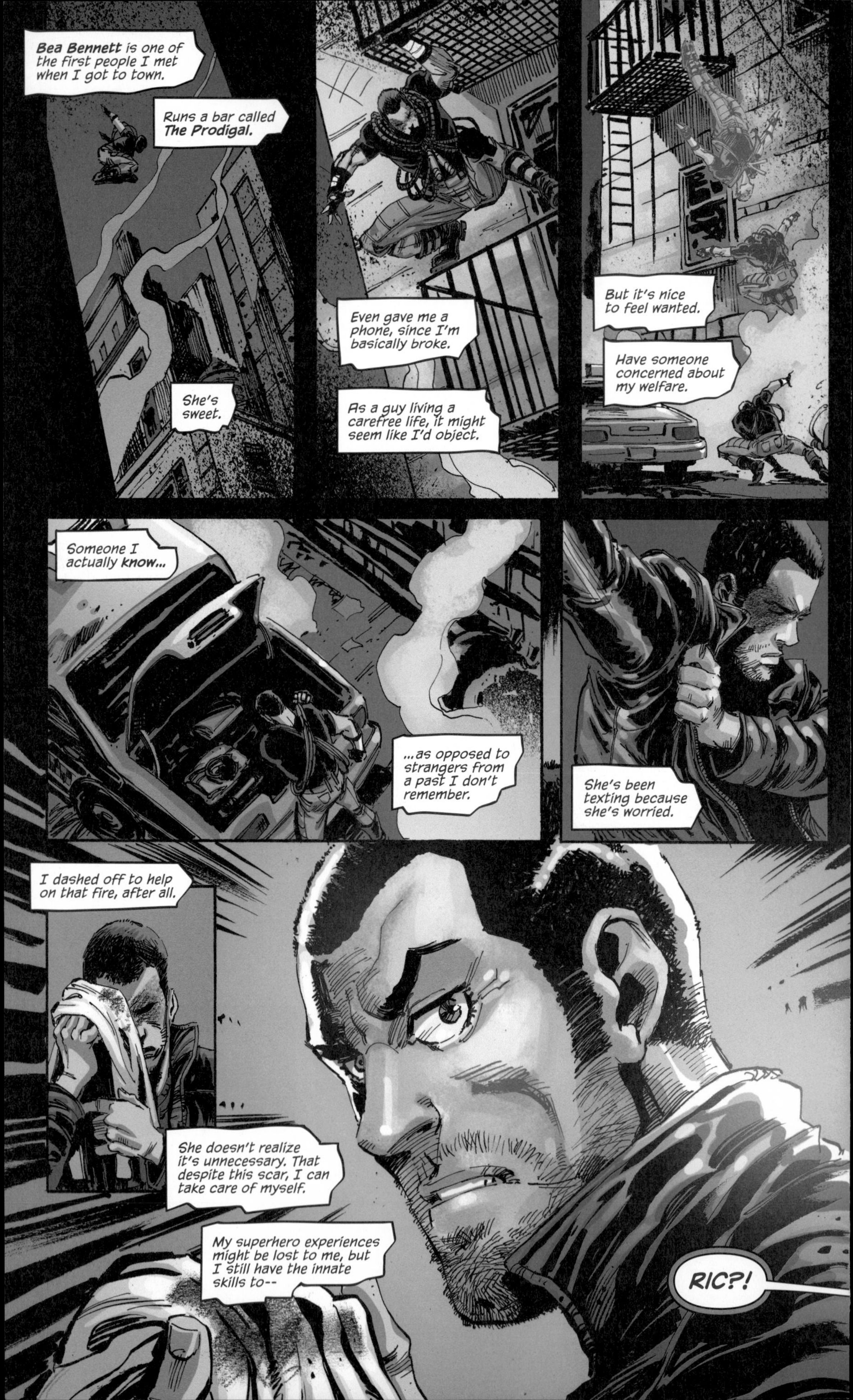
Bea Bennett is one of the first people I met when I got to town.
Runs a bar called The Prodigal.
She's sweet.
Even gave me a phone, since I'm basically broke.
As a guy living a carefree life, it might seem like I'd object.
But it's nice to feel wanted.
Have someone concerned about my welfare.
Someone I actually know...
...as opposed to strangers from a past I don't remember.
She's been texting because she's worried.
I dashed off to help on that fire, after all.
She doesn't realize it's unnecessary. That despite this scar, I can take care of myself.
My superhero experiences might be lost to me, but I still have the innate skills to--
RIC?!

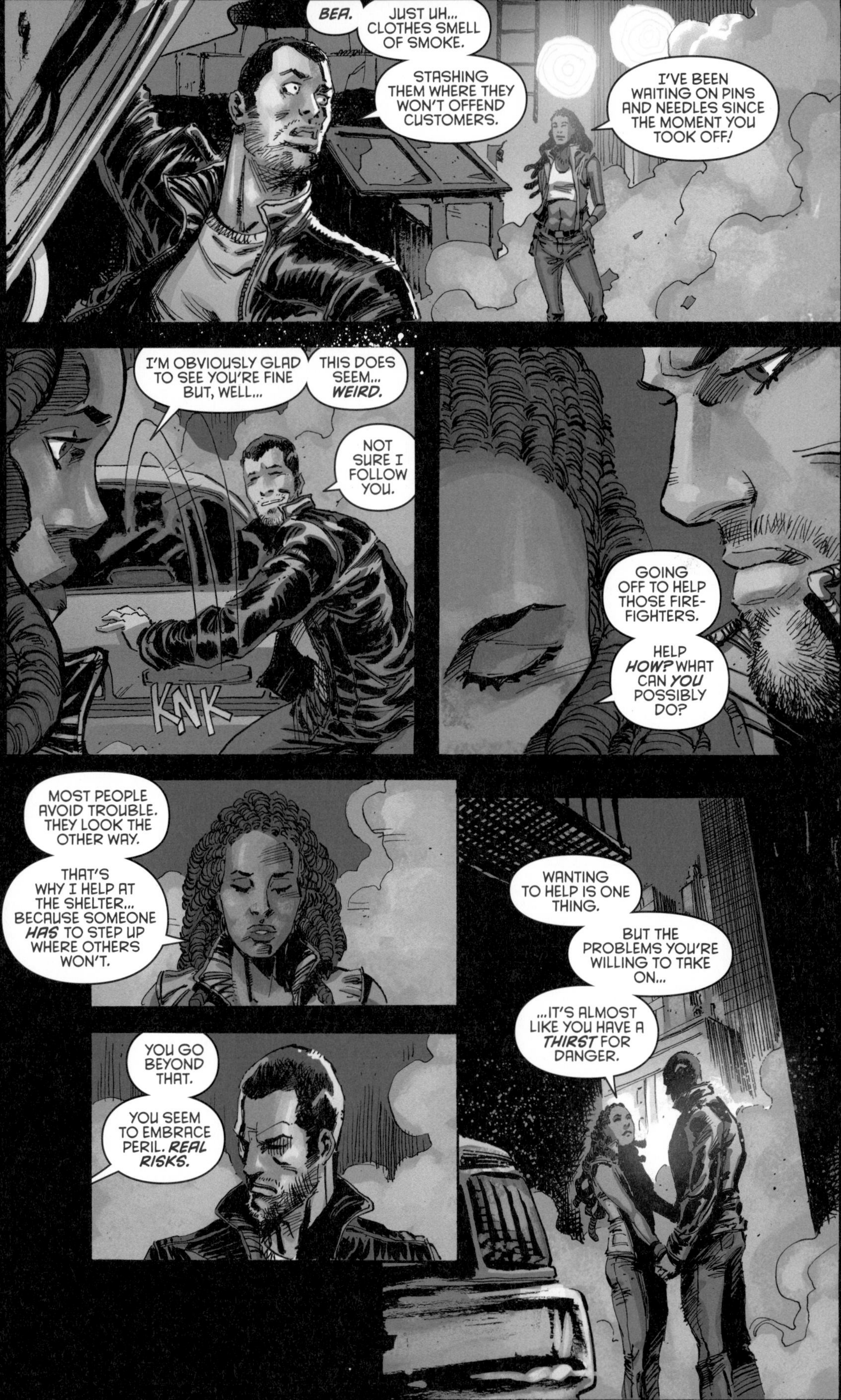
BEA.
JUST UH... CLOTHES SMELL OF SMOKE.
STASHING THEM WHERE THEY WON'T OFFEND CUSTOMERS.
I'VE BEEN WAITING ON PINS AND NEEDLES SINCE THE MOMENT YOU TOOK OFF!
I'M OBVIOUSLY GLAD TO SEE YOU'RE FINE BUT, WELL...
THIS DOES SEEM... WEIRD.
NOT SURE I FOLLOW YOU.
KNK
GOING OFF TO HELP THOSE FIRE-FIGHTERS.
HELP HOW? WHAT CAN YOU POSSIBLY DO?
MOST PEOPLE AVOID TROUBLE. THEY LOOK THE OTHER WAY.
THAT'S WHY I HELP AT THE SHELTER... BECAUSE SOMEONE HAS TO STEP UP WHERE OTHERS WON'T.
YOU GO BEYOND THAT.
YOU SEEM TO EMBRACE PERIL. REAL RISKS.
WANTING TO HELP IS ONE THING.
BUT THE PROBLEMS YOU'RE WILLING TO TAKE ON...
...IT'S ALMOST LIKE YOU HAVE A THIRST FOR DANGER.

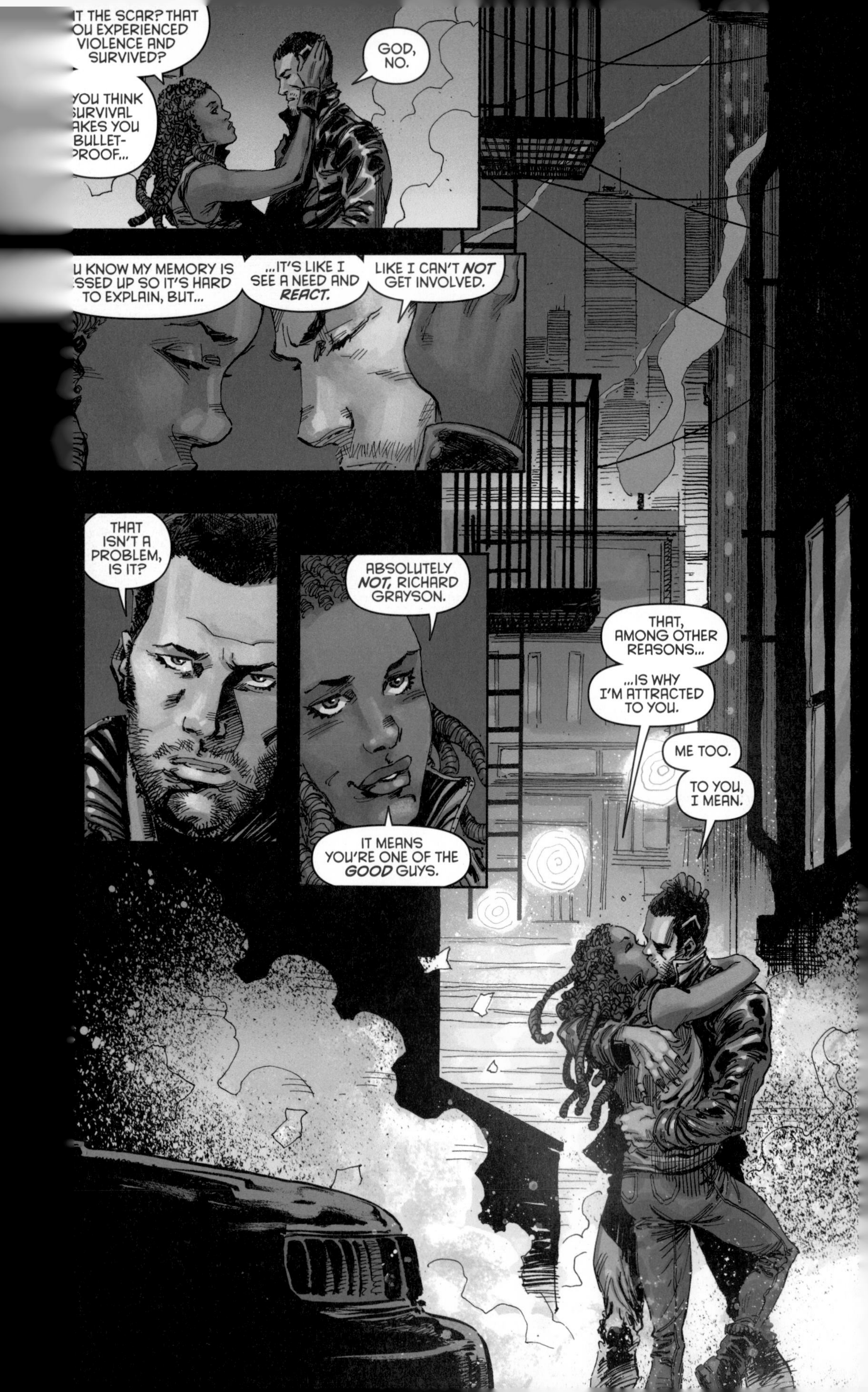
IT THE SCAR? THAT OU EXPERIENCED VIOLENCE AND SURVIVED?
YOU THINK SURVIVAL AKES YOU BULLET-PROOF...
GOD, NO.
U KNOW MY MEMORY IS SSED UP SO IT'S HARD TO EXPLAIN, BUT...
...IT'S LIKE I SEE A NEED AND *REACT.*
LIKE I CAN'T ***NOT*** GET INVOLVED.
THAT ISN'T A PROBLEM, IS IT?
ABSOLUTELY ***NOT,*** RICHARD GRAYSON.
IT MEANS YOU'RE ONE OF THE ***GOOD*** GUYS.
THAT, AMONG OTHER REASONS...
...IS WHY I'M ATTRACTED TO YOU.
ME TOO.
TO YOU, I MEAN.

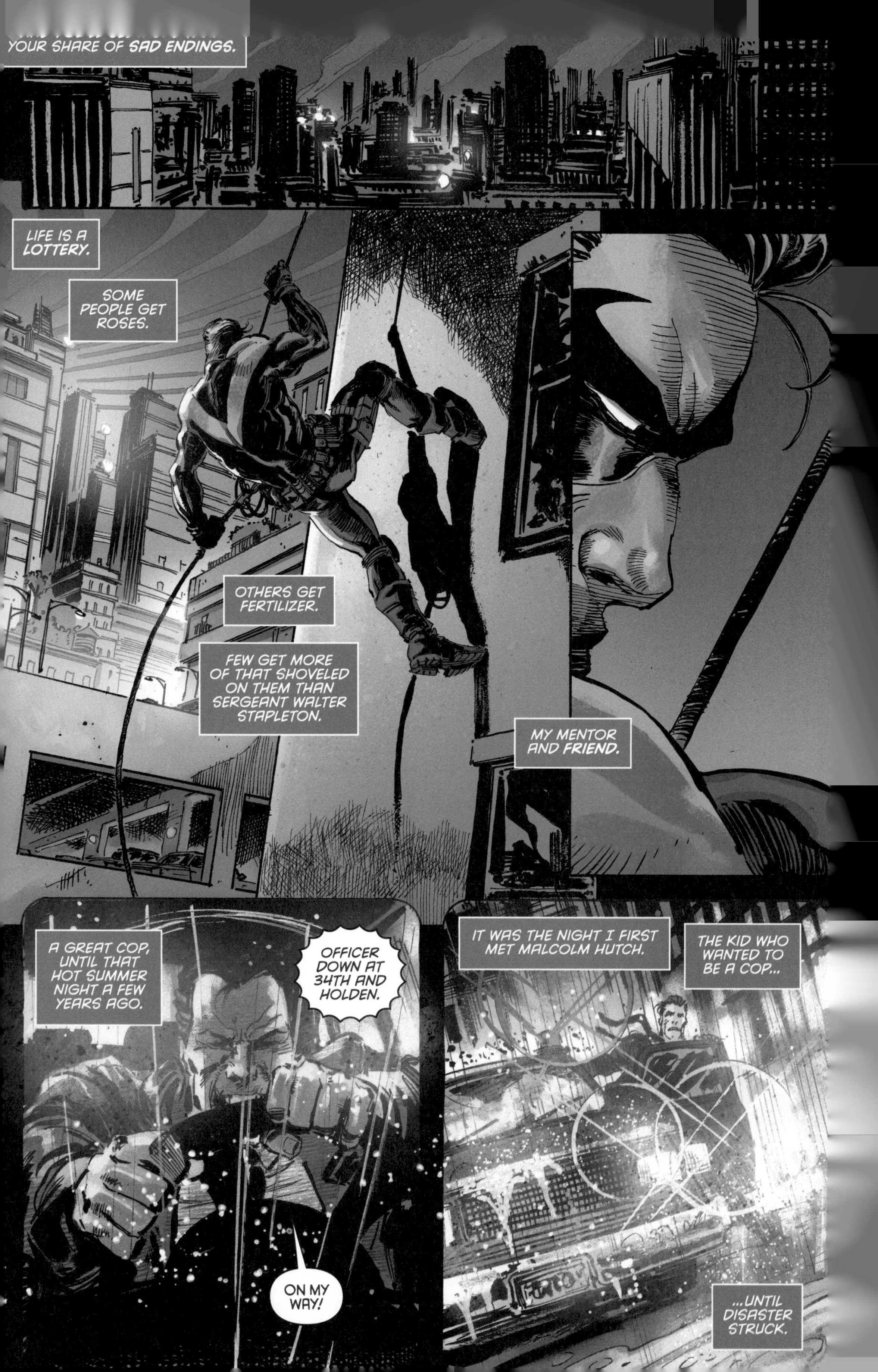
YOUR SHARE OF SAD ENDINGS.
LIFE IS A LOTTERY.
SOME PEOPLE GET ROSES.
OTHERS GET FERTILIZER.
FEW GET MORE OF THAT SHOVELED ON THEM THAN SERGEANT WALTER STAPLETON.
MY MENTOR AND FRIEND.
A GREAT COP, UNTIL THAT HOT SUMMER NIGHT A FEW YEARS AGO.
OFFICER DOWN AT 34TH AND HOLDEN.
ON MY WAY!
IT WAS THE NIGHT I FIRST MET MALCOLM HUTCH.
THE KID WHO WANTED TO BE A COP...
...UNTIL DISASTER STRUCK.

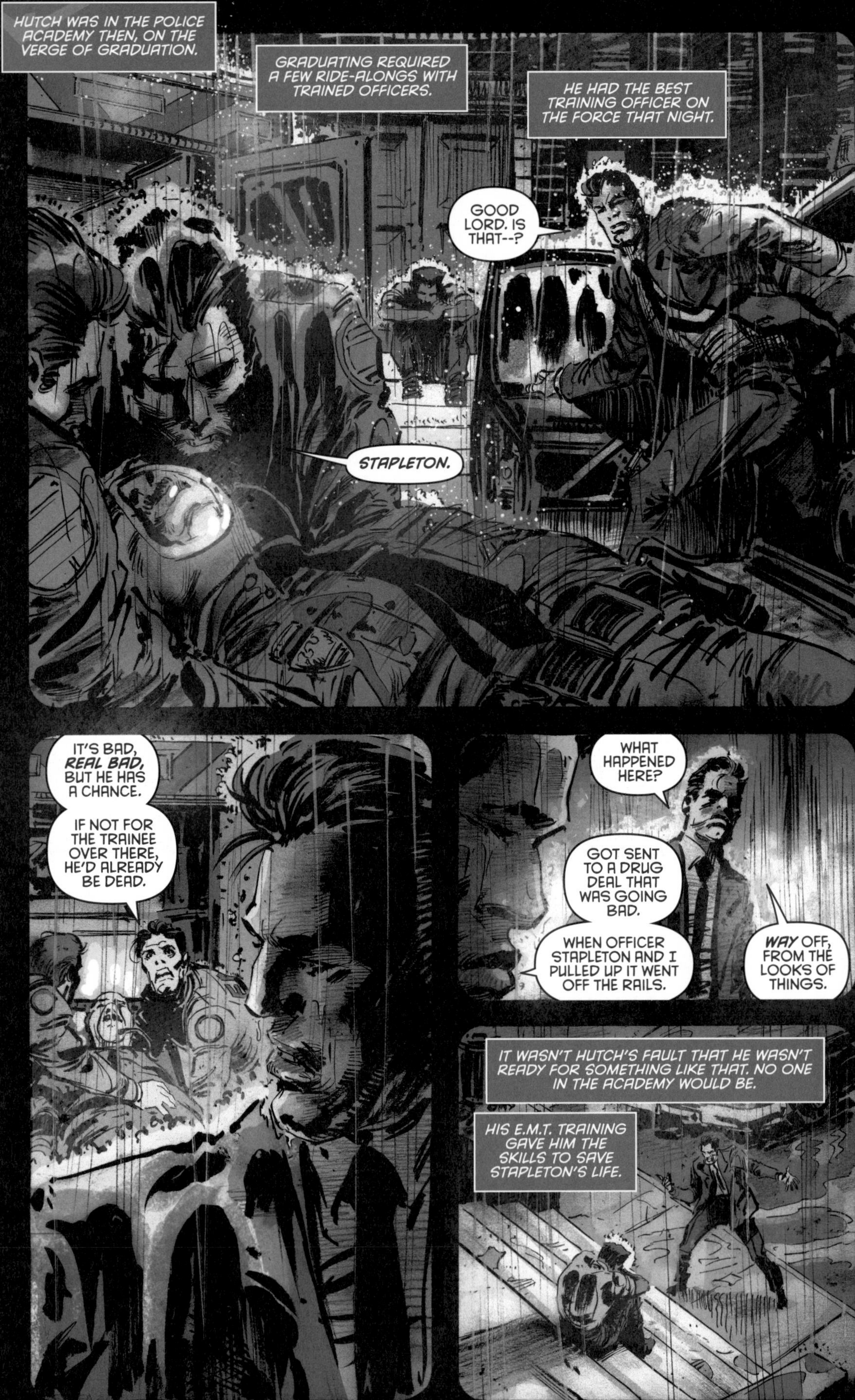
HUTCH WAS IN THE POLICE ACADEMY THEN, ON THE VERGE OF GRADUATION.
GRADUATING REQUIRED A FEW RIDE-ALONGS WITH TRAINED OFFICERS.
HE HAD THE BEST TRAINING OFFICER ON THE FORCE THAT NIGHT.
GOOD LORD. IS THAT--?
STAPLETON.
IT'S BAD, REAL BAD, BUT HE HAS A CHANCE.
IF NOT FOR THE TRAINEE OVER THERE, HE'D ALREADY BE DEAD.
WHAT HAPPENED HERE?
GOT SENT TO A DRUG DEAL THAT WAS GOING BAD.
WHEN OFFICER STAPLETON AND I PULLED UP IT WENT OFF THE RAILS.
WAY OFF, FROM THE LOOKS OF THINGS.
IT WASN'T HUTCH'S FAULT THAT HE WASN'T READY FOR SOMETHING LIKE THAT. NO ONE IN THE ACADEMY WOULD BE.
HIS E.M.T. TRAINING GAVE HIM THE SKILLS TO SAVE STAPLETON'S LIFE.

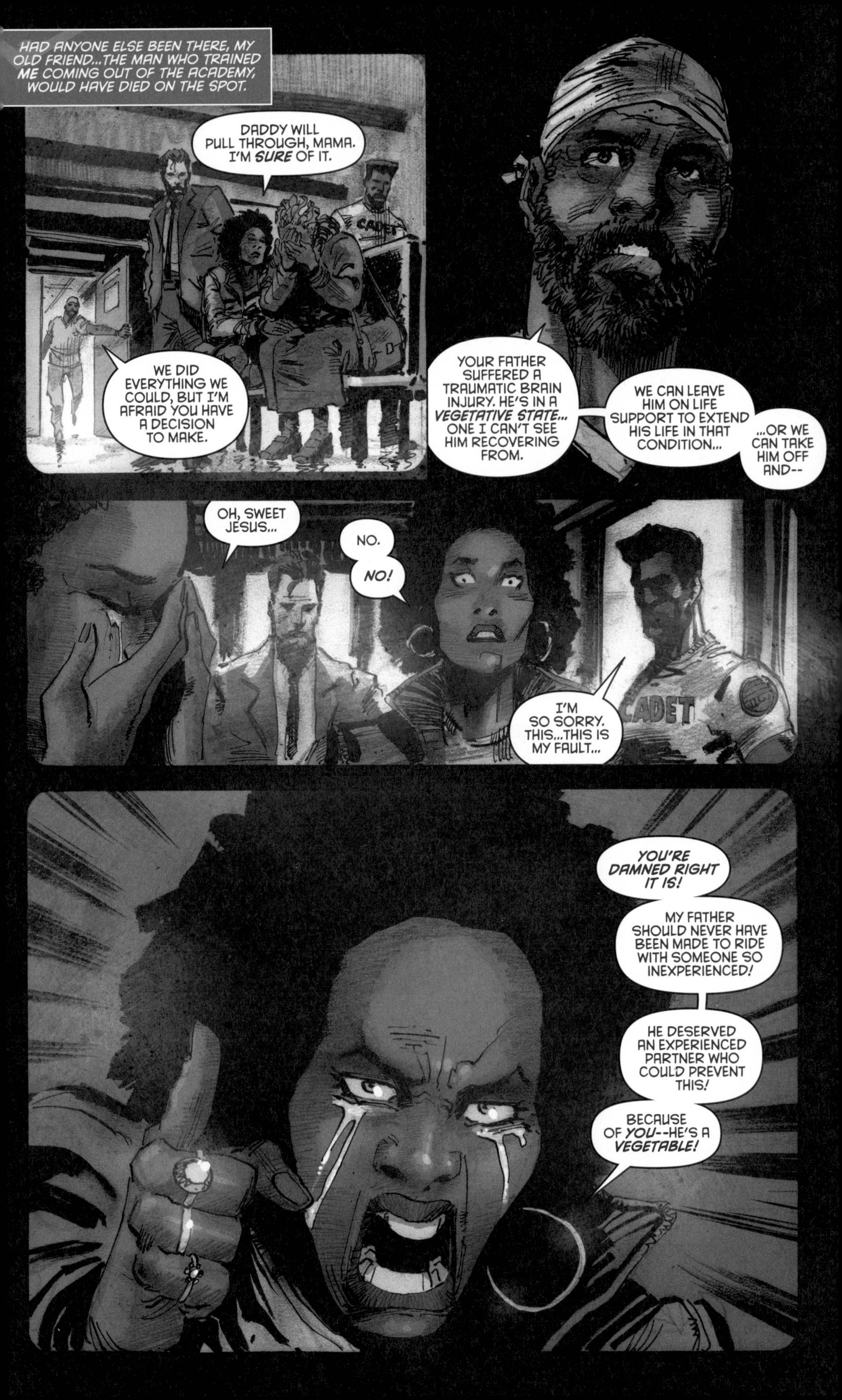
HAD ANYONE ELSE BEEN THERE, MY OLD FRIEND...THE MAN WHO TRAINED ME COMING OUT OF THE ACADEMY, WOULD HAVE DIED ON THE SPOT.
DADDY WILL PULL THROUGH, MAMA. I'M SURE OF IT.
CADET
WE DID EVERYTHING WE COULD, BUT I'M AFRAID YOU HAVE A DECISION TO MAKE.
YOUR FATHER SUFFERED A TRAUMATIC BRAIN INJURY. HE'S IN A VEGETATIVE STATE... ONE I CAN'T SEE HIM RECOVERING FROM.
WE CAN LEAVE HIM ON LIFE SUPPORT TO EXTEND HIS LIFE IN THAT CONDITION...
...OR WE CAN TAKE HIM OFF AND--
OH, SWEET JESUS...
NO.
NO!
CADET
I'M SO SORRY. THIS...THIS IS MY FAULT...
YOU'RE DAMNED RIGHT IT IS!
MY FATHER SHOULD NEVER HAVE BEEN MADE TO RIDE WITH SOMEONE SO INEXPERIENCED!
HE DESERVED AN EXPERIENCED PARTNER WHO COULD PREVENT THIS!
BECAUSE OF YOU--HE'S A VEGETABLE!

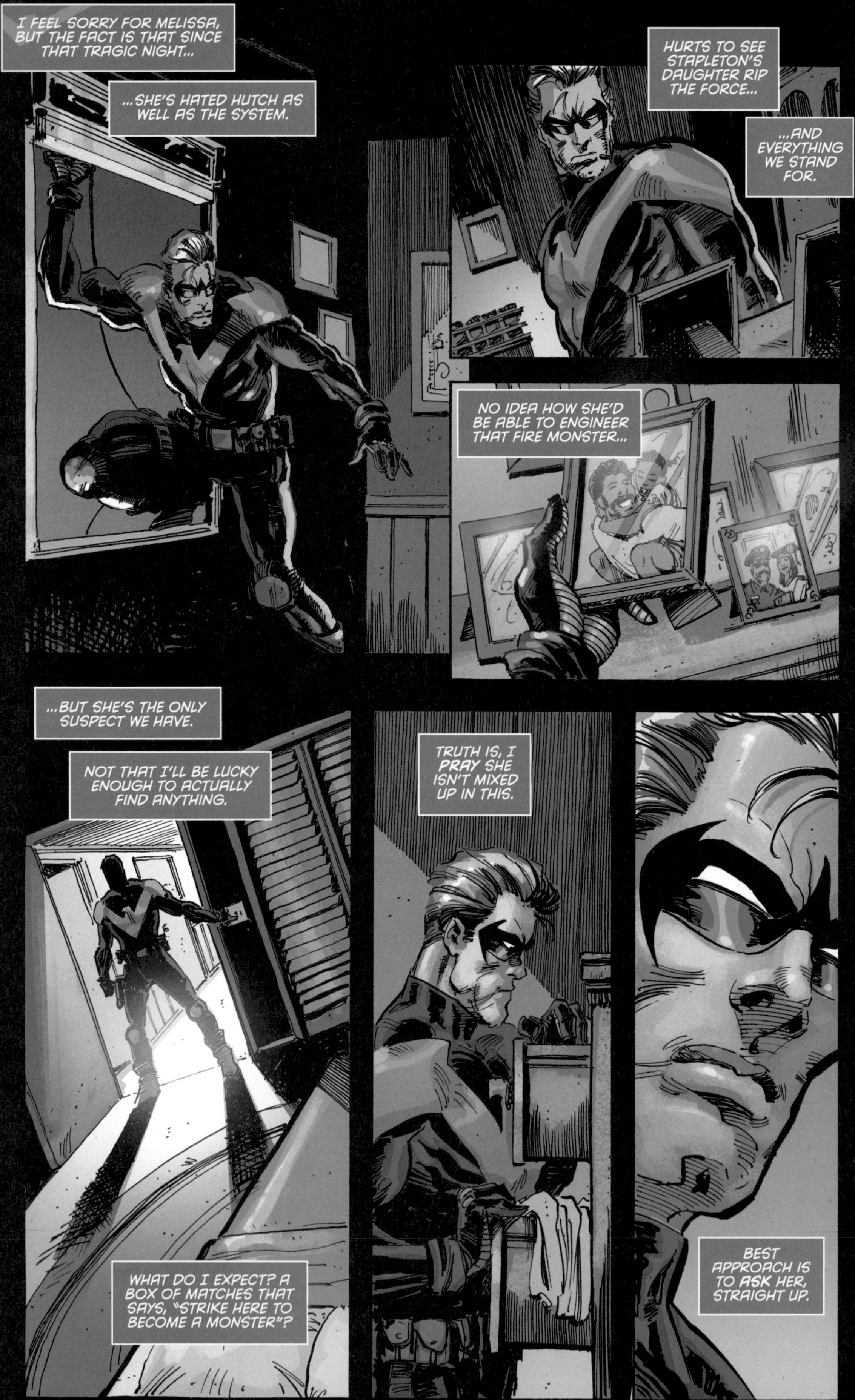
I FEEL SORRY FOR MELISSA, BUT THE FACT IS THAT SINCE THAT TRAGIC NIGHT...
...SHE'S HATED HUTCH AS WELL AS THE SYSTEM.
HURTS TO SEE STAPLETON'S DAUGHTER RIP THE FORCE...
...AND EVERYTHING WE STAND FOR.
NO IDEA HOW SHE'D BE ABLE TO ENGINEER THAT FIRE MONSTER...
...BUT SHE'S THE ONLY SUSPECT WE HAVE.
NOT THAT I'LL BE LUCKY ENOUGH TO ACTUALLY FIND ANYTHING.
WHAT DO I EXPECT? A BOX OF MATCHES THAT SAYS, "STRIKE HERE TO BECOME A MONSTER"?
TRUTH IS, I **PRAY** SHE ISN'T MIXED UP IN THIS.
BEST APPROACH IS TO **ASK** HER, STRAIGHT UP.

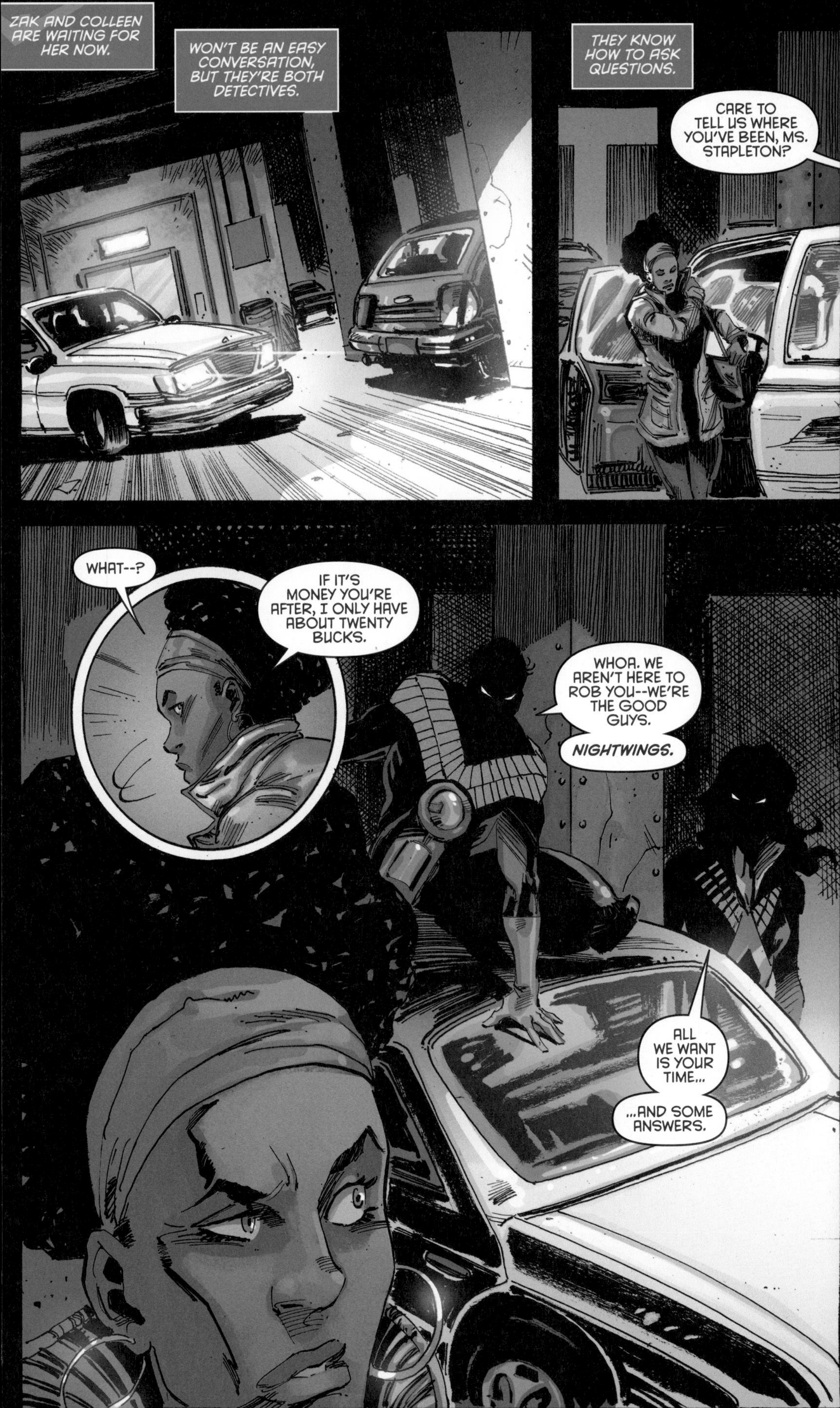
ZAK AND COLLEEN ARE WAITING FOR HER NOW.
WON'T BE AN EASY CONVERSATION, BUT THEY'RE BOTH DETECTIVES.
THEY KNOW HOW TO ASK QUESTIONS.
CARE TO TELL US WHERE YOU'VE BEEN, MS. STAPLETON?
WHAT--?
IF IT'S MONEY YOU'RE AFTER, I ONLY HAVE ABOUT TWENTY BUCKS.
WHOA. WE AREN'T HERE TO ROB YOU--WE'RE THE GOOD GUYS.
NIGHTWINGS.
ALL WE WANT IS YOUR TIME...
...AND SOME ANSWERS.

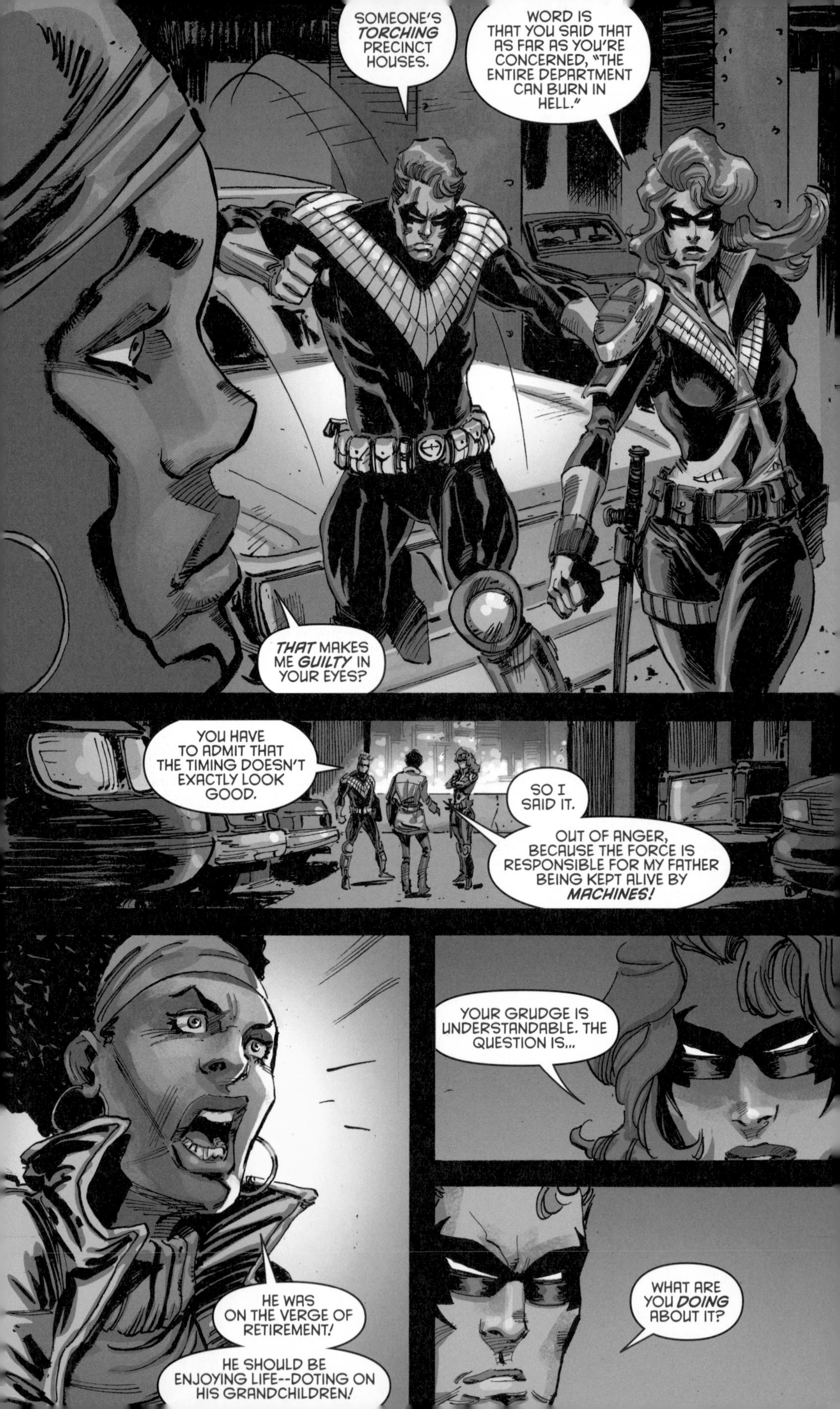
SOMEONE'S *TORCHING* PRECINCT HOUSES.
WORD IS THAT YOU SAID THAT AS FAR AS YOU'RE CONCERNED, "THE ENTIRE DEPARTMENT CAN BURN IN HELL."
THAT MAKES ME *GUILTY* IN YOUR EYES?
YOU HAVE TO ADMIT THAT THE TIMING DOESN'T EXACTLY LOOK GOOD.
SO I SAID IT.
OUT OF ANGER, BECAUSE THE FORCE IS RESPONSIBLE FOR MY FATHER BEING KEPT ALIVE BY *MACHINES!*
HE WAS ON THE VERGE OF RETIREMENT!
HE SHOULD BE ENJOYING LIFE--DOTING ON HIS GRANDCHILDREN!
YOUR GRUDGE IS UNDERSTANDABLE. THE QUESTION IS...
WHAT ARE YOU *DOING* ABOUT IT?

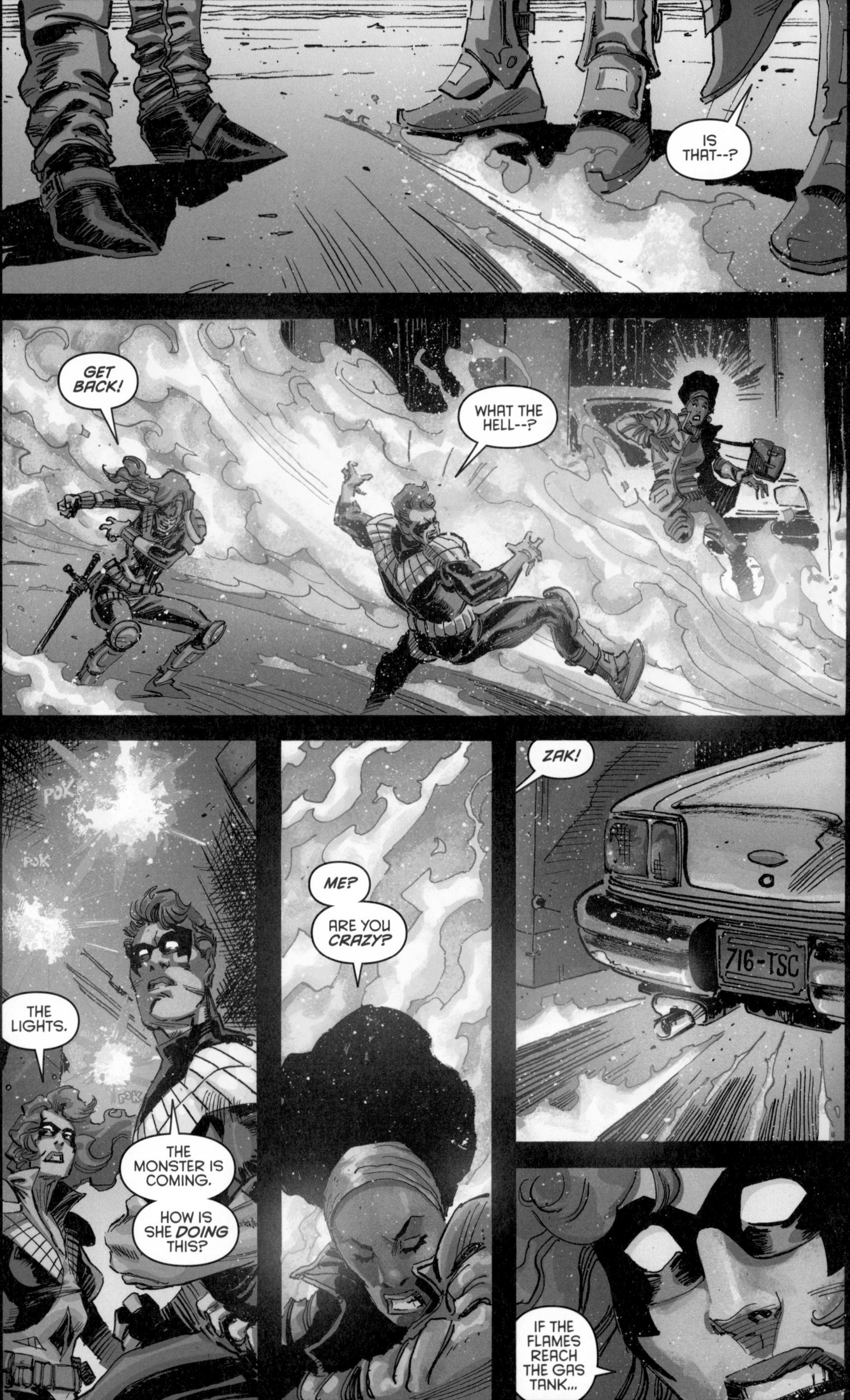
IS THAT--?
GET BACK!
WHAT THE HELL--?
POK
POK
THE LIGHTS.
POK
THE MONSTER IS COMING.
HOW IS SHE *DOING* THIS?
ME?
ARE YOU *CRAZY?*
ZAK!
716-TSC
IF THE FLAMES REACH THE GAS TANK...

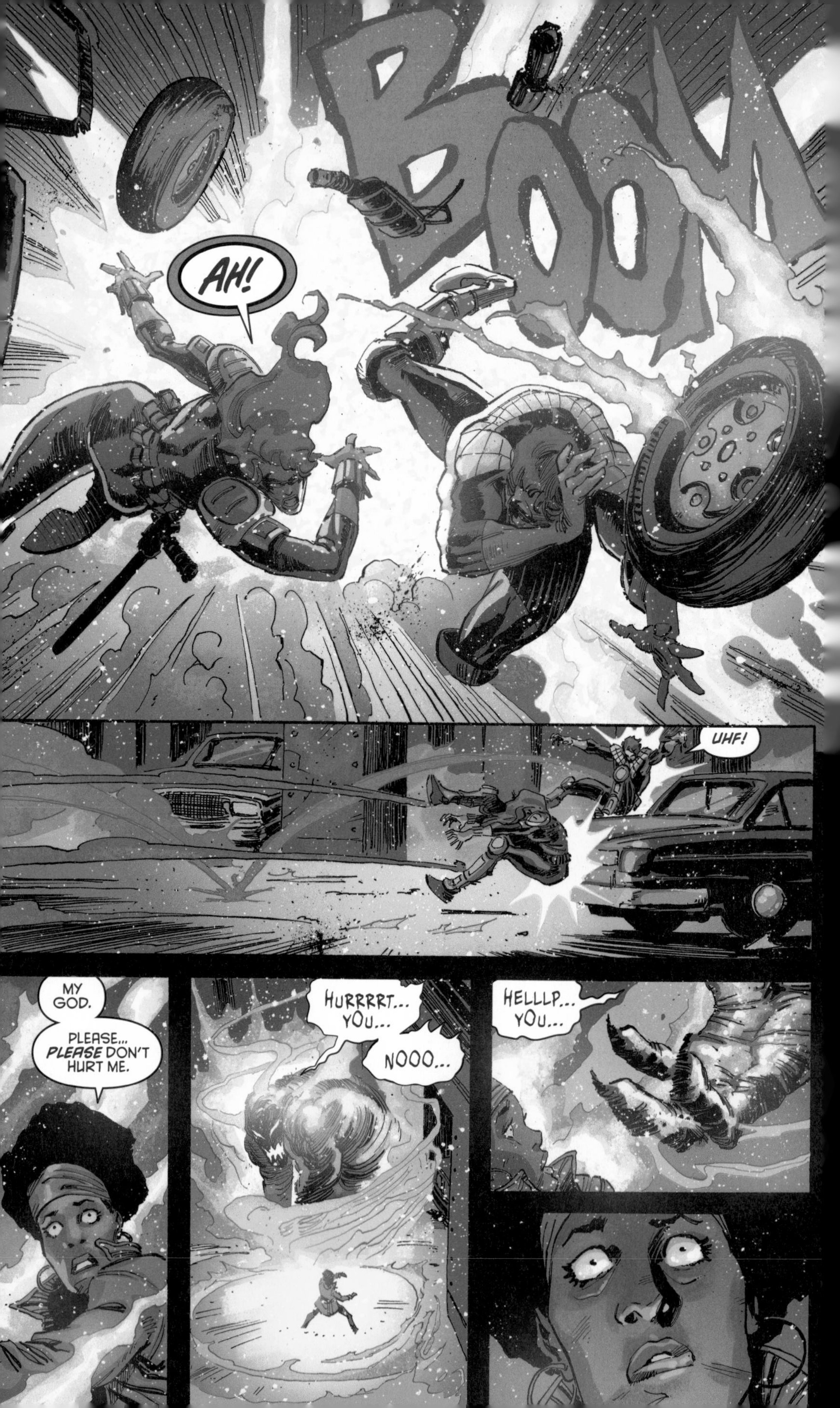
BOOM
AH!
UHF!
MY GOD.
PLEASE... PLEASE DON'T HURT ME.
HURRRRT... YOU...
NOOO...
HELLLP... YOU...

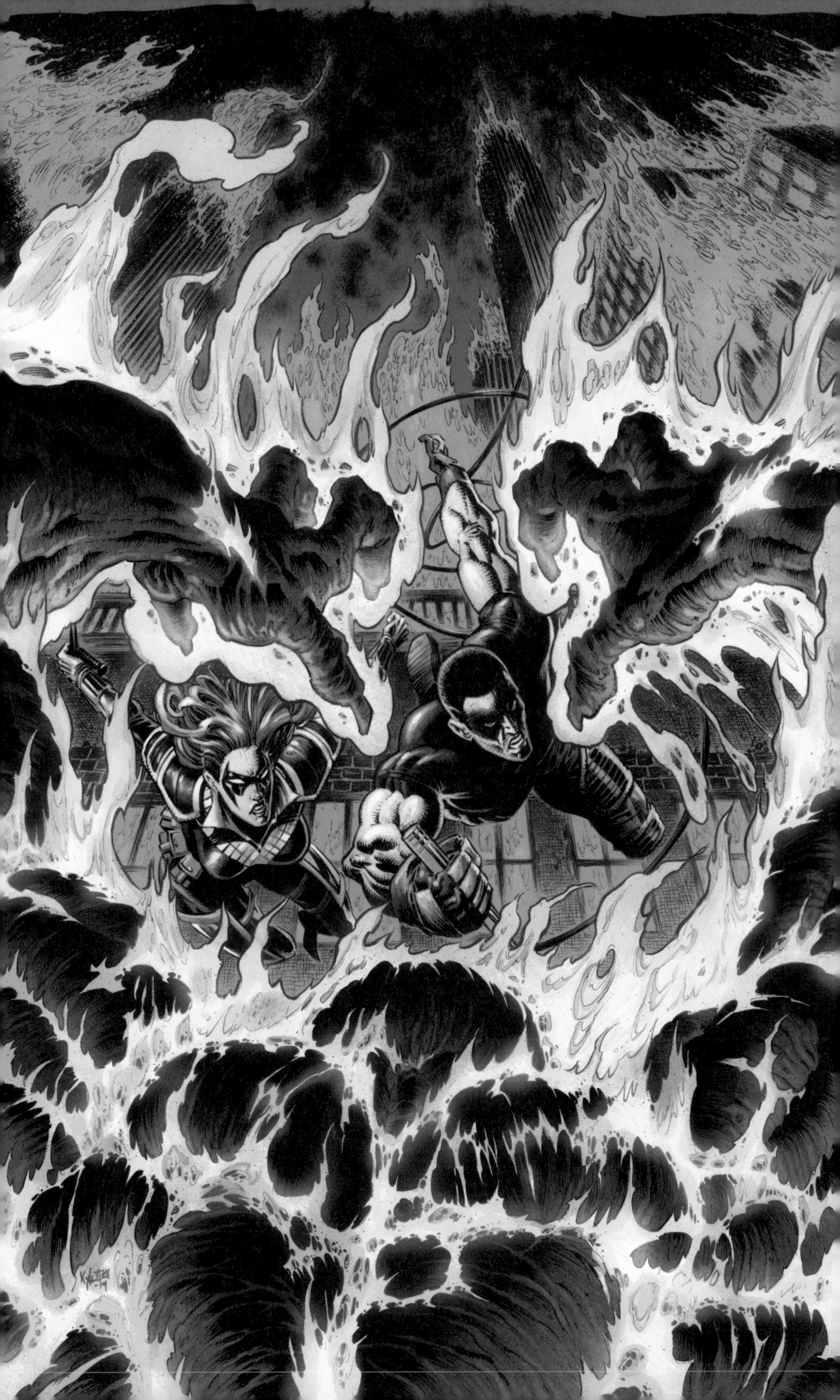

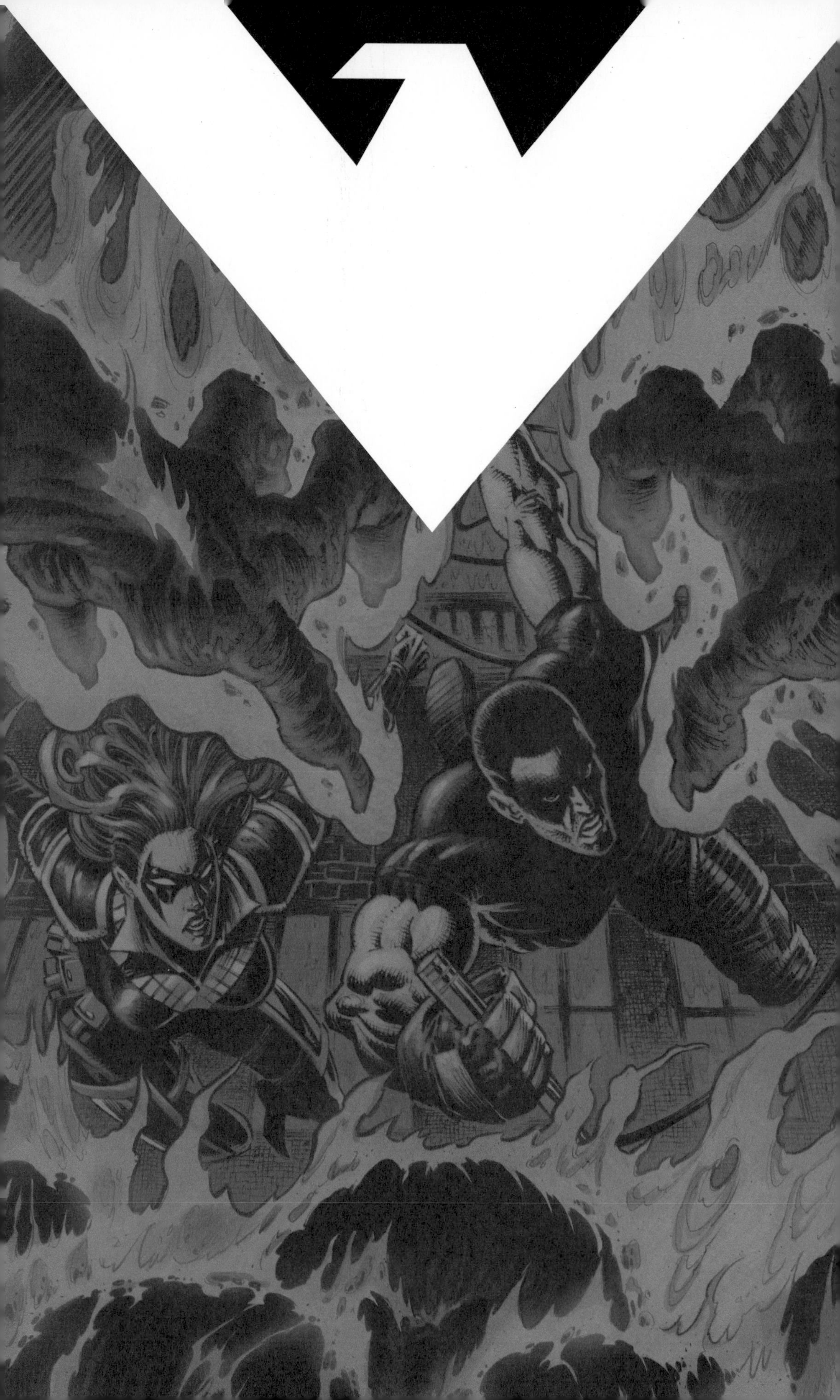

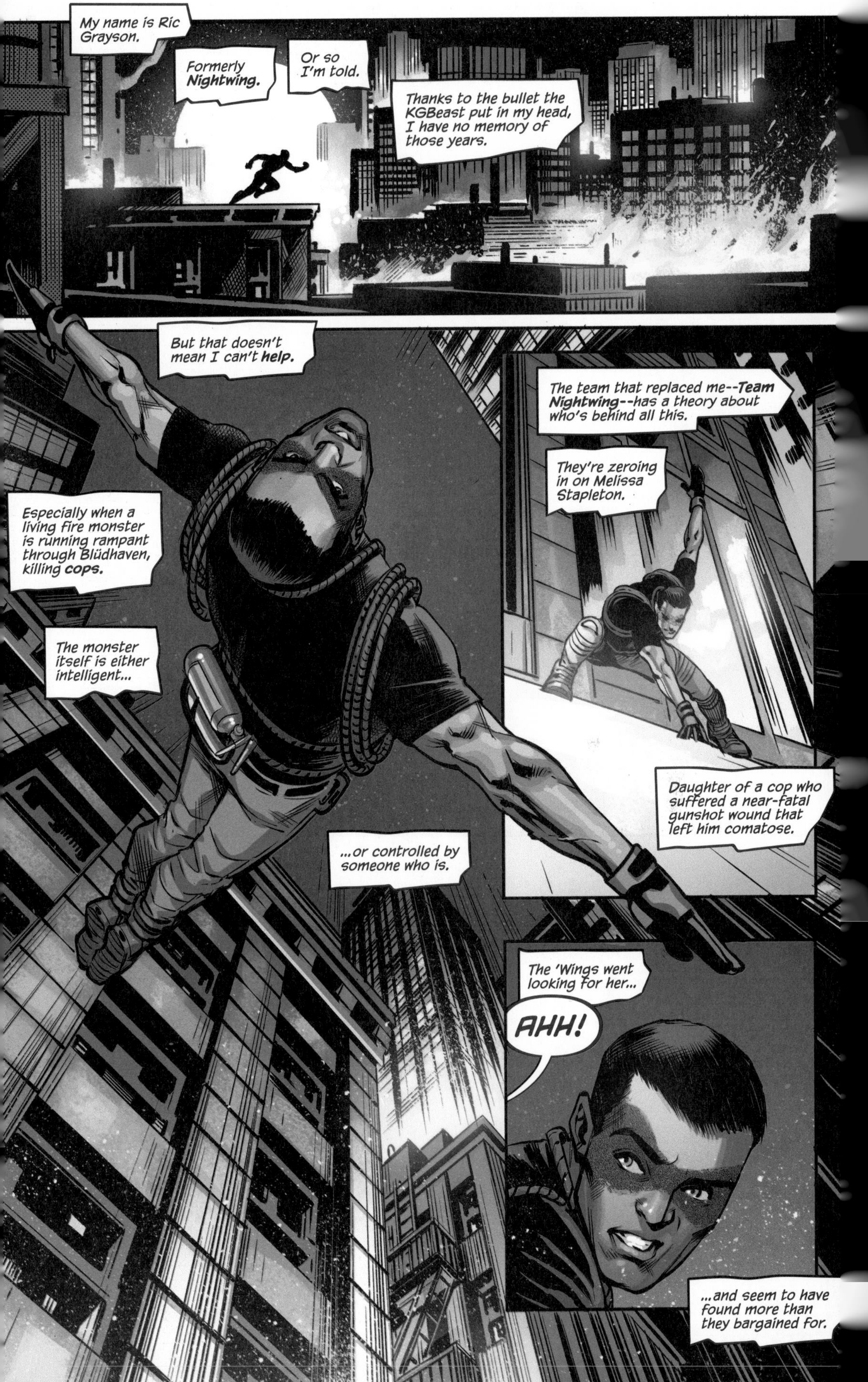

My name is Ric Grayson.
Formerly Nightwing.
Or so I'm told.
Thanks to the bullet the KGBeast put in my head, I have no memory of those years.
But that doesn't mean I can't help.
Especially when a living fire monster is running rampant through Blüdhaven, killing cops.
The monster itself is either intelligent...
...or controlled by someone who is.
The team that replaced me--Team Nightwing--has a theory about who's behind all this.
They're zeroing in on Melissa Stapleton.
Daughter of a cop who suffered a near-fatal gunshot wound that left him comatose.
The 'Wings went looking for her...
AHH!
...and seem to have found more than they bargained for.

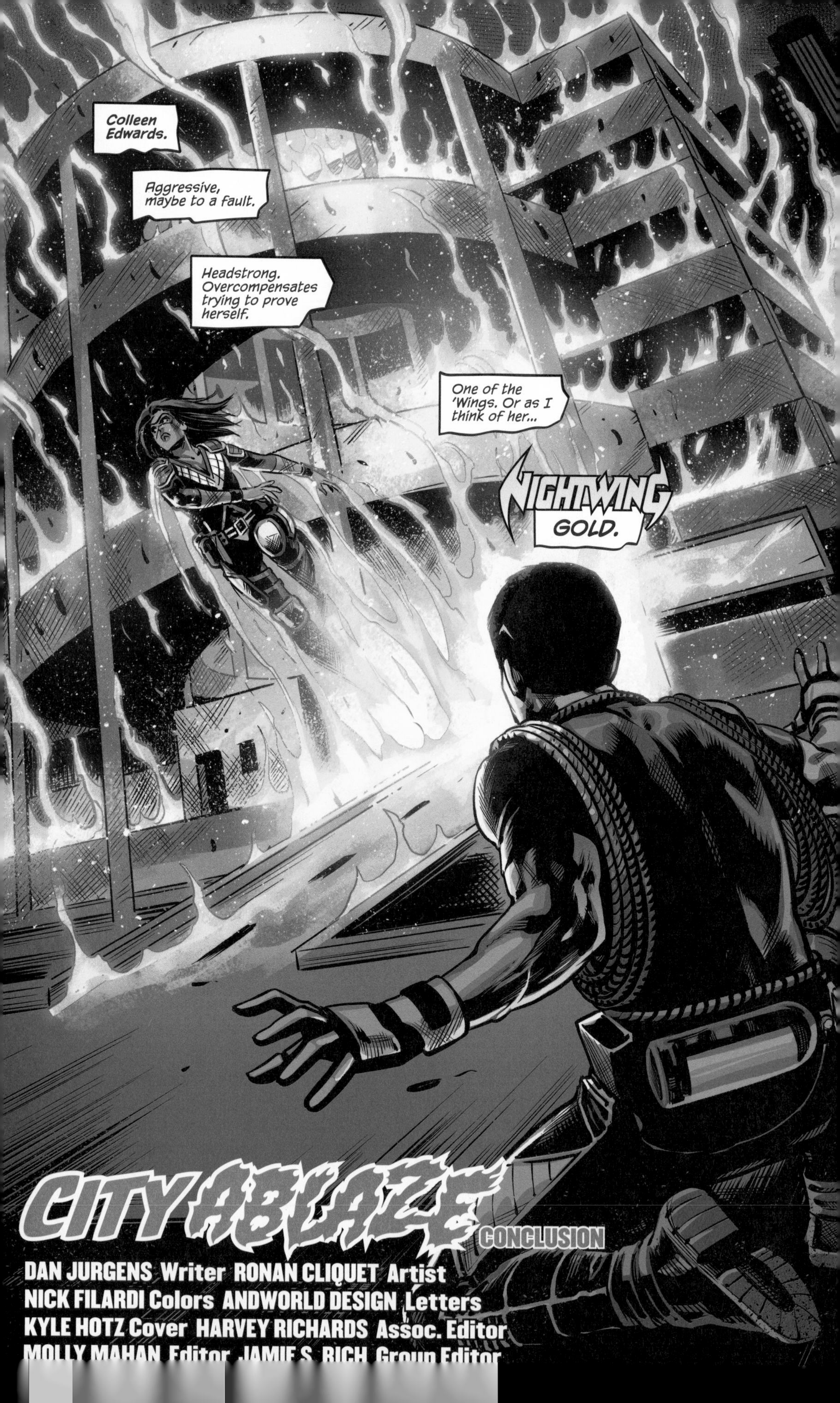

Colleen Edwards.
Aggressive, maybe to a fault.
Headstrong. Overcompensates trying to prove herself.
One of the 'Wings. Or as I think of her...
NIGHTWING
GOLD.
CITY ABLAZE
CONCLUSION
DAN JURGENS Writer RONAN CLIQUET Artist
NICK FILARDI Colors ANDWORLD DESIGN Letters
KYLE HOTZ Cover HARVEY RICHARDS Assoc. Editor
MOLLY MAHAN Editor JAMIE S. RICH Group Editor

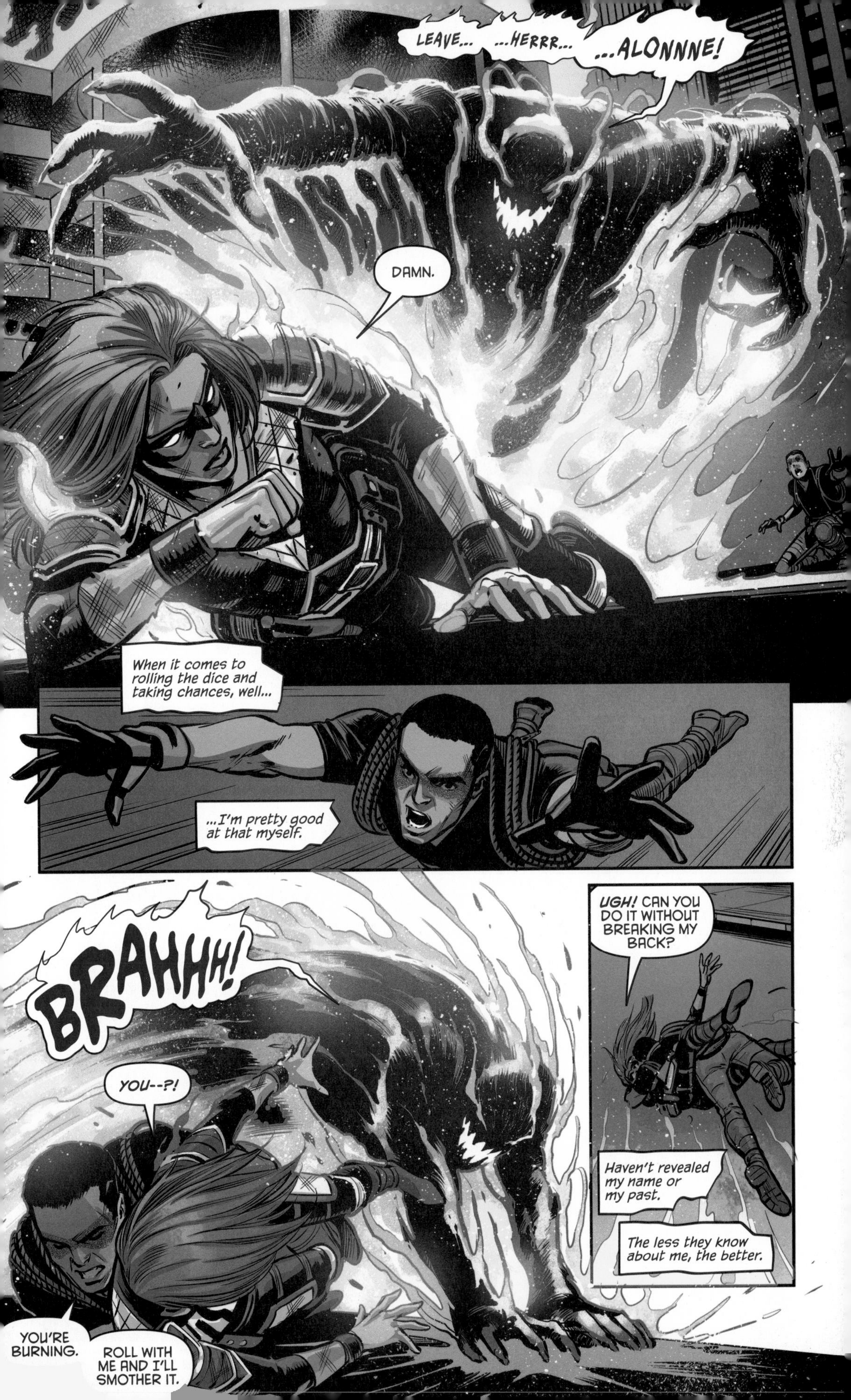
LEAVE... ...HERRR... ...ALONNNE!
DAMN.
When it comes to rolling the dice and taking chances, well...
...I'm pretty good at that myself.
BRAHHH!
YOU--?!
YOU'RE BURNING.
ROLL WITH ME AND I'LL SMOTHER IT.
UGH! CAN YOU DO IT WITHOUT BREAKING MY BACK?
Haven't revealed my name or my past.
The less they know about me, the better.

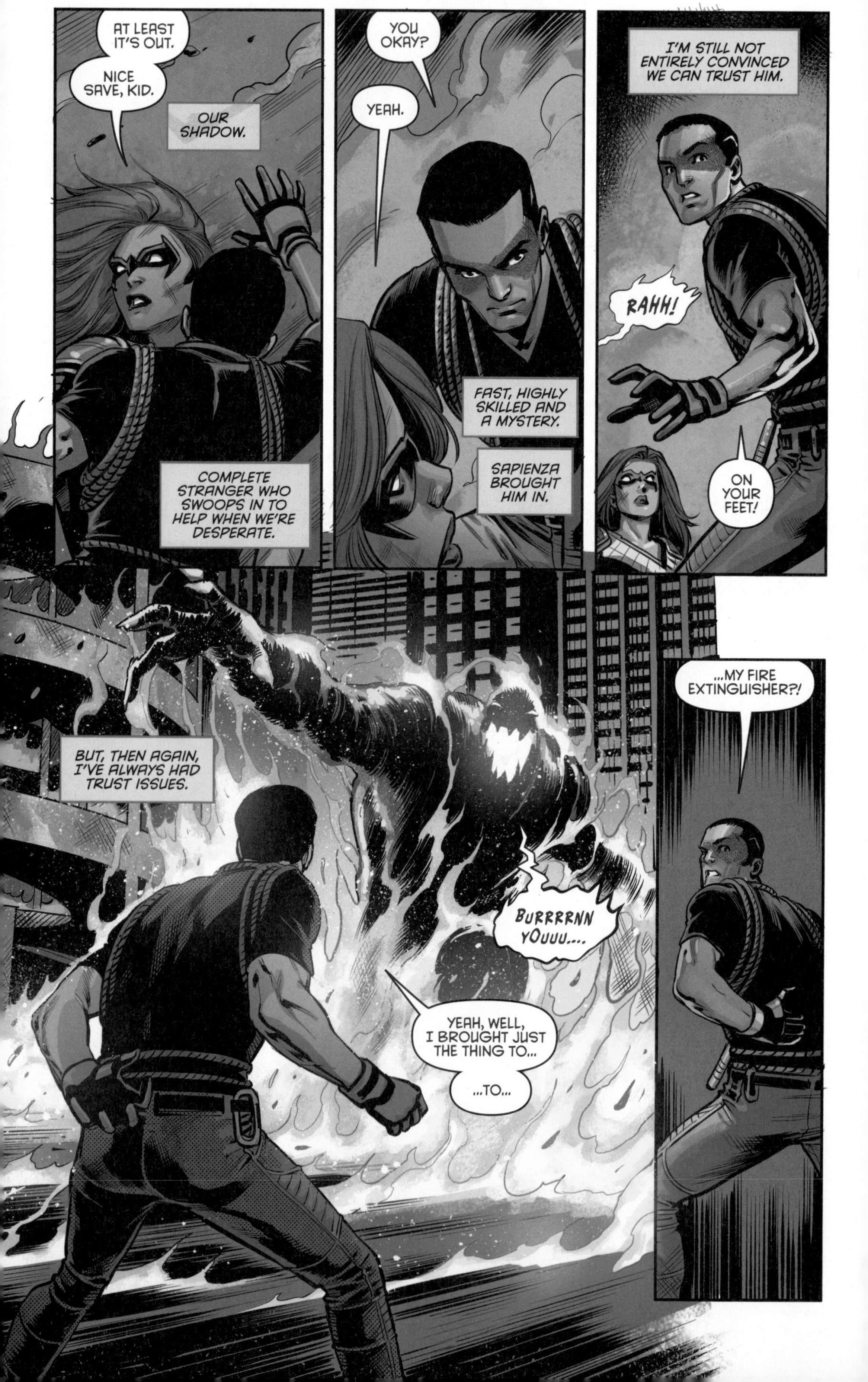
AT LEAST IT'S OUT.
NICE SAVE, KID.
OUR SHADOW.
COMPLETE STRANGER WHO SWOOPS IN TO HELP WHEN WE'RE DESPERATE.
YOU OKAY?
YEAH.
FAST, HIGHLY SKILLED AND A MYSTERY.
SAPIENZA BROUGHT HIM IN.
I'M STILL NOT ENTIRELY CONVINCED WE CAN TRUST HIM.
RAHH!
ON YOUR FEET!
BUT, THEN AGAIN, I'VE ALWAYS HAD TRUST ISSUES.
BURRRRNN YOUUU....
YEAH, WELL, I BROUGHT JUST THE THING TO...
...TO...
...MY FIRE EXTINGUISHER?!

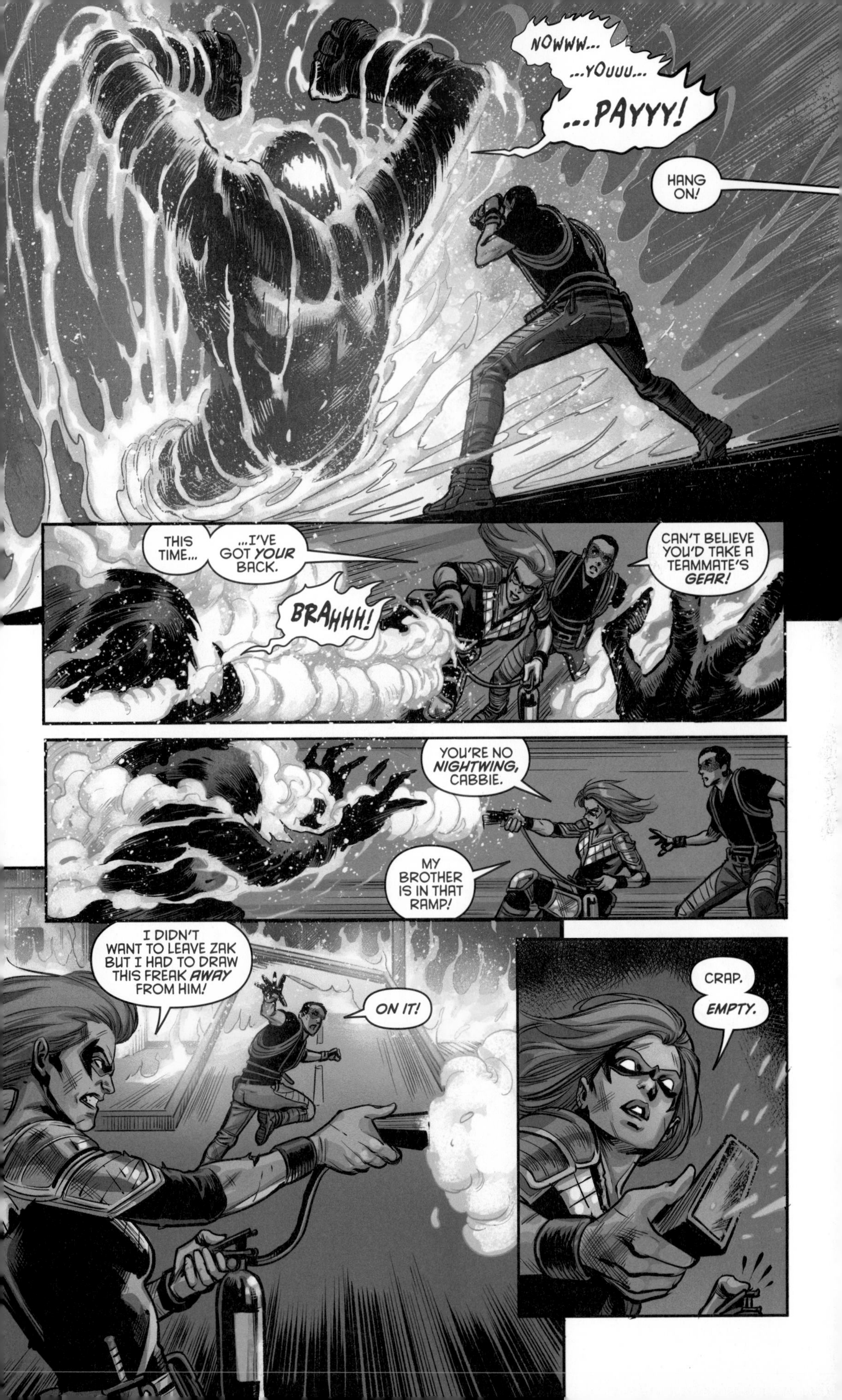
NOWWW...
...YOUUU...
...PAYYY!
HANG ON!
THIS TIME...
...I'VE GOT YOUR BACK.
CAN'T BELIEVE YOU'D TAKE A TEAMMATE'S GEAR!
BRAHHH!
YOU'RE NO NIGHTWING, CABBIE.
MY BROTHER IS IN THAT RAMP!
I DIDN'T WANT TO LEAVE ZAK BUT I HAD TO DRAW THIS FREAK AWAY FROM HIM!
ON IT!
CRAP.
EMPTY.

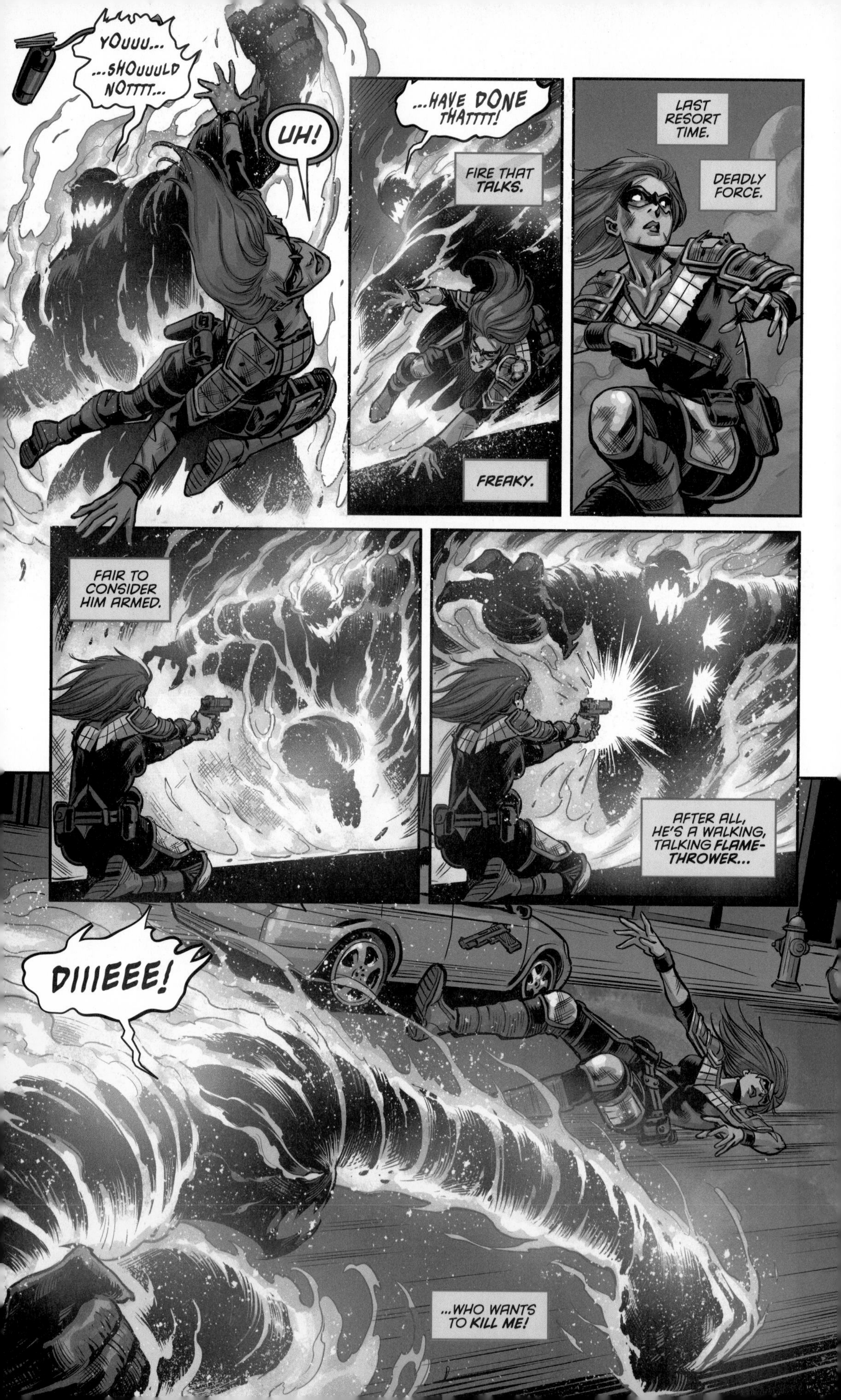
YOUUU...
...SHOUUULD
NOTTTT...
UH!
...HAVE DONE
THATTTT!
FIRE THAT
TALKS.
FREAKY.
LAST
RESORT
TIME.
DEADLY
FORCE.
FAIR TO
CONSIDER
HIM ARMED.
AFTER ALL,
HE'S A WALKING,
TALKING FLAME-
THROWER...
DIIIEEE!
...WHO WANTS
TO KILL ME!

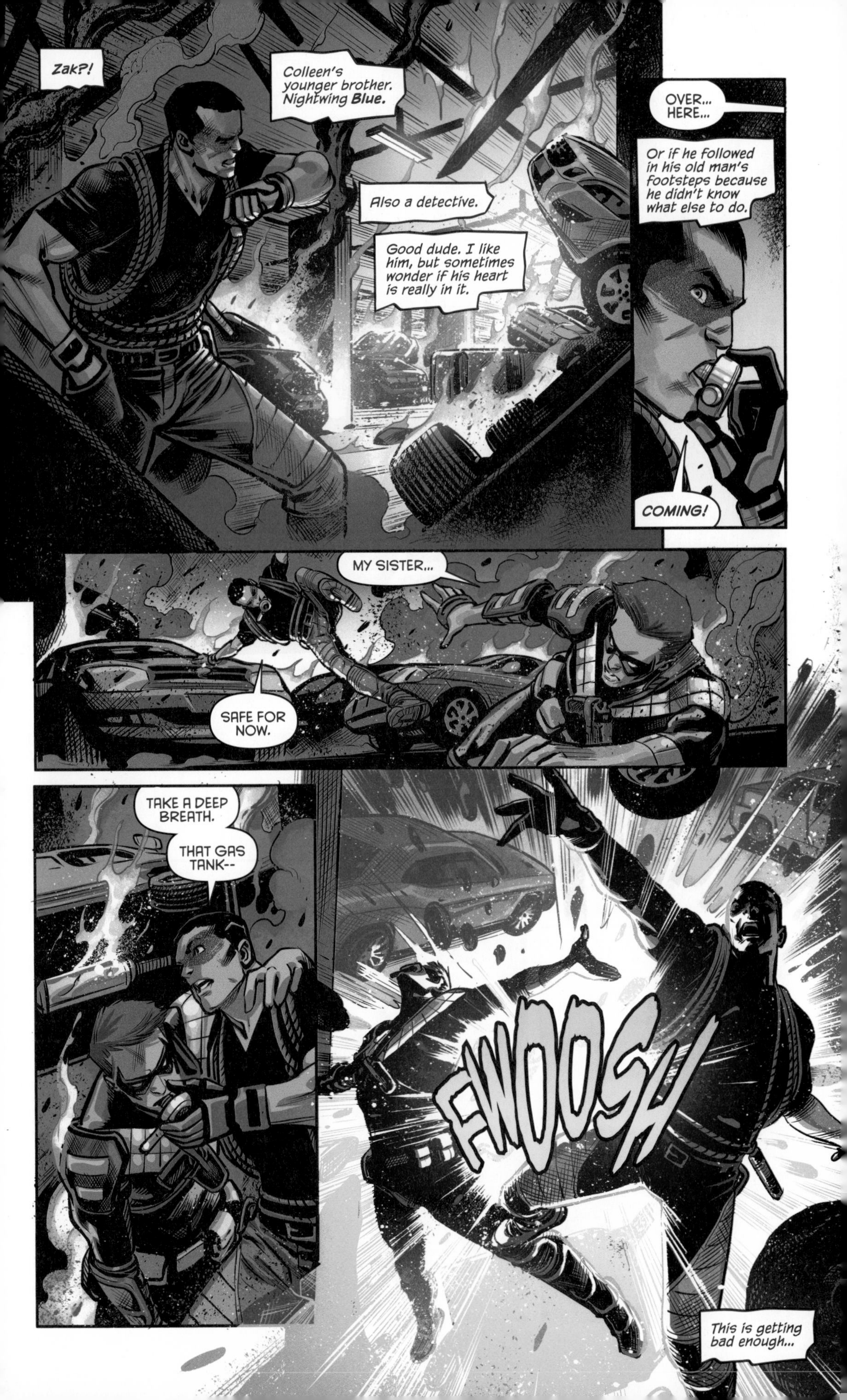
Zak?!
Colleen's younger brother. Nightwing **Blue.**
Also a detective.
Good dude. I like him, but sometimes wonder if his heart is really in it.
OVER... HERE...
Or if he followed in his old man's footsteps because he didn't know what else to do.
COMING!
MY SISTER...
SAFE FOR NOW.
TAKE A DEEP BREATH.
THAT GAS TANK--
FWOOSH
This is getting bad enough...

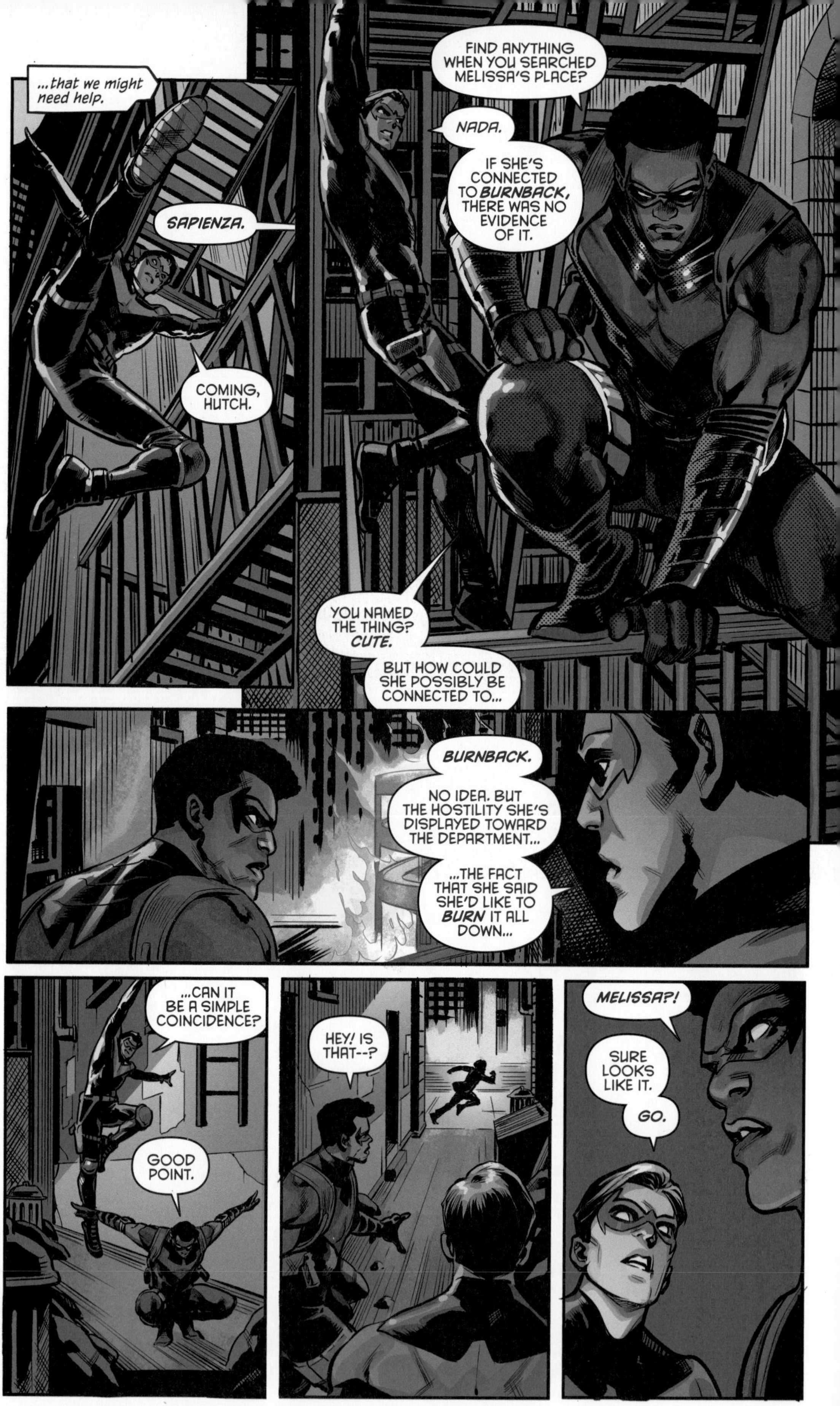
...that we might need help.
SAPIENZA.
COMING, HUTCH.
FIND ANYTHING WHEN YOU SEARCHED MELISSA'S PLACE?
NADA.
IF SHE'S CONNECTED TO BURNBACK, THERE WAS NO EVIDENCE OF IT.
YOU NAMED THE THING? CUTE.
BUT HOW COULD SHE POSSIBLY BE CONNECTED TO...
BURNBACK.
NO IDEA. BUT THE HOSTILITY SHE'S DISPLAYED TOWARD THE DEPARTMENT...
...THE FACT THAT SHE SAID SHE'D LIKE TO BURN IT ALL DOWN...
...CAN IT BE A SIMPLE COINCIDENCE?
GOOD POINT.
HEY! IS THAT--?
MELISSA?!
SURE LOOKS LIKE IT.
GO.

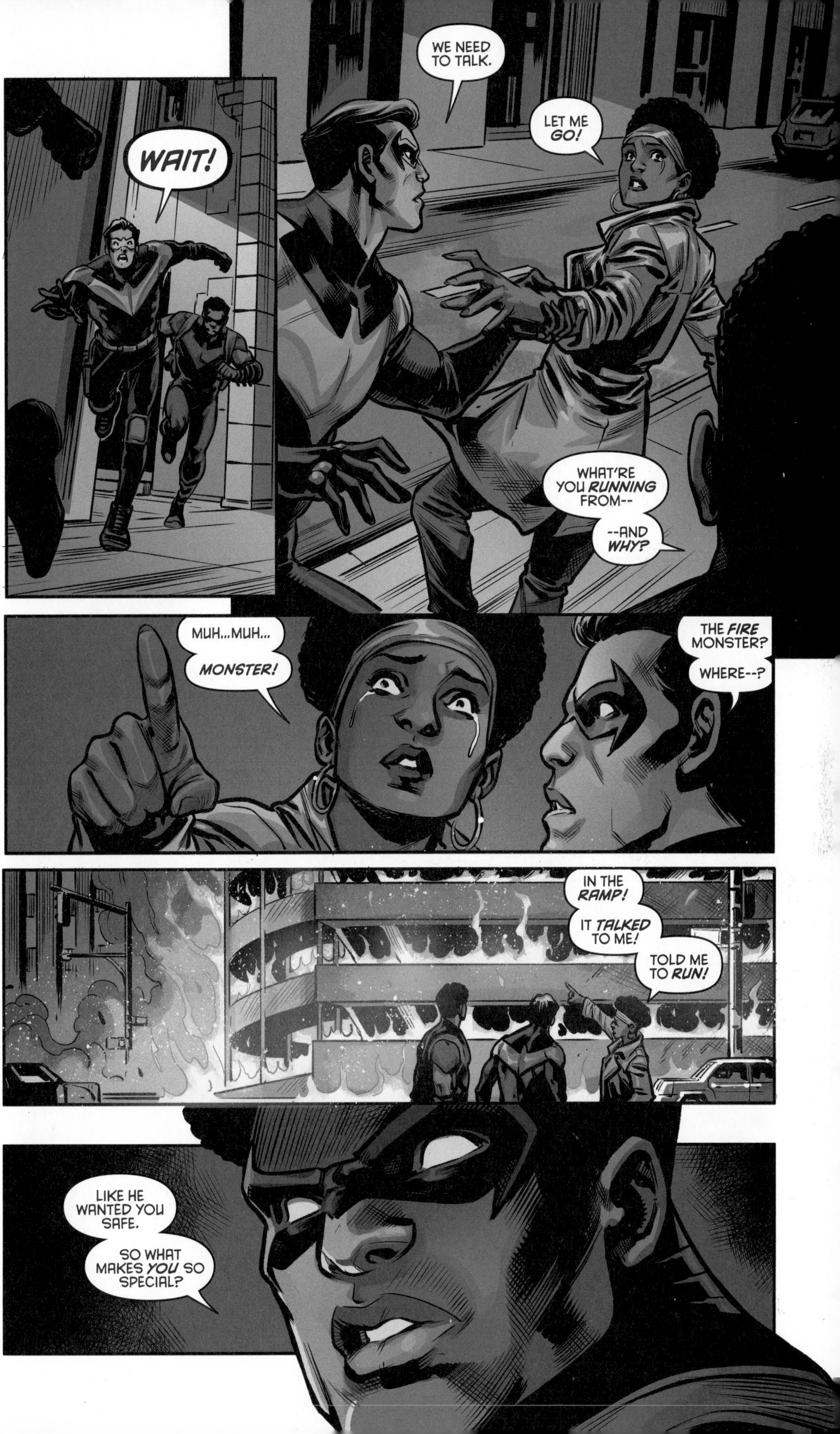
WAIT!
WE NEED TO TALK.
LET ME GO!
WHAT'RE YOU RUNNING FROM--
--AND WHY?
MUH...MUH...
MONSTER!
THE FIRE MONSTER?
WHERE--?
IN THE RAMP!
IT TALKED TO ME!
TOLD ME TO RUN!
LIKE HE WANTED YOU SAFE.
SO WHAT MAKES YOU SO SPECIAL?

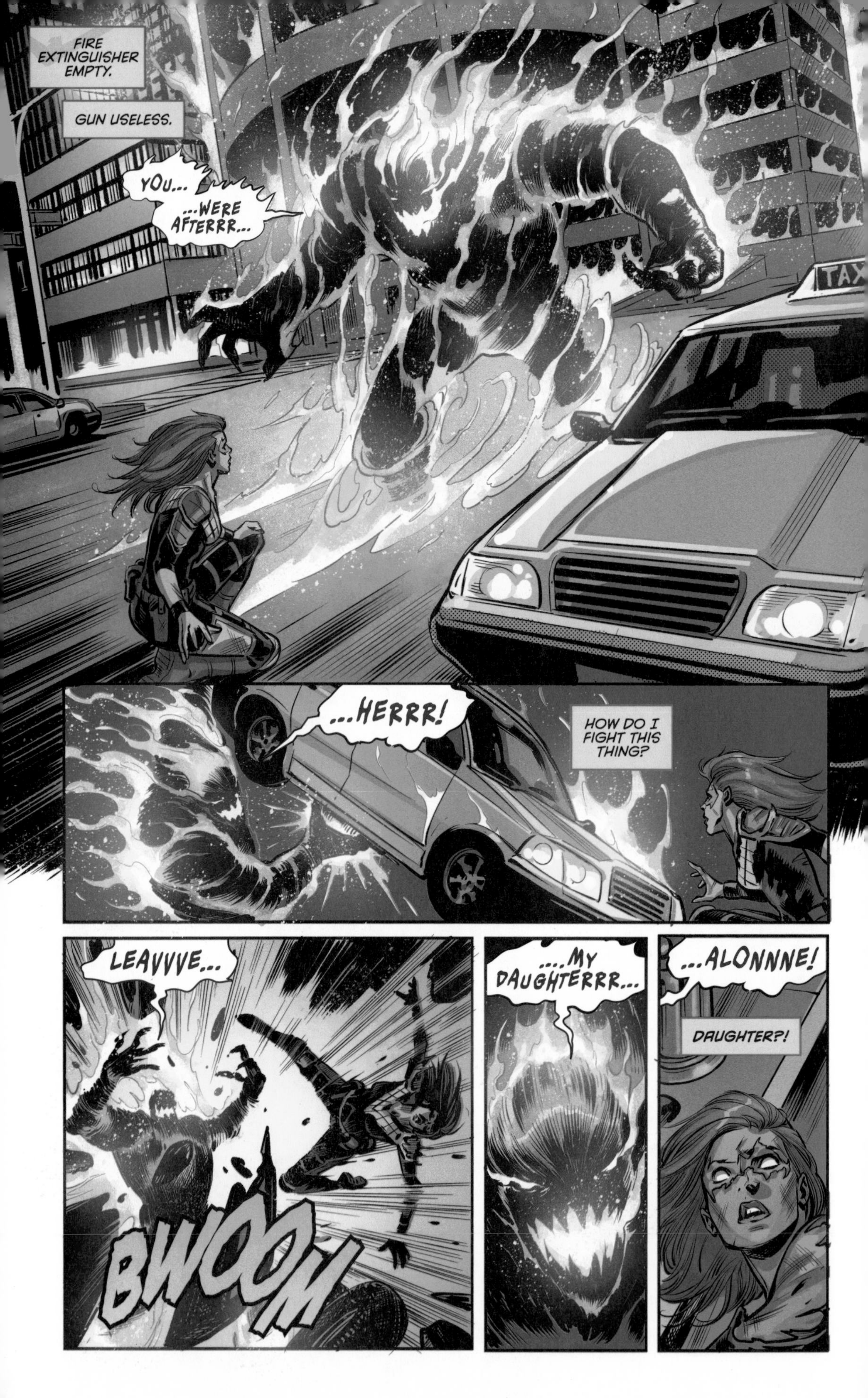
FIRE EXTINGUISHER EMPTY.
GUN USELESS.
YOU...
...WERE AFTERRR...
TAX
...HERRR!
HOW DO I FIGHT THIS THING?
LEAVVVE...
BWOOM
....MY DAUGHTERRR...
...ALONNNE!
DAUGHTER?!

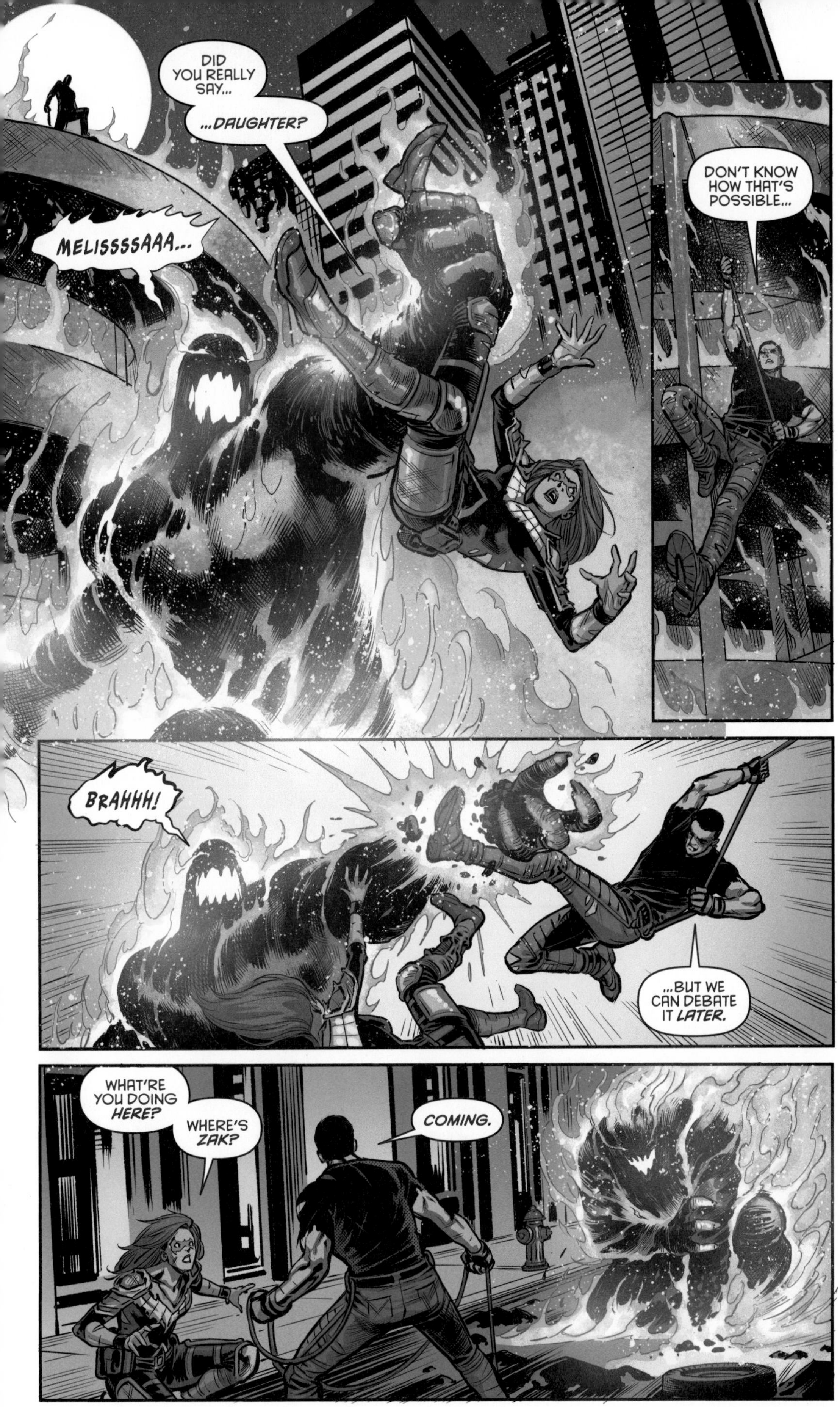
DID YOU REALLY SAY...
...DAUGHTER?
MELISSSSAAA...
DON'T KNOW HOW THAT'S POSSIBLE...
BRAHHH!
...BUT WE CAN DEBATE IT LATER.
WHAT'RE YOU DOING HERE?
WHERE'S ZAK?
COMING.

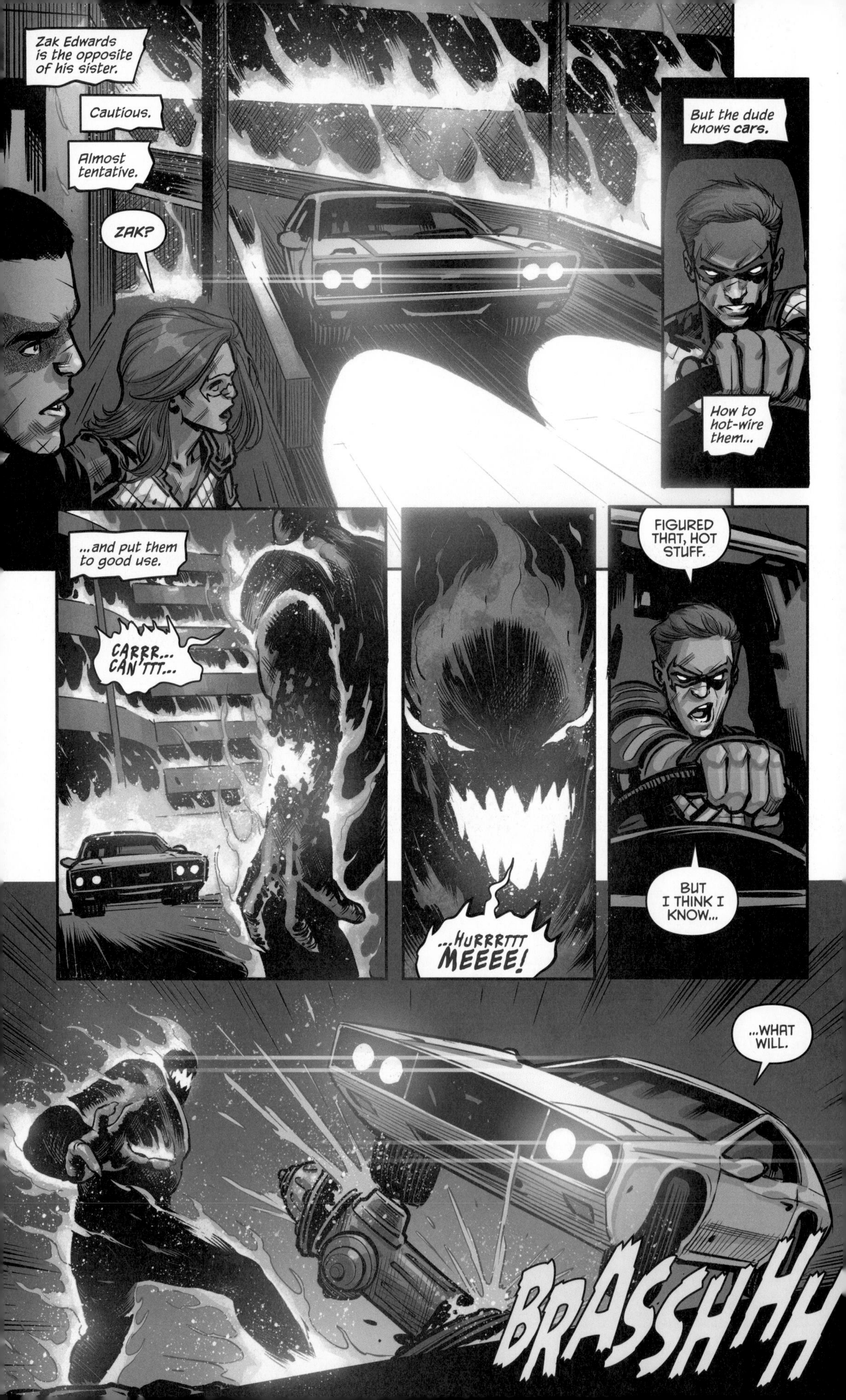
Zak Edwards is the opposite of his sister.
Cautious.
Almost tentative.
ZAK?
But the dude knows cars.
How to hot-wire them...
...and put them to good use.
CARRR... CAN'TTT...
...HURRRTTT MEEEE!
FIGURED THAT, HOT STUFF.
BUT I THINK I KNOW...
...WHAT WILL.
BRASSHHH

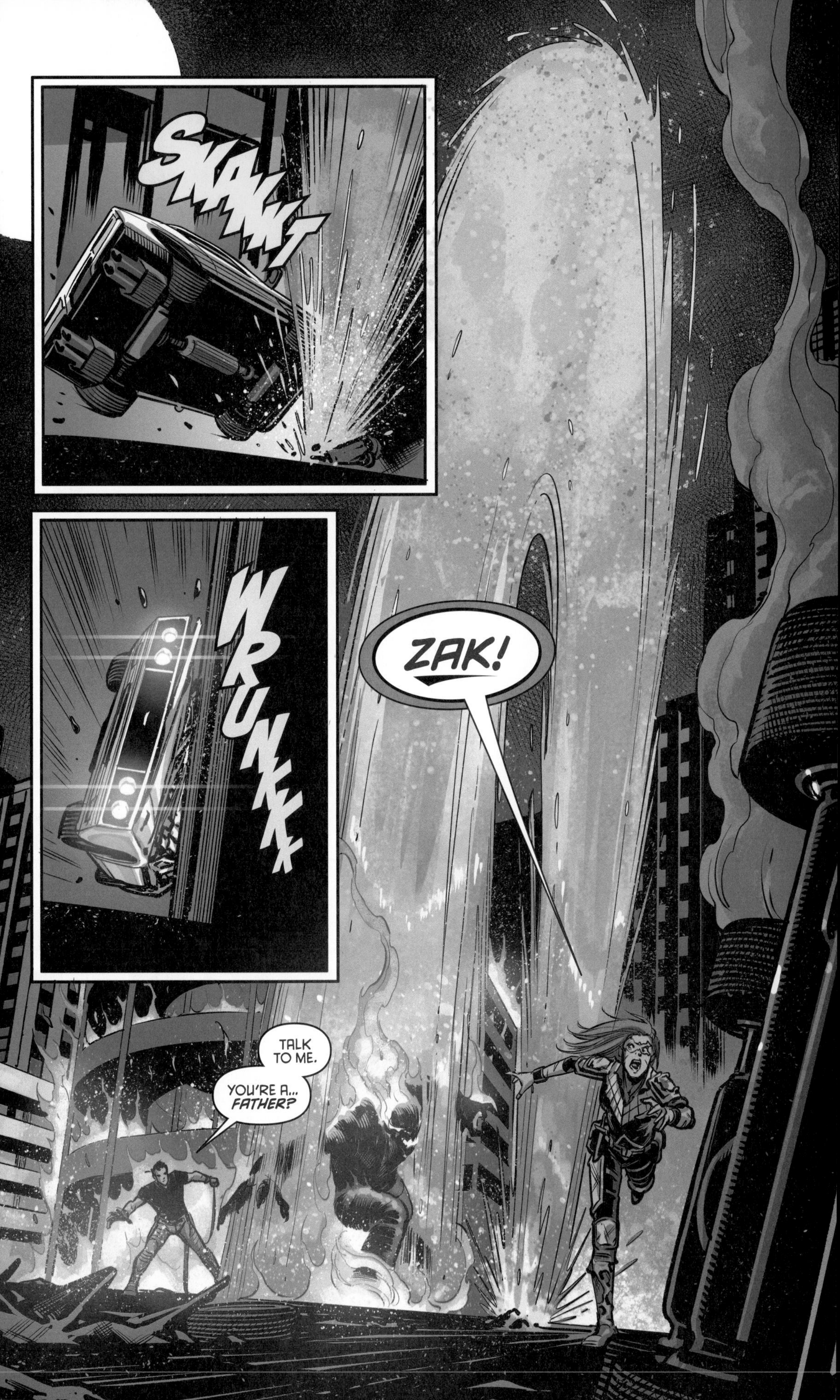

SKANK T
WRUNKKK
ZAK!
TALK TO ME.
YOU'RE A... *FATHER?*

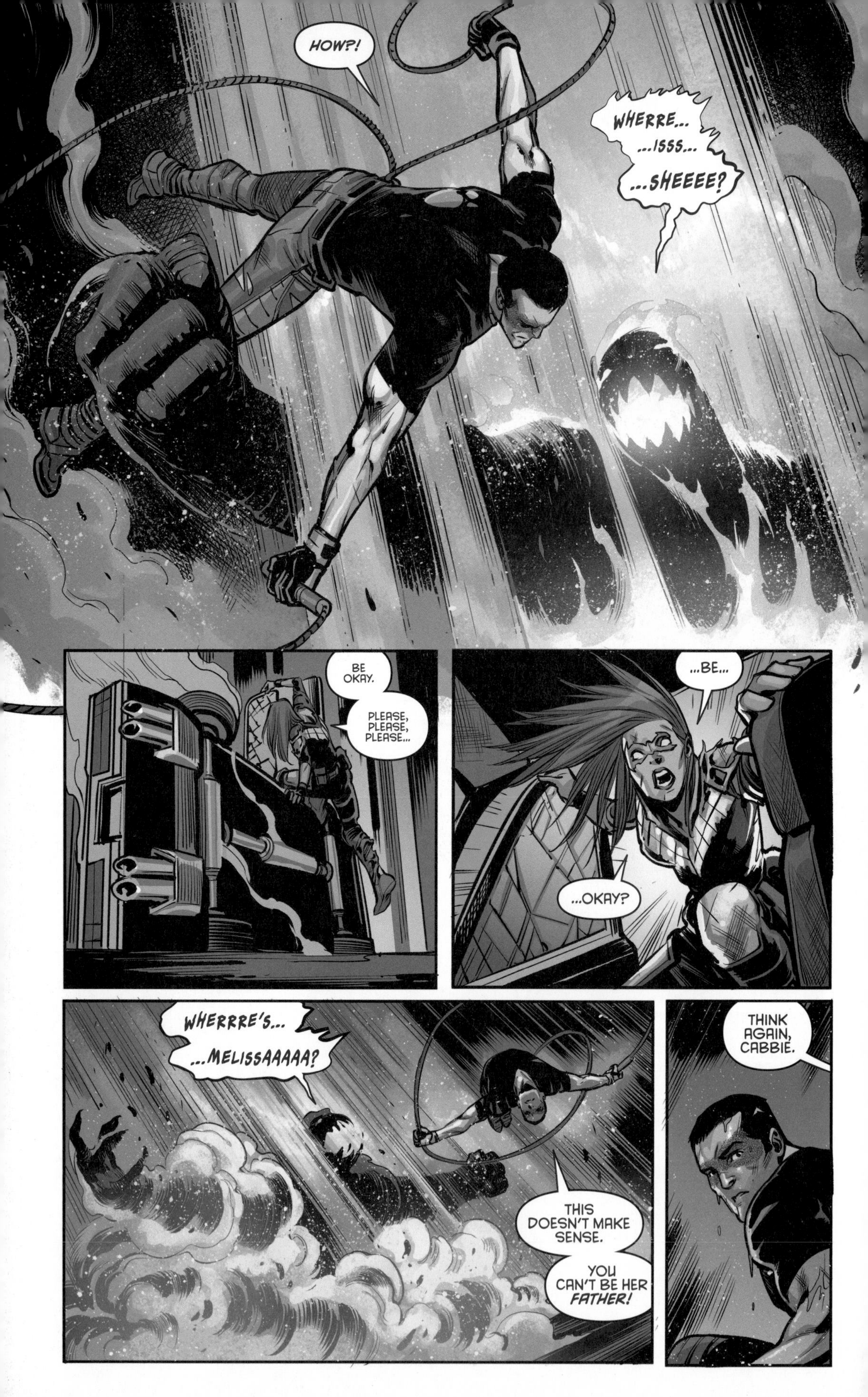
HOW?!
WHERRE... ...ISSS... ...SHEEEE?
BE OKAY.
PLEASE, PLEASE, PLEASE...
...BE...
...OKAY?
WHERRRE'S... ...MELISSAAAAA?
THIS DOESN'T MAKE SENSE.
YOU CAN'T BE HER *FATHER!*
THINK AGAIN, CABBIE.

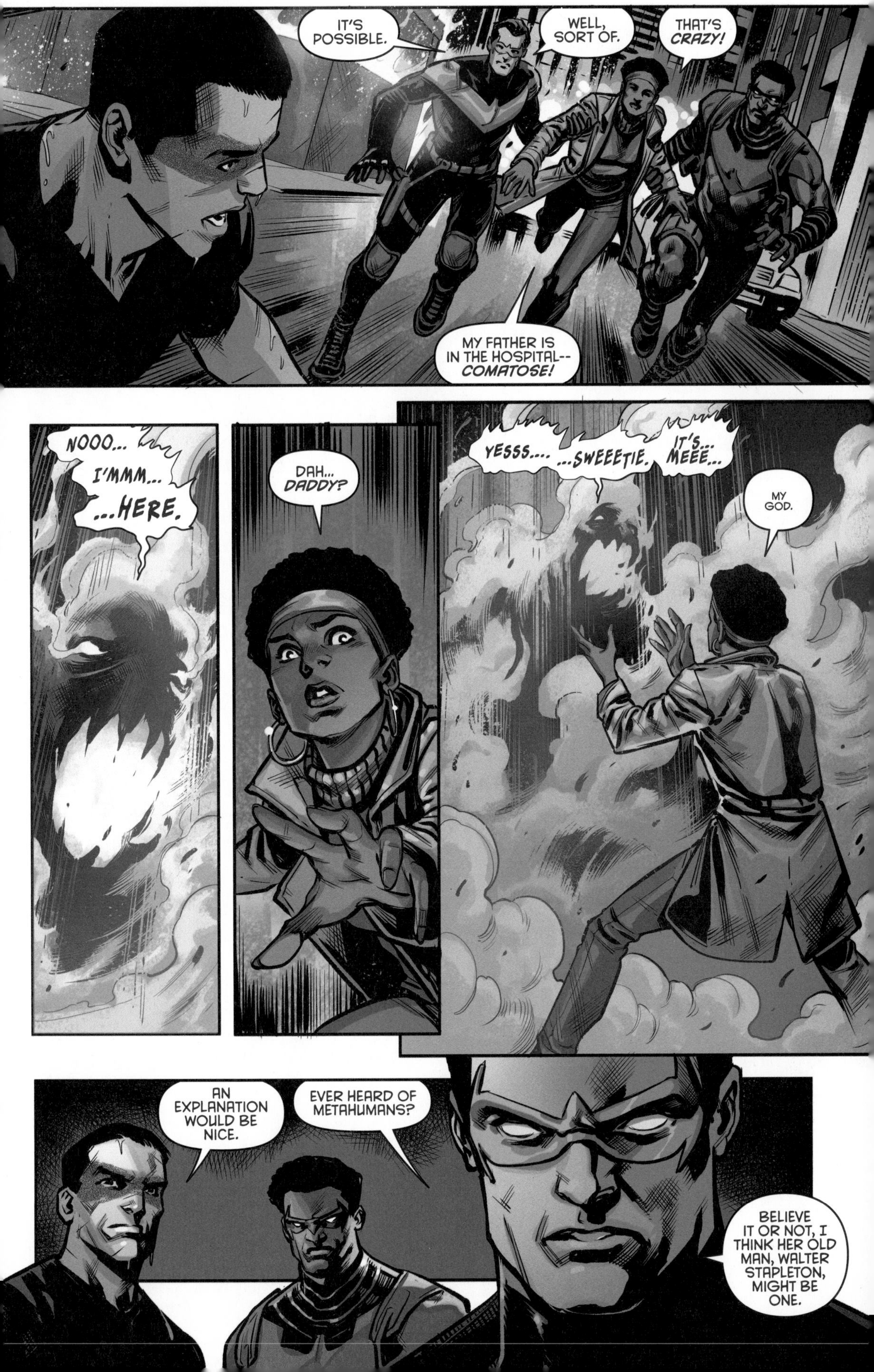

IT'S POSSIBLE.
WELL, SORT OF.
THAT'S *CRAZY!*
MY FATHER IS IN THE HOSPITAL-- *COMATOSE!*
NOOO... I'MMM... ...HERE.
DAH... *DADDY?*
YESSS.... ...SWEEETIE. IT'S... MEEE...
MY GOD.
AN EXPLANATION WOULD BE NICE.
EVER HEARD OF METAHUMANS?
BELIEVE IT OR NOT, I THINK HER OLD MAN, WALTER STAPLETON, MIGHT BE ONE.

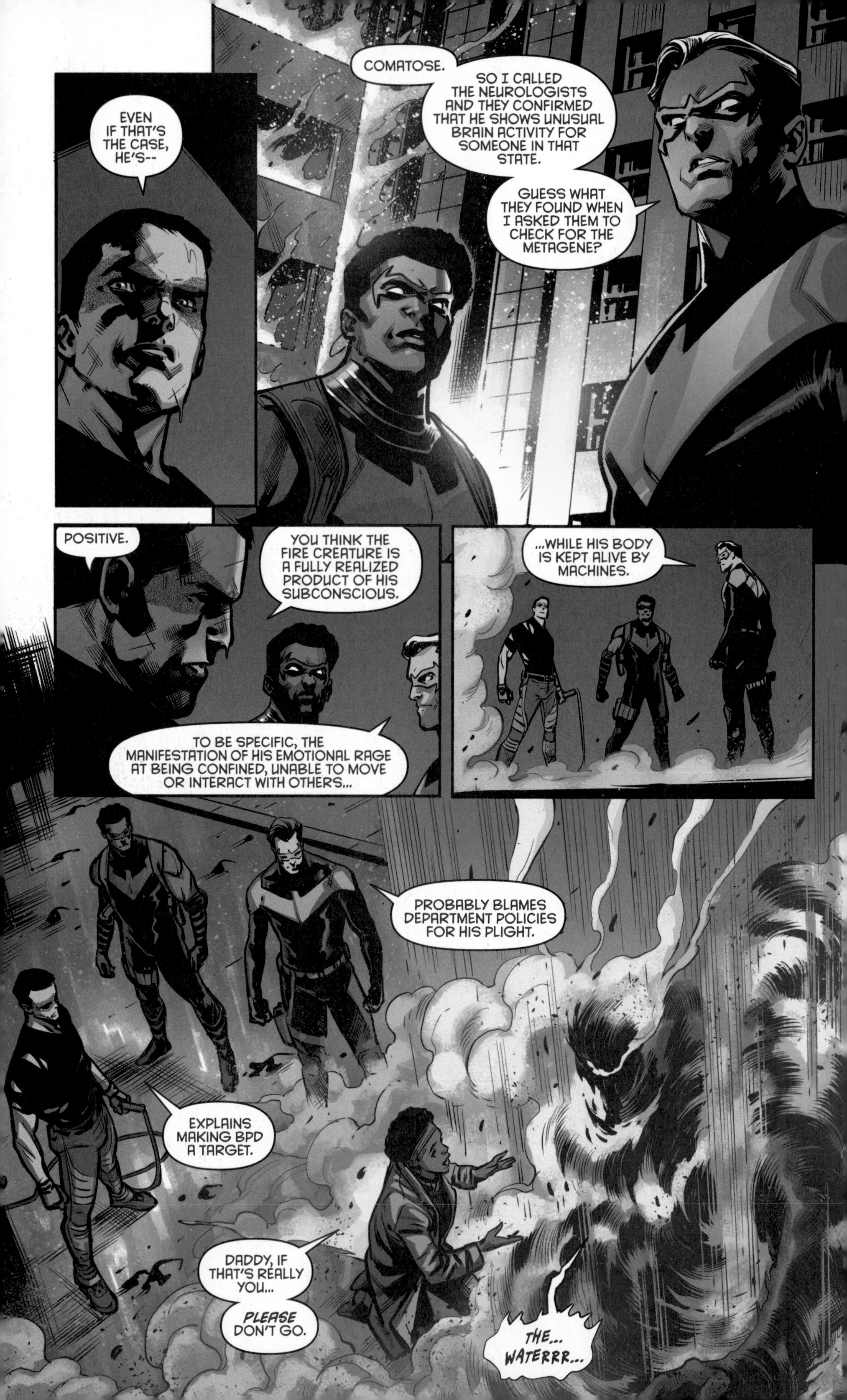
EVEN IF THAT'S THE CASE, HE'S--
COMATOSE.
SO I CALLED THE NEUROLOGISTS AND THEY CONFIRMED THAT HE SHOWS UNUSUAL BRAIN ACTIVITY FOR SOMEONE IN THAT STATE.
GUESS WHAT THEY FOUND WHEN I ASKED THEM TO CHECK FOR THE METAGENE?
POSITIVE.
YOU THINK THE FIRE CREATURE IS A FULLY REALIZED PRODUCT OF HIS SUBCONSCIOUS.
TO BE SPECIFIC, THE MANIFESTATION OF HIS EMOTIONAL RAGE AT BEING CONFINED, UNABLE TO MOVE OR INTERACT WITH OTHERS...
...WHILE HIS BODY IS KEPT ALIVE BY MACHINES.
PROBABLY BLAMES DEPARTMENT POLICIES FOR HIS PLIGHT.
EXPLAINS MAKING BPD A TARGET.
DADDY, IF THAT'S REALLY YOU...
PLEASE DON'T GO.
THE... WATERRR...

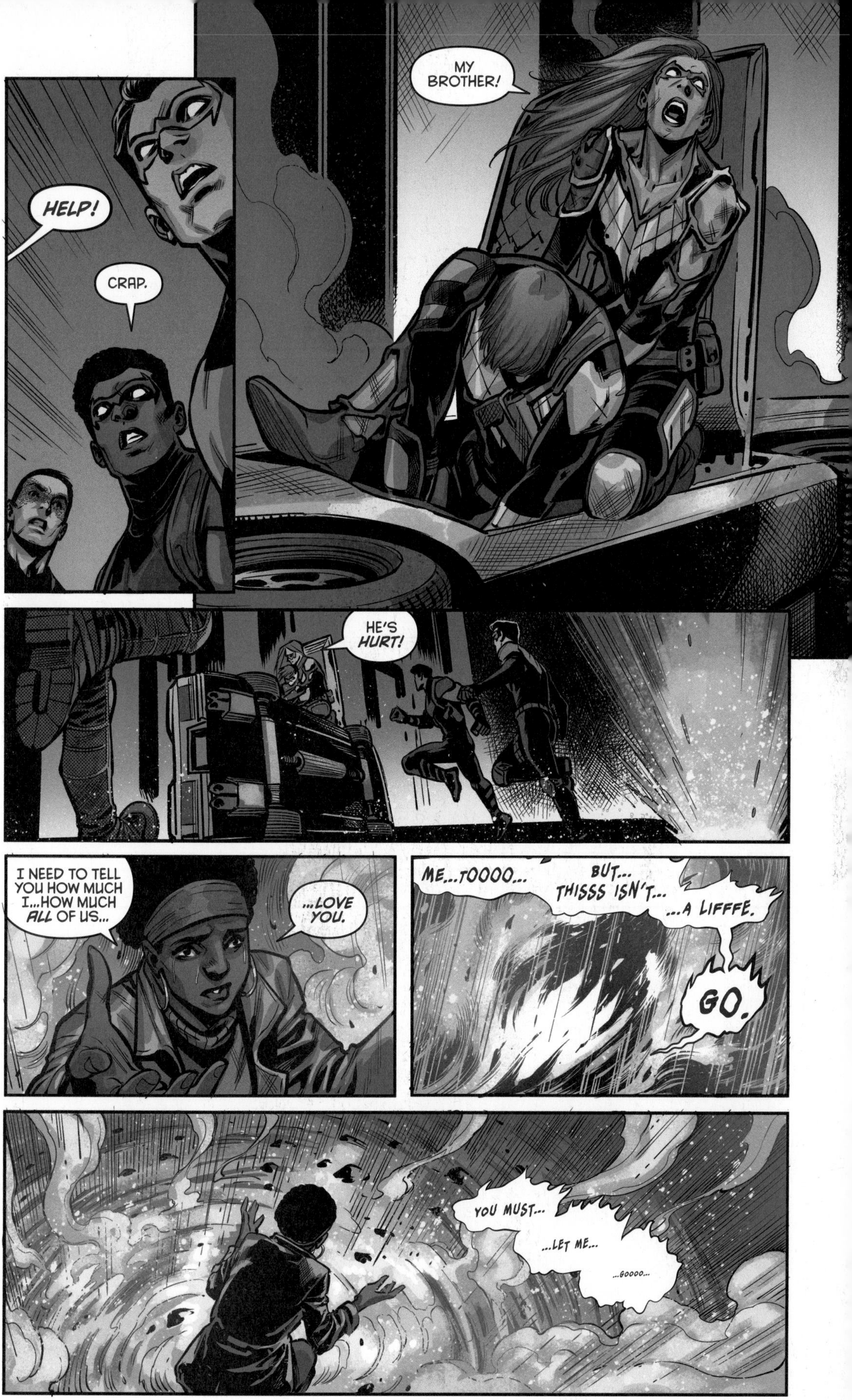
MY BROTHER!
HELP!
CRAP.
HE'S *HURT!*
I NEED TO TELL YOU HOW MUCH I...HOW MUCH *ALL* OF US...
...LOVE YOU.
ME...TOOOO...
BUT... THISSS ISN'T...
...A LIFFFE.
GO.
YOU MUST...
...LET ME...
...GOOOO...

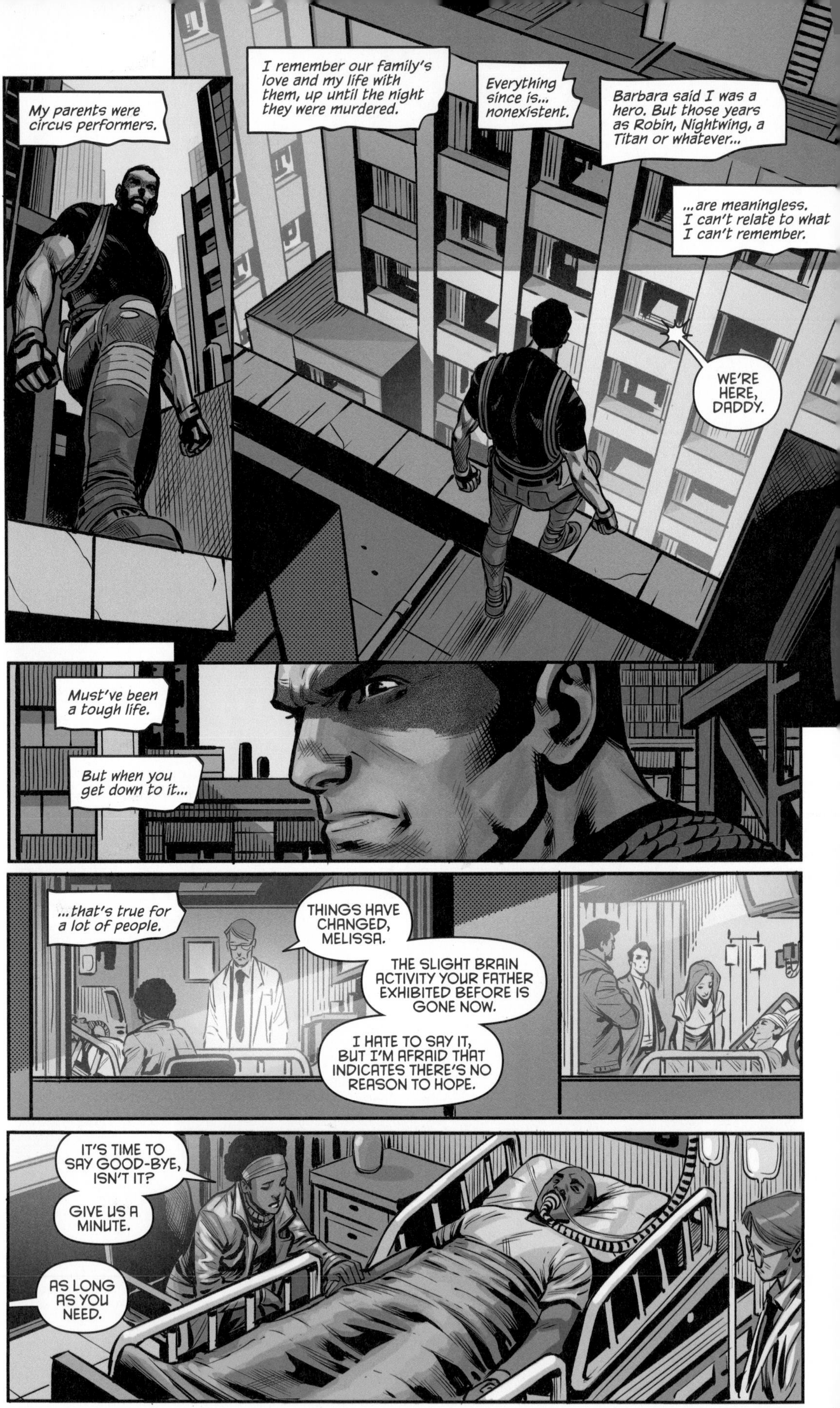
My parents were circus performers.
I remember our family's love and my life with them, up until the night they were murdered.
Everything since is... nonexistent.
Barbara said I was a hero. But those years as Robin, Nightwing, a Titan or whatever...
...are meaningless. I can't relate to what I can't remember.
WE'RE HERE, DADDY.
Must've been a tough life.
But when you get down to it...
...that's true for a lot of people.
THINGS HAVE CHANGED, MELISSA.
THE SLIGHT BRAIN ACTIVITY YOUR FATHER EXHIBITED BEFORE IS GONE NOW.
I HATE TO SAY IT, BUT I'M AFRAID THAT INDICATES THERE'S NO REASON TO HOPE.
IT'S TIME TO SAY GOOD-BYE, ISN'T IT?
GIVE US A MINUTE.
AS LONG AS YOU NEED.

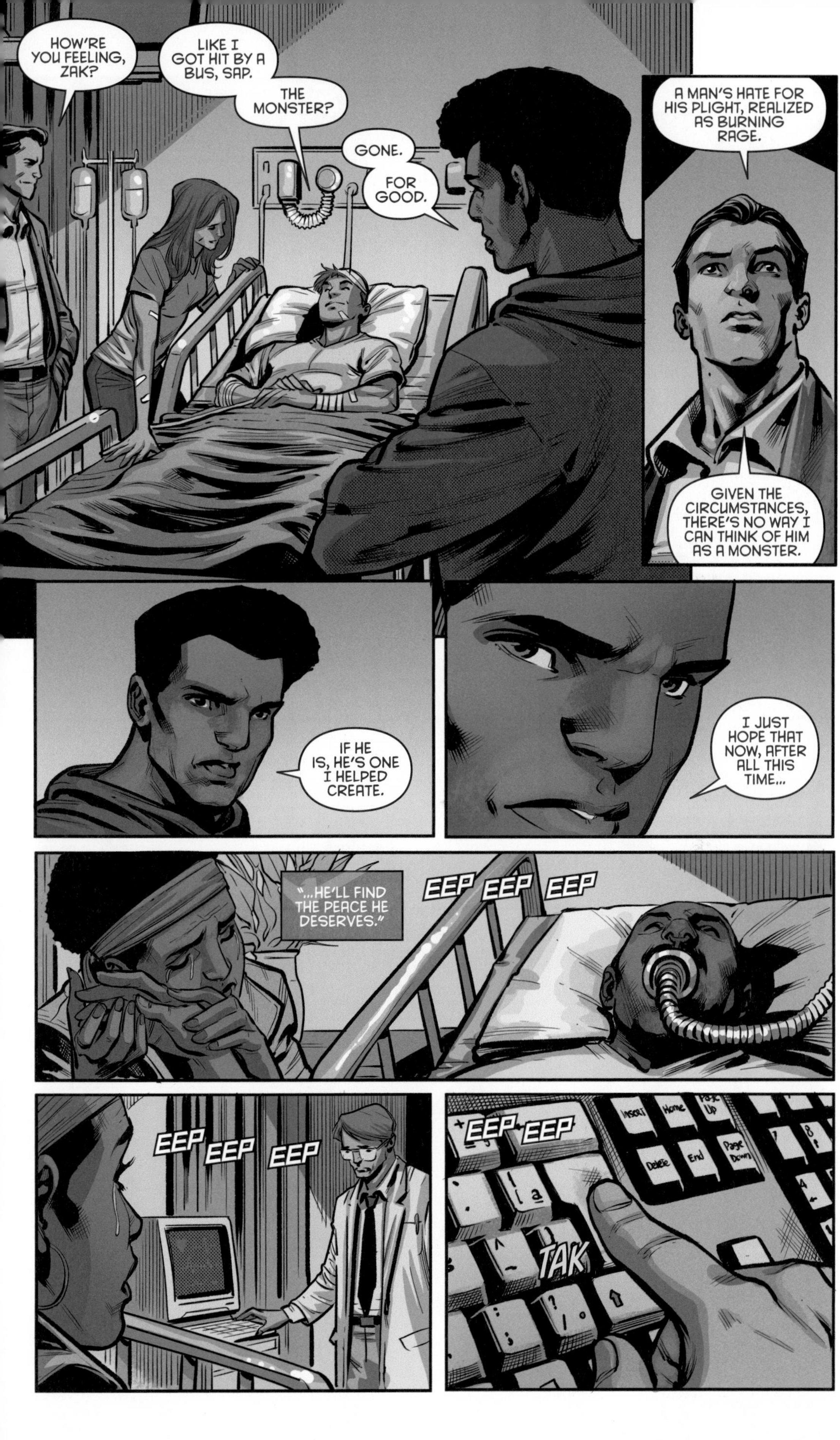
HOW'RE YOU FEELING, ZAK?
LIKE I GOT HIT BY A BUS, SAP.
THE MONSTER?
GONE.
FOR GOOD.
A MAN'S HATE FOR HIS PLIGHT, REALIZED AS BURNING RAGE.
GIVEN THE CIRCUMSTANCES, THERE'S NO WAY I CAN THINK OF HIM AS A MONSTER.
IF HE IS, HE'S ONE I HELPED CREATE.
I JUST HOPE THAT NOW, AFTER ALL THIS TIME...
"...HE'LL FIND THE PEACE HE DESERVES."
EEP EEP EEP
EEP EEP EEP
EEP EEP
TAK

BREEEEEEEEEEEEEEEEEET.

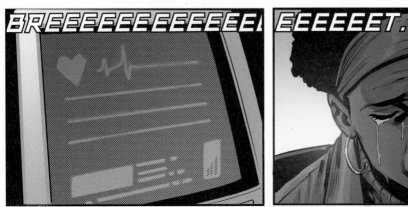

Like I said, I don't remember my years as a hero.

If they were filled with days like this...

...I consider that a blessing.

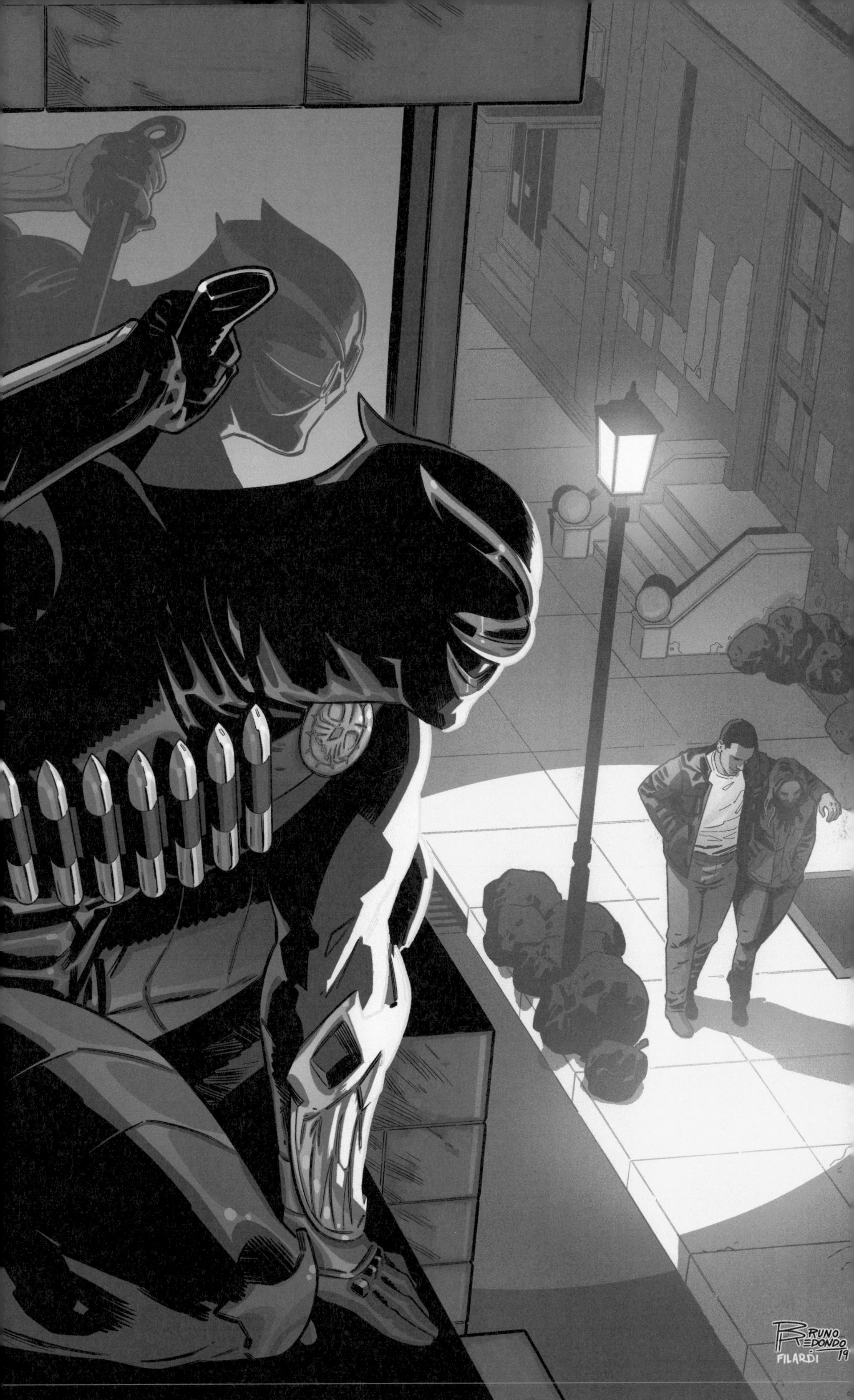
BRUNO REDONDO '19
FILARDI

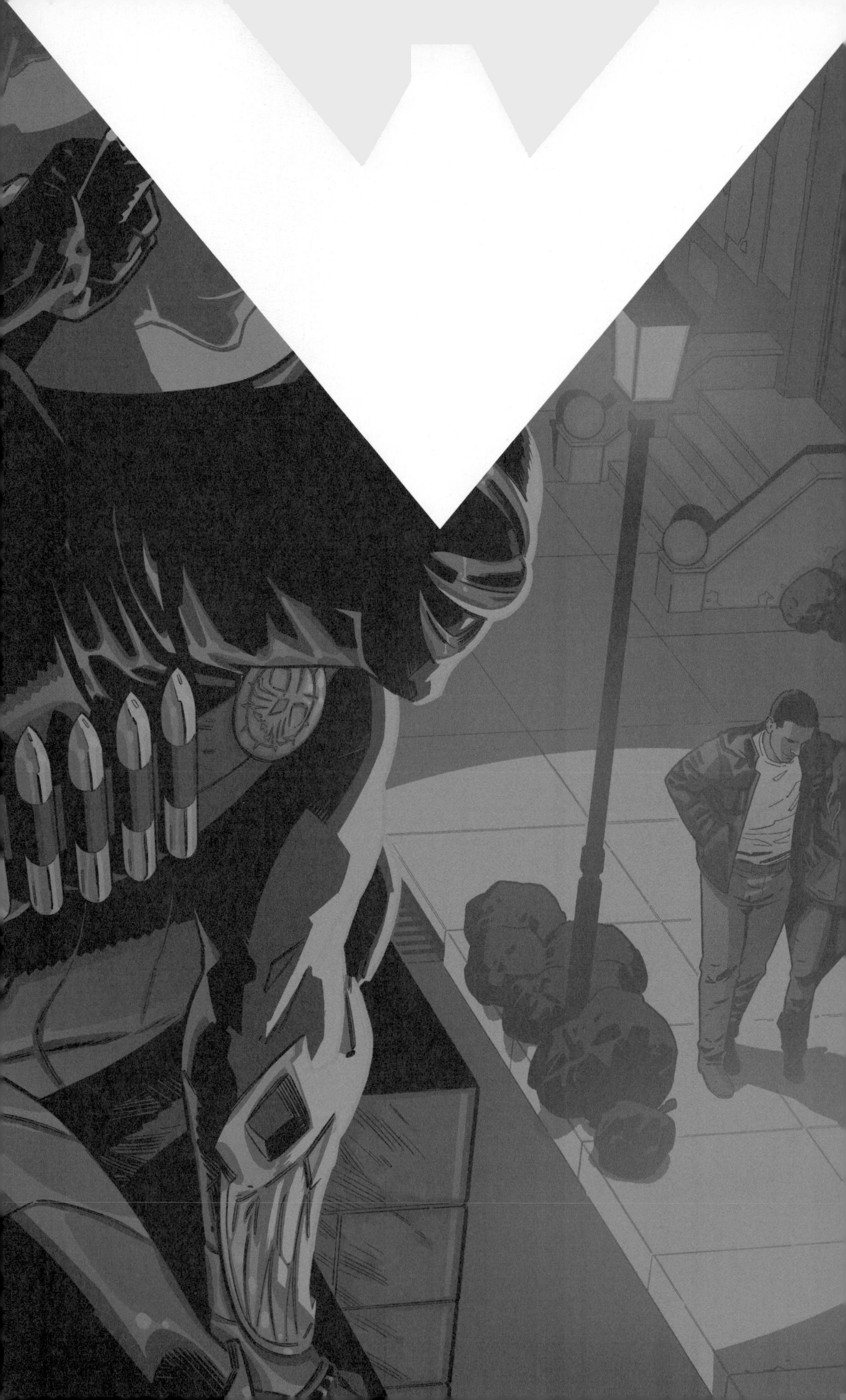

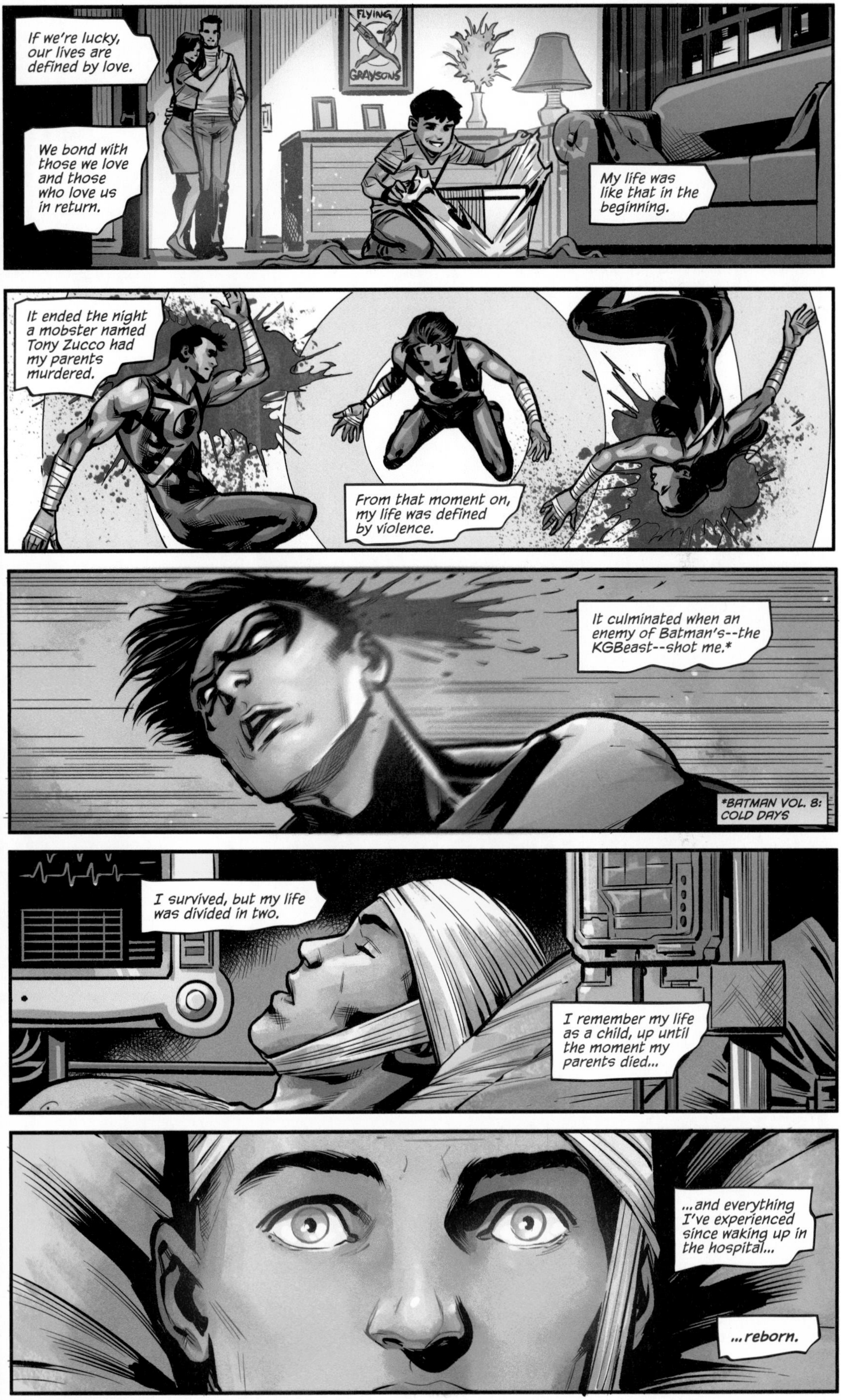

If we're lucky, our lives are defined by love.
FLYING GRAYSONS
We bond with those we love and those who love us in return.
My life was like that in the beginning.
It ended the night a mobster named Tony Zucco had my parents murdered.
From that moment on, my life was defined by violence.
It culminated when an enemy of Batman's--the KGBeast--shot me.*
*BATMAN VOL. 8: COLD DAYS
I survived, but my life was divided in two.
I remember my life as a child, up until the moment my parents died...
...and everything I've experienced since waking up in the hospital...
...reborn.

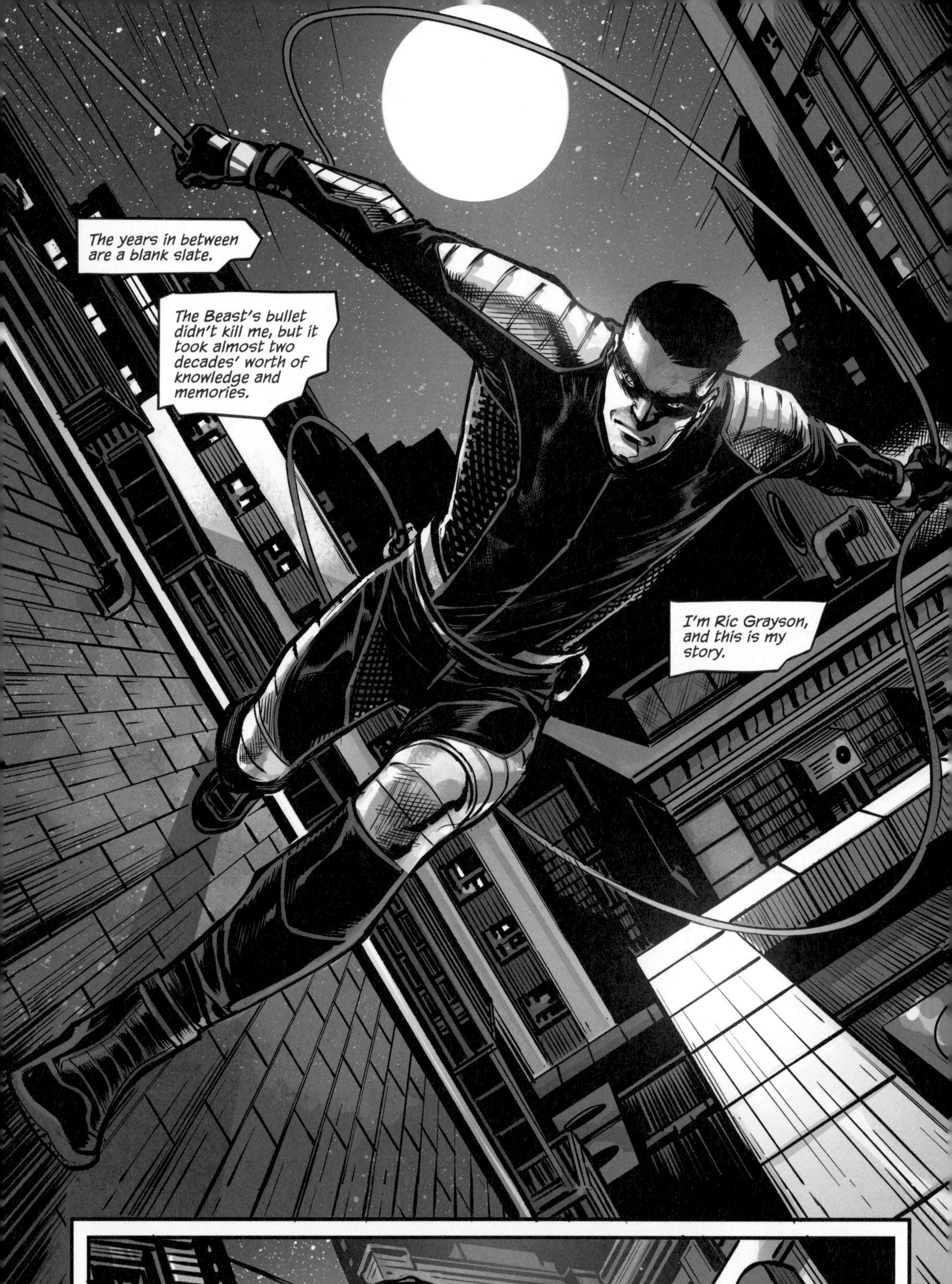

The years in between are a blank slate.
The Beast's bullet didn't kill me, but it took almost two decades' worth of knowledge and memories.
I'm Ric Grayson, and this is my story.

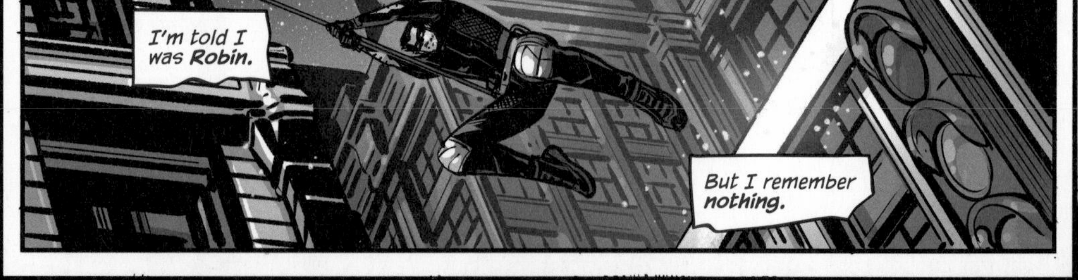

I'm told I was **Robin.**
But I remember **nothing.**

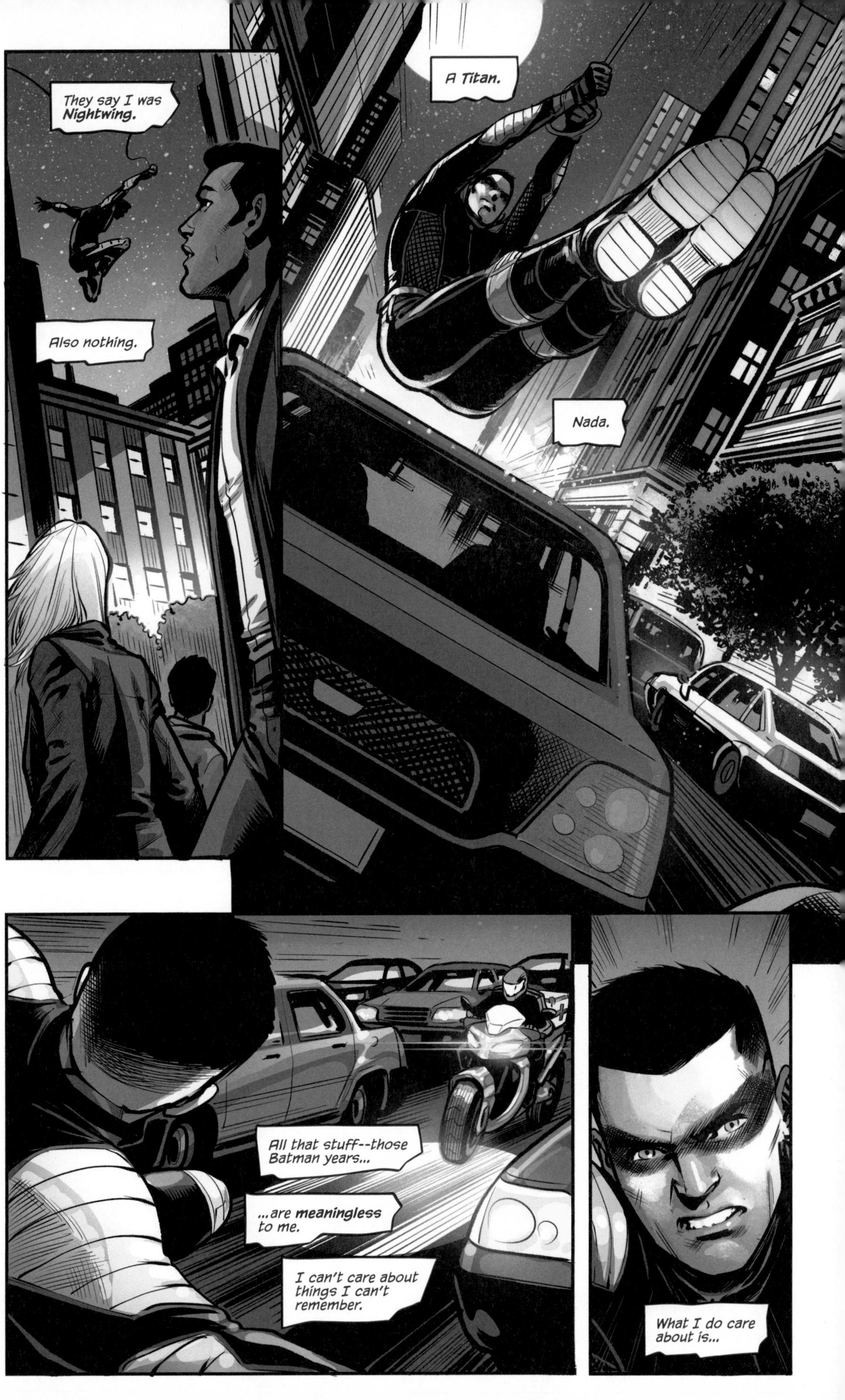
They say I was Nightwing.
Also nothing.
A Titan.
Nada.
All that stuff--those Batman years...
...are meaningless to me.
I can't care about things I can't remember.
What I do care about is...

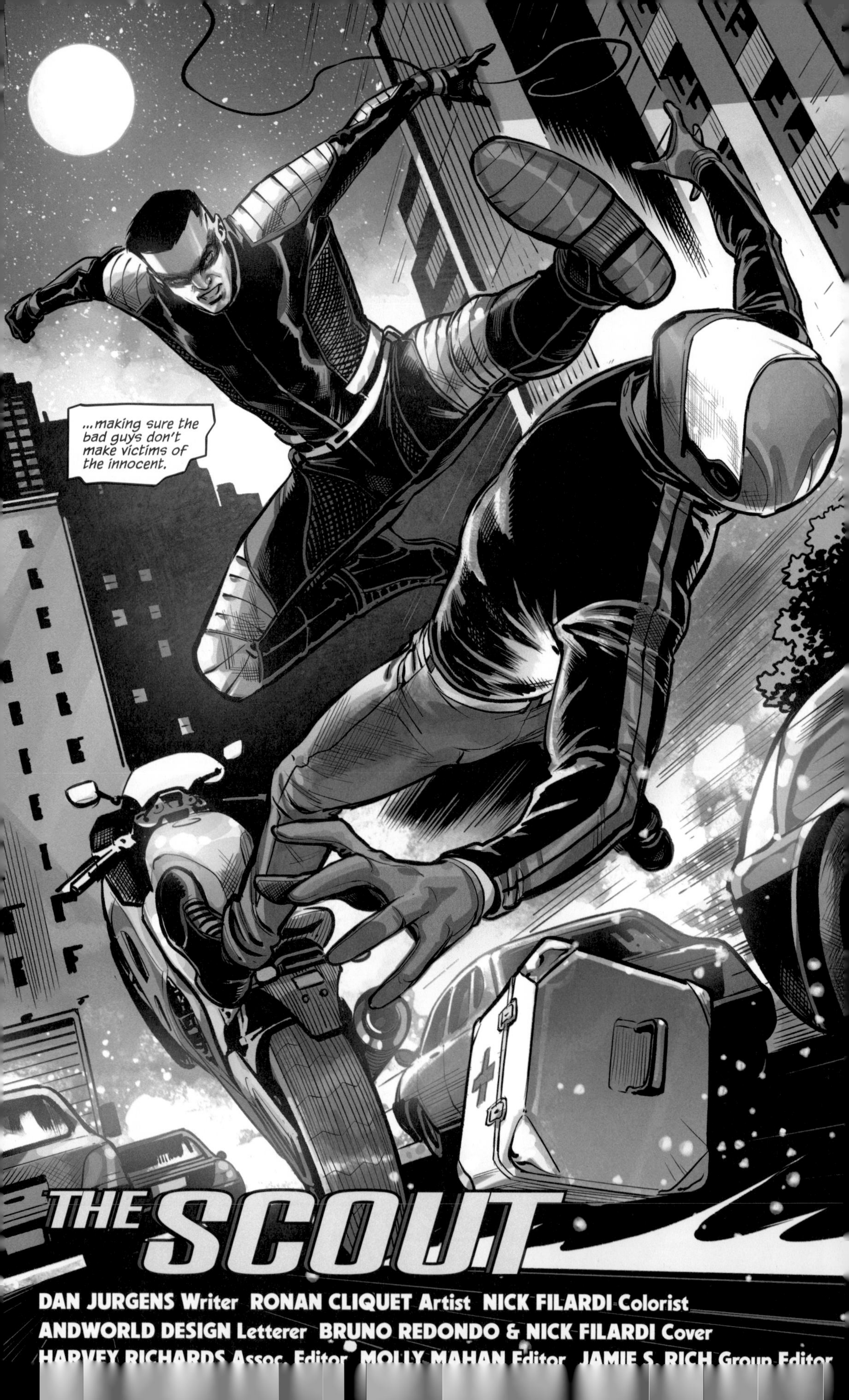
...making sure the bad guys don't make victims of the innocent.
THE SCOUT
DAN JURGENS Writer RONAN CLIQUET Artist NICK FILARDI Colorist
ANDWORLD DESIGN Letterer BRUNO REDONDO & NICK FILARDI Cover
HARVEY RICHARDS Assoc. Editor MOLLY MAHAN Editor JAMIE S. RICH Group Editor

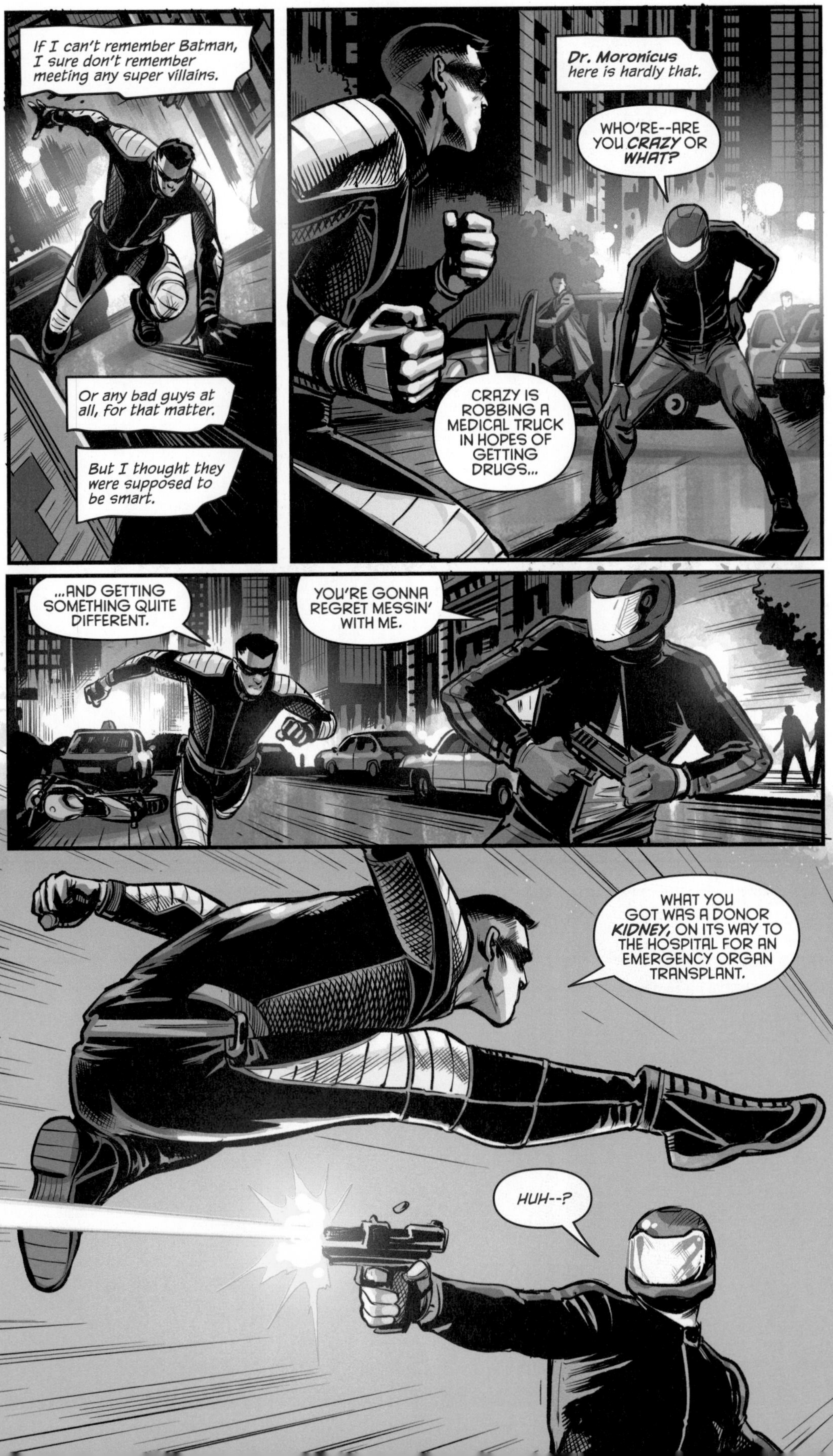

If I can't remember Batman, I sure don't remember meeting any super villains.
Or any bad guys at all, for that matter.
But I thought they were supposed to be smart.
Dr. Moronicus here is hardly that.
WHO'RE--ARE YOU CRAZY OR WHAT?
CRAZY IS ROBBING A MEDICAL TRUCK IN HOPES OF GETTING DRUGS...
...AND GETTING SOMETHING QUITE DIFFERENT.
YOU'RE GONNA REGRET MESSIN' WITH ME.
WHAT YOU GOT WAS A DONOR KIDNEY, ON ITS WAY TO THE HOSPITAL FOR AN EMERGENCY ORGAN TRANSPLANT.
HUH--?

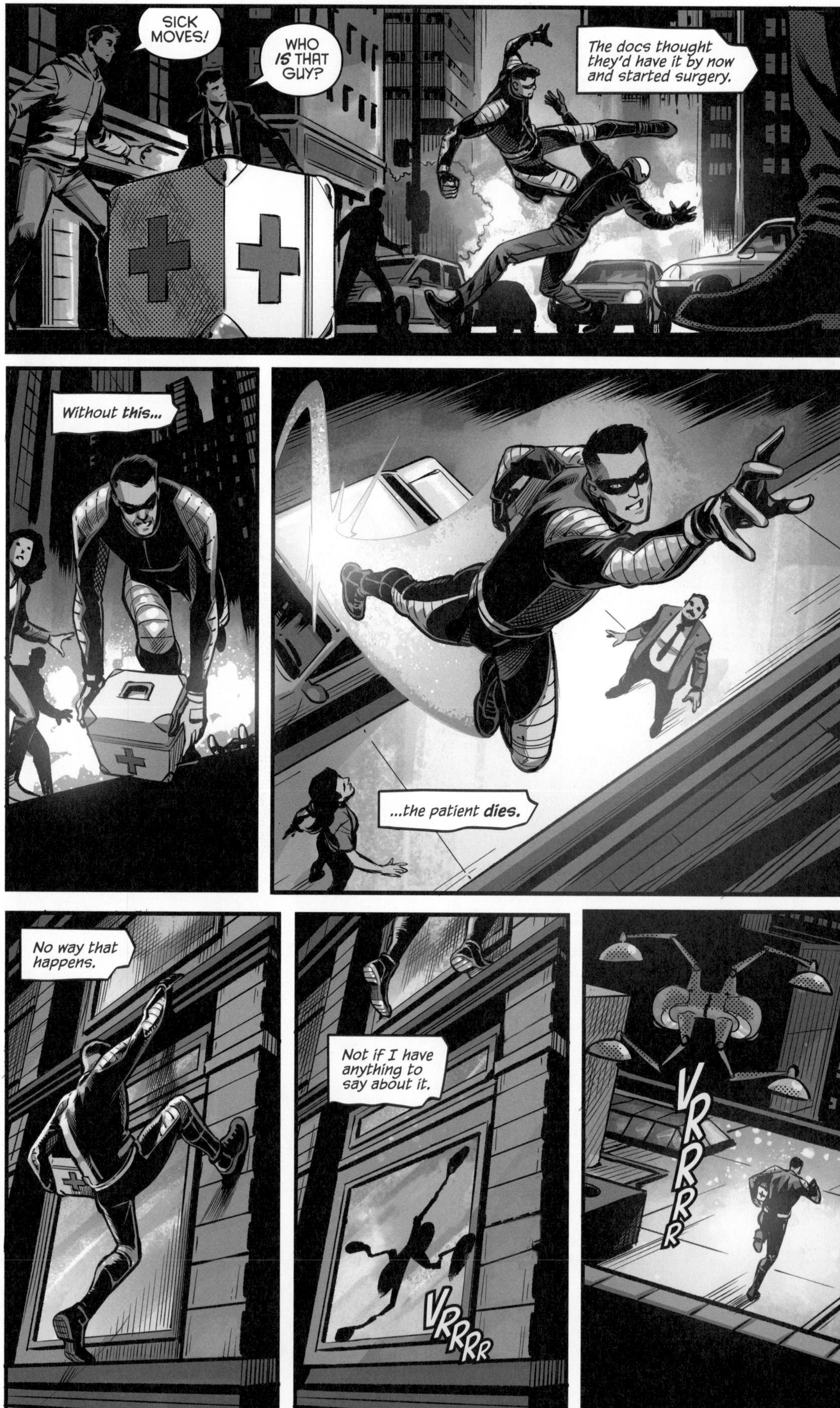

SICK MOVES!
WHO IS THAT GUY?
The docs thought they'd have it by now and started surgery.
Without this...
...the patient dies.
No way that happens.
Not if I have anything to say about it.
VRRRR
VRRRR

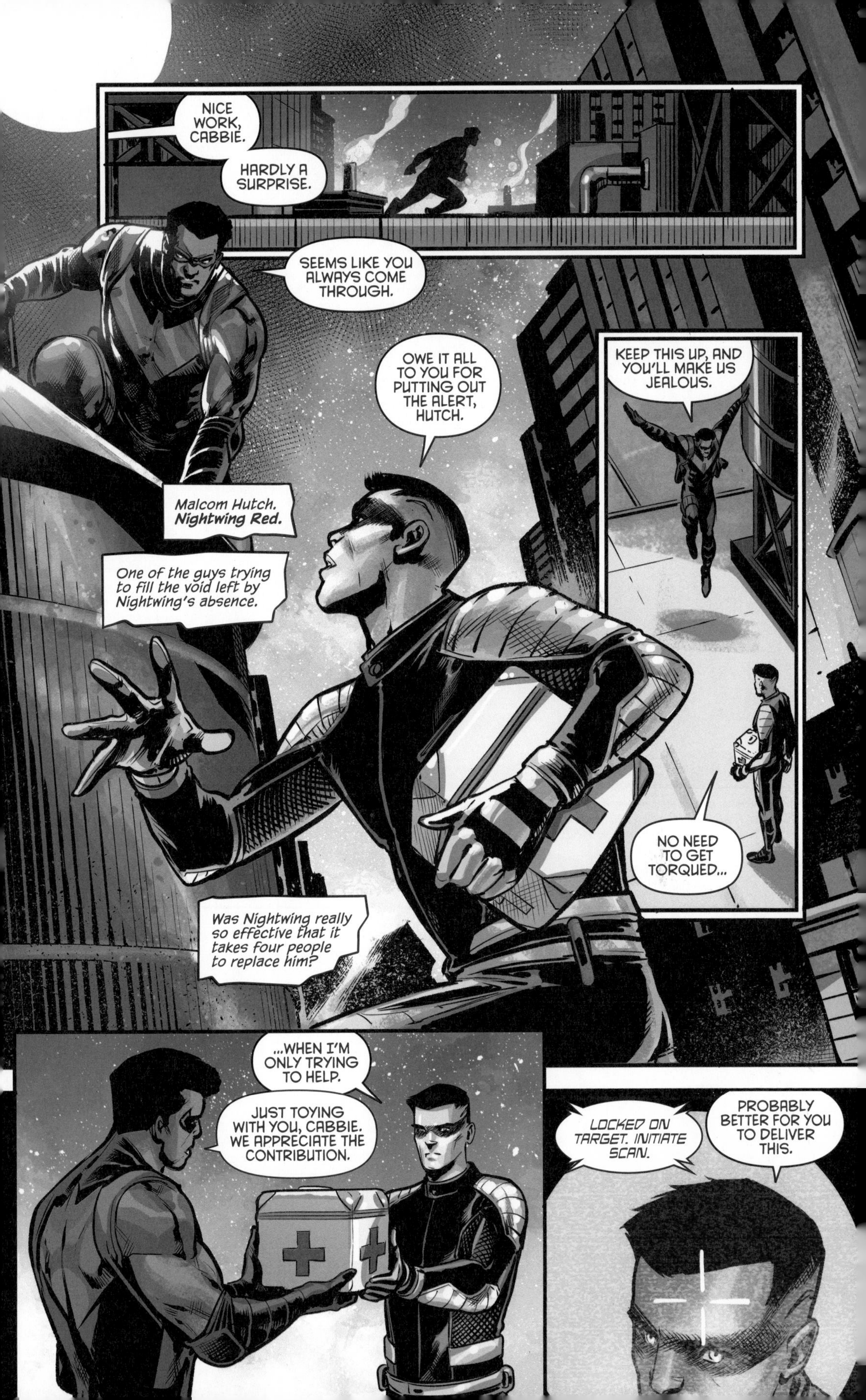
NICE WORK, CABBIE.
HARDLY A SURPRISE.
SEEMS LIKE YOU ALWAYS COME THROUGH.
OWE IT ALL TO YOU FOR PUTTING OUT THE ALERT, HUTCH.
Malcom Hutch. Nightwing Red.
One of the guys trying to fill the void left by Nightwing's absence.
Was Nightwing really so effective that it takes four people to replace him?
KEEP THIS UP, AND YOU'LL MAKE US JEALOUS.
NO NEED TO GET TORQUED...
...WHEN I'M ONLY TRYING TO HELP.
JUST TOYING WITH YOU, CABBIE. WE APPRECIATE THE CONTRIBUTION.
LOCKED ON TARGET. INITIATE SCAN.
PROBABLY BETTER FOR YOU TO DELIVER THIS.

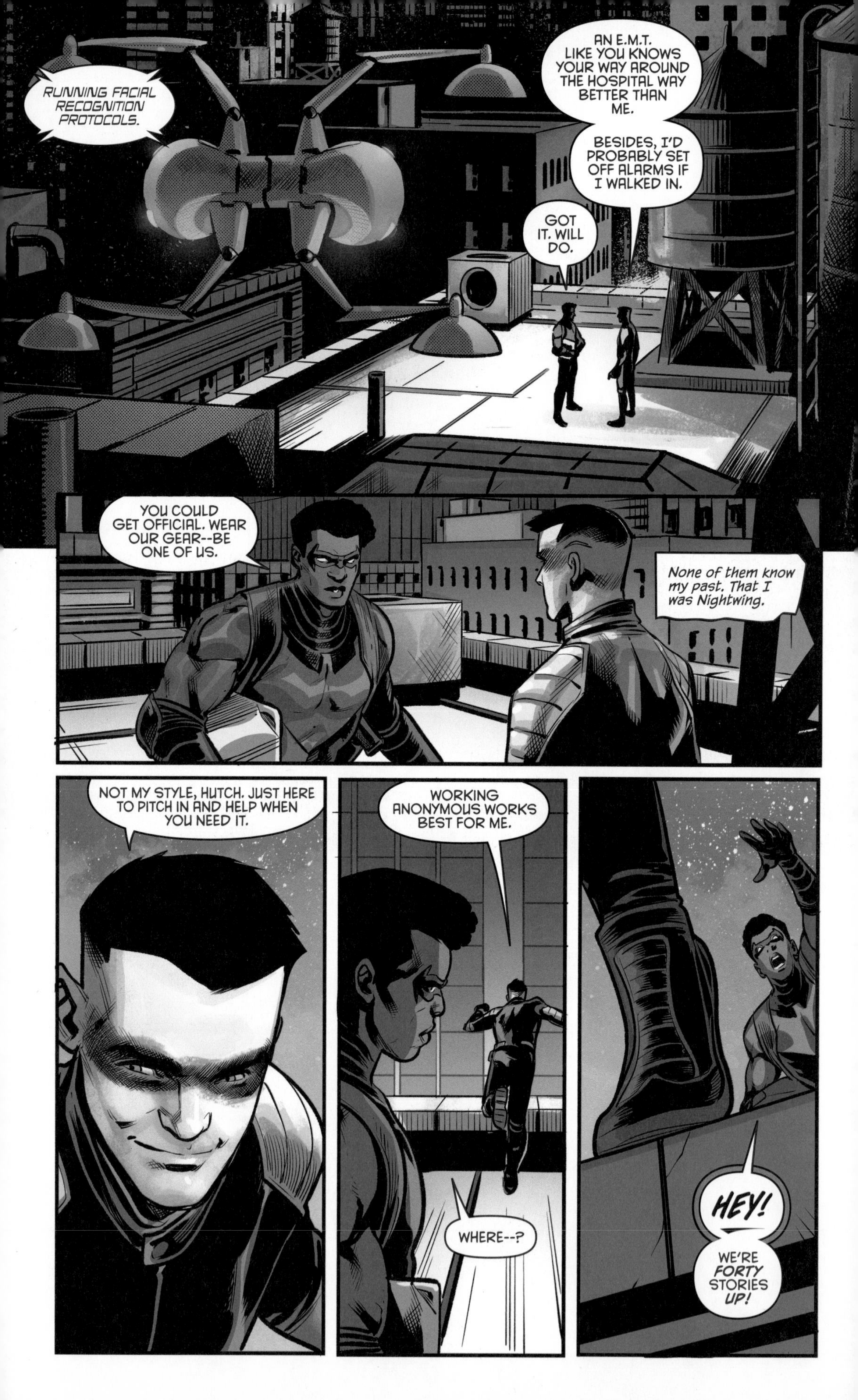
RUNNING FACIAL RECOGNITION PROTOCOLS.
AN E.M.T. LIKE YOU KNOWS YOUR WAY AROUND THE HOSPITAL WAY BETTER THAN ME.
BESIDES, I'D PROBABLY SET OFF ALARMS IF I WALKED IN.
GOT IT. WILL DO.
YOU COULD GET OFFICIAL. WEAR OUR GEAR--BE ONE OF US.
None of them know my past. That I was Nightwing.
NOT MY STYLE, HUTCH. JUST HERE TO PITCH IN AND HELP WHEN YOU NEED IT.
WORKING ANONYMOUS WORKS BEST FOR ME.
WHERE--?
HEY!
WE'RE FORTY STORIES UP!

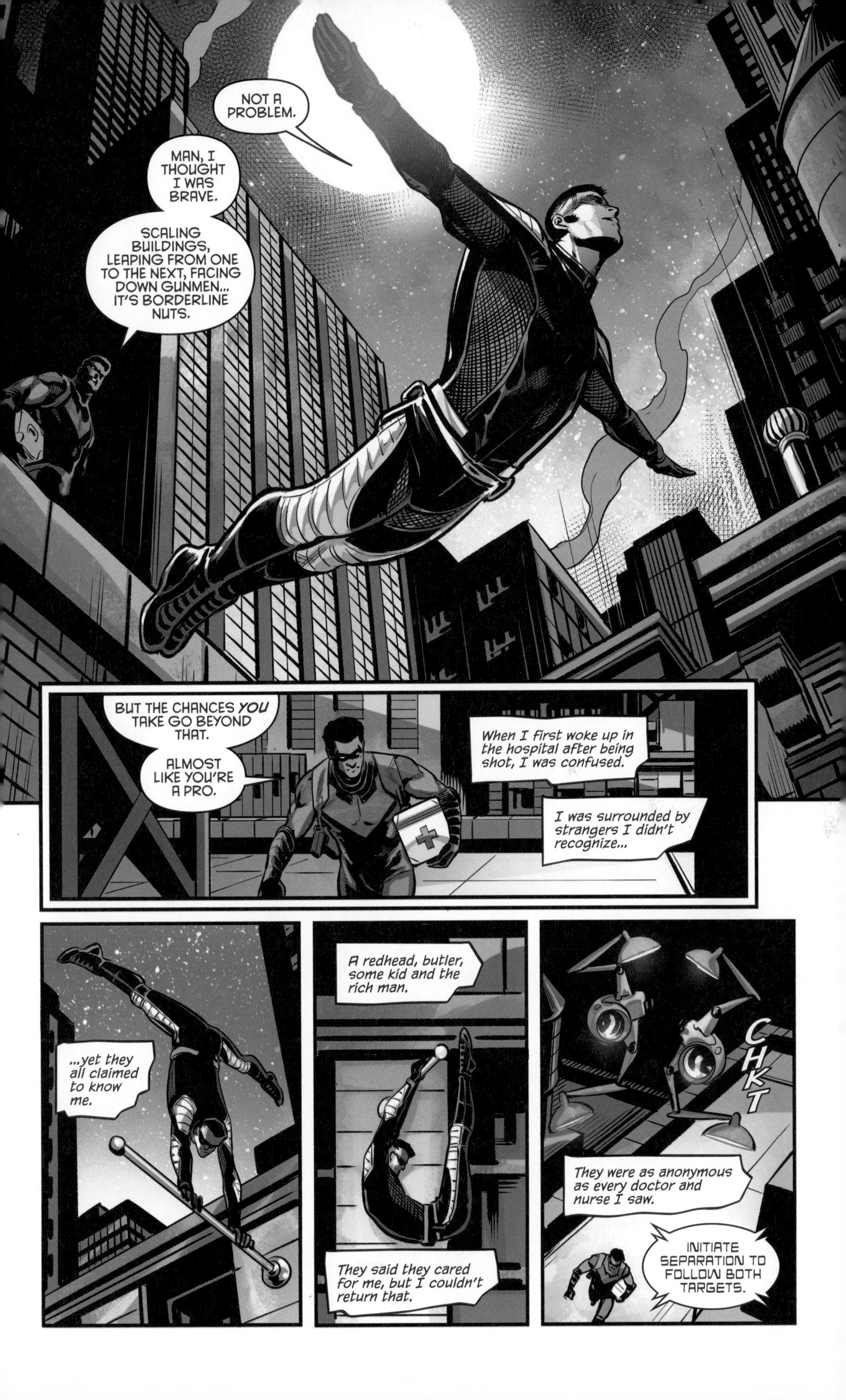
NOT A PROBLEM.
MAN, I THOUGHT I WAS BRAVE.
SCALING BUILDINGS, LEAPING FROM ONE TO THE NEXT, FACING DOWN GUNMEN... IT'S BORDERLINE NUTS.
BUT THE CHANCES YOU TAKE GO BEYOND THAT.
ALMOST LIKE YOU'RE A PRO.
When I first woke up in the hospital after being shot, I was confused.
I was surrounded by strangers I didn't recognize...
...yet they all claimed to know me.
A redhead, butler, some kid and the rich man.
They said they cared for me, but I couldn't return that.
CHKT
They were as anonymous as every doctor and nurse I saw.
INITIATE SEPARATION TO FOLLOW BOTH TARGETS.

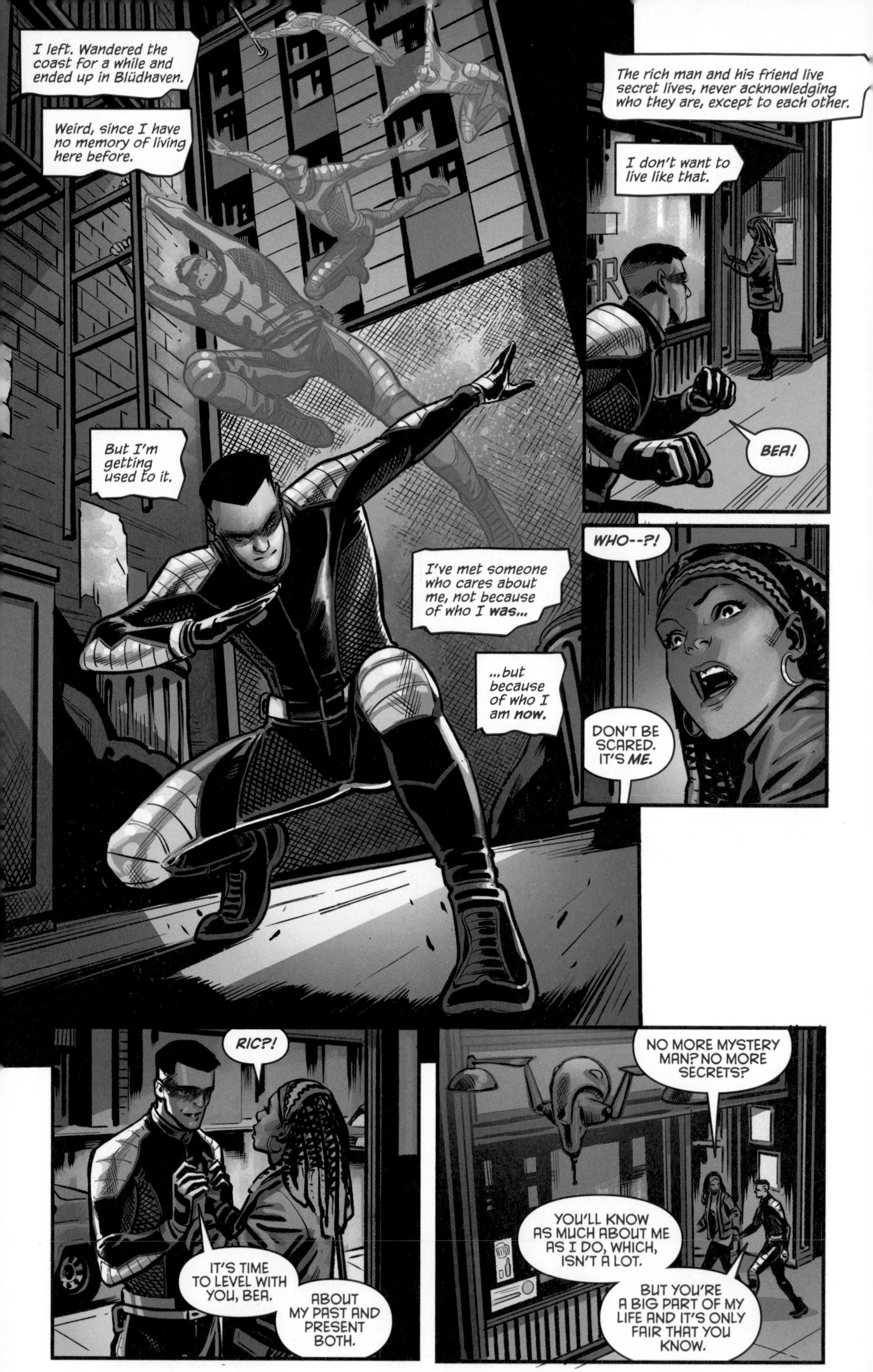

I left. Wandered the coast for a while and ended up in Blüdhaven.
Weird, since I have no memory of living here before.
But I'm getting used to it.
I've met someone who cares about me, not because of who I was...
...but because of who I am *now.*
The rich man and his friend live secret lives, never acknowledging who they are, except to each other.
I don't want to live like that.
BEA!
WHO--?!
DON'T BE SCARED. IT'S *ME.*
RIC?!
IT'S TIME TO LEVEL WITH YOU, BEA.
ABOUT MY PAST AND PRESENT BOTH.
NO MORE MYSTERY MAN? NO MORE SECRETS?
YOU'LL KNOW AS MUCH ABOUT ME AS I DO, WHICH, ISN'T A LOT.
BUT YOU'RE A BIG PART OF MY LIFE AND IT'S ONLY FAIR THAT YOU KNOW.

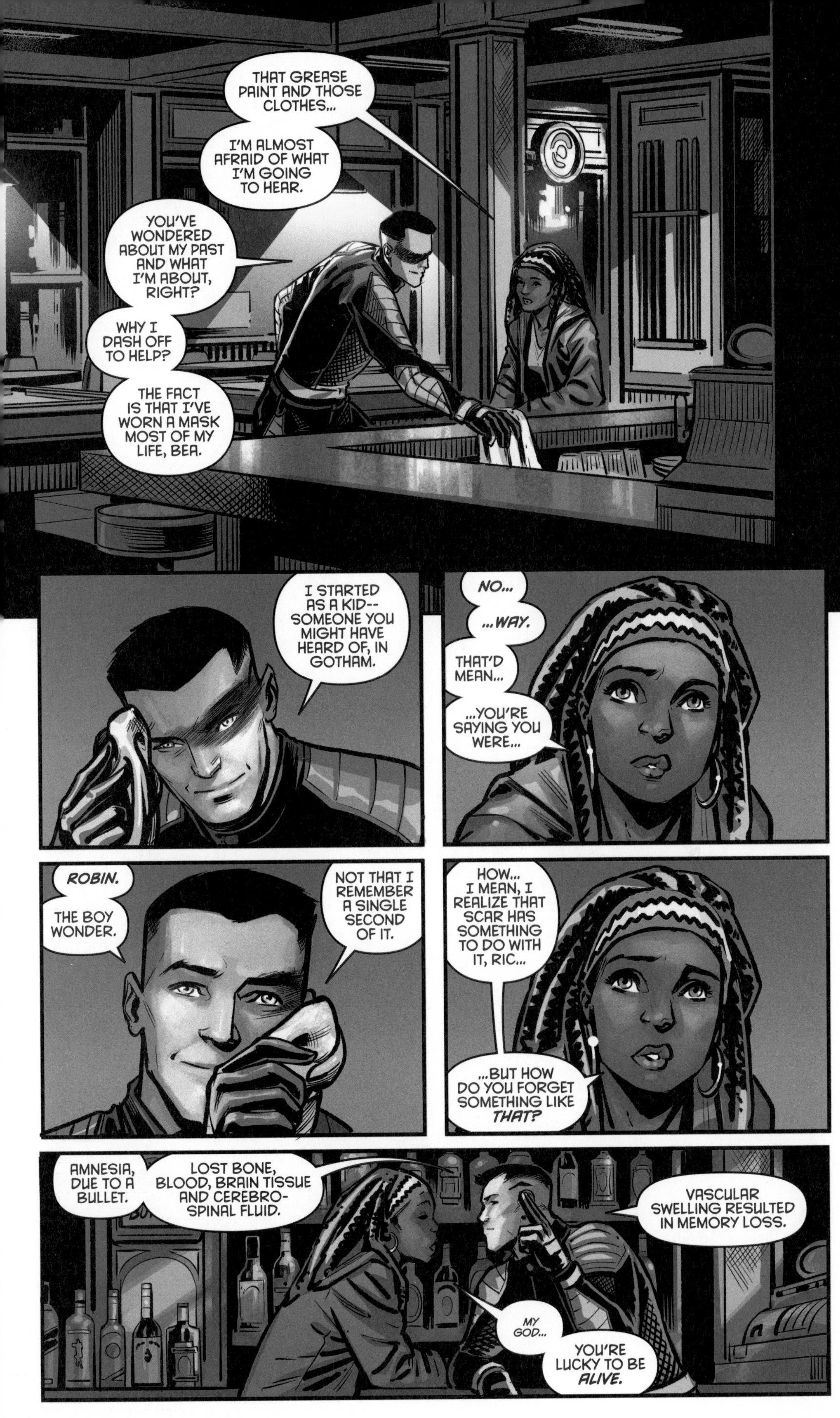

THAT GREASE PAINT AND THOSE CLOTHES...
I'M ALMOST AFRAID OF WHAT I'M GOING TO HEAR.
YOU'VE WONDERED ABOUT MY PAST AND WHAT I'M ABOUT, RIGHT?
WHY I DASH OFF TO HELP?
THE FACT IS THAT I'VE WORN A MASK MOST OF MY LIFE, BEA.
I STARTED AS A KID-- SOMEONE YOU MIGHT HAVE HEARD OF, IN GOTHAM.
NO...
...WAY.
THAT'D MEAN...
...YOU'RE SAYING YOU WERE...
ROBIN.
THE BOY WONDER.
NOT THAT I REMEMBER A SINGLE SECOND OF IT.
HOW... I MEAN, I REALIZE THAT SCAR HAS SOMETHING TO DO WITH IT, RIC...
...BUT HOW DO YOU FORGET SOMETHING LIKE THAT?
AMNESIA, DUE TO A BULLET.
LOST BONE, BLOOD, BRAIN TISSUE AND CEREBRO-SPINAL FLUID.
VASCULAR SWELLING RESULTED IN MEMORY LOSS.
MY GOD...
YOU'RE LUCKY TO BE ALIVE.

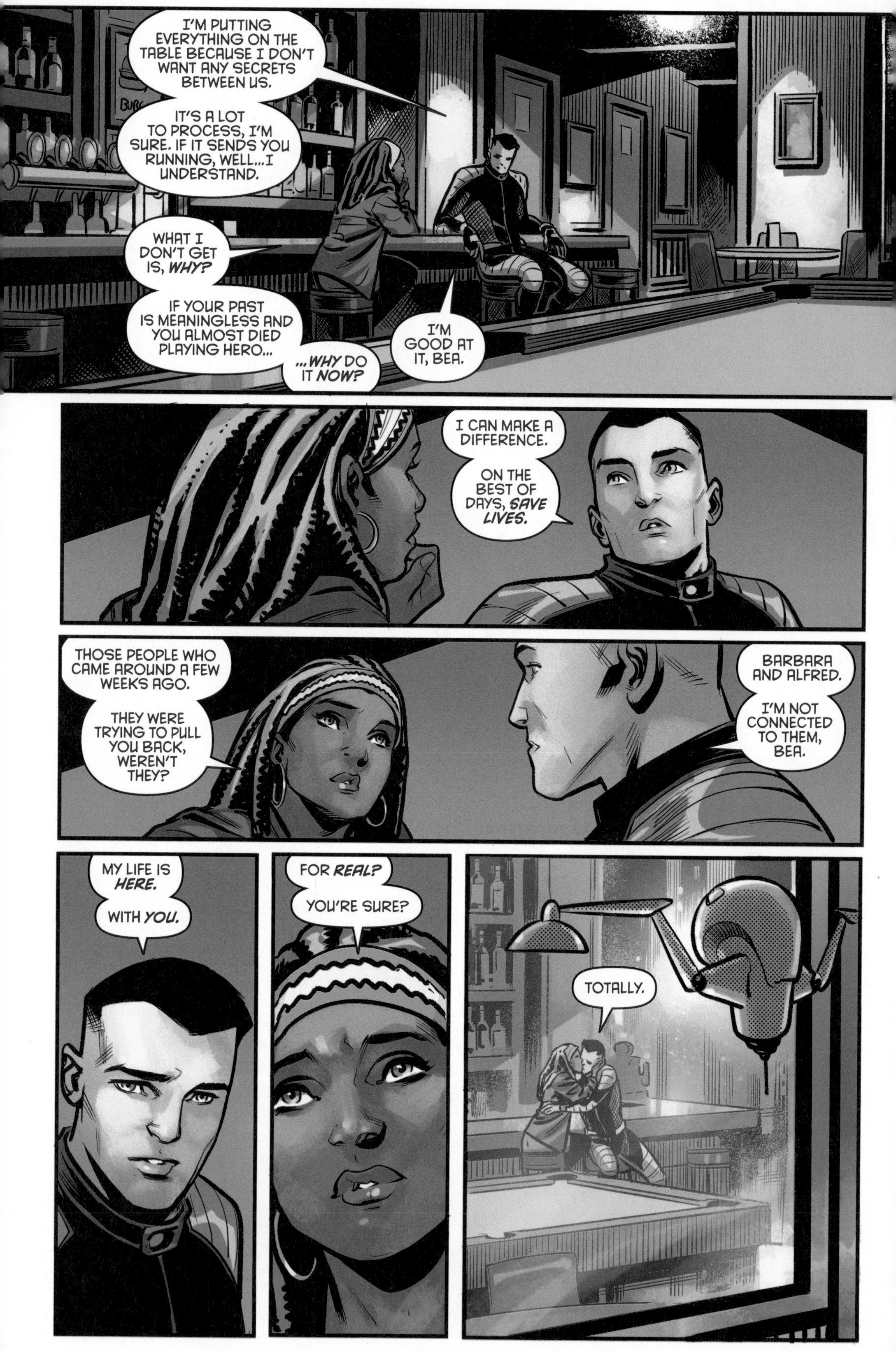
I'M PUTTING EVERYTHING ON THE TABLE BECAUSE I DON'T WANT ANY SECRETS BETWEEN US.
IT'S A LOT TO PROCESS, I'M SURE. IF IT SENDS YOU RUNNING, WELL...I UNDERSTAND.
WHAT I DON'T GET IS, WHY?
IF YOUR PAST IS MEANINGLESS AND YOU ALMOST DIED PLAYING HERO...
...WHY DO IT NOW?
I'M GOOD AT IT, BEA.
I CAN MAKE A DIFFERENCE.
ON THE BEST OF DAYS, SAVE LIVES.
THOSE PEOPLE WHO CAME AROUND A FEW WEEKS AGO.
THEY WERE TRYING TO PULL YOU BACK, WEREN'T THEY?
BARBARA AND ALFRED.
I'M NOT CONNECTED TO THEM, BEA.
MY LIFE IS HERE.
WITH YOU.
FOR REAL?
YOU'RE SURE?
TOTALLY.

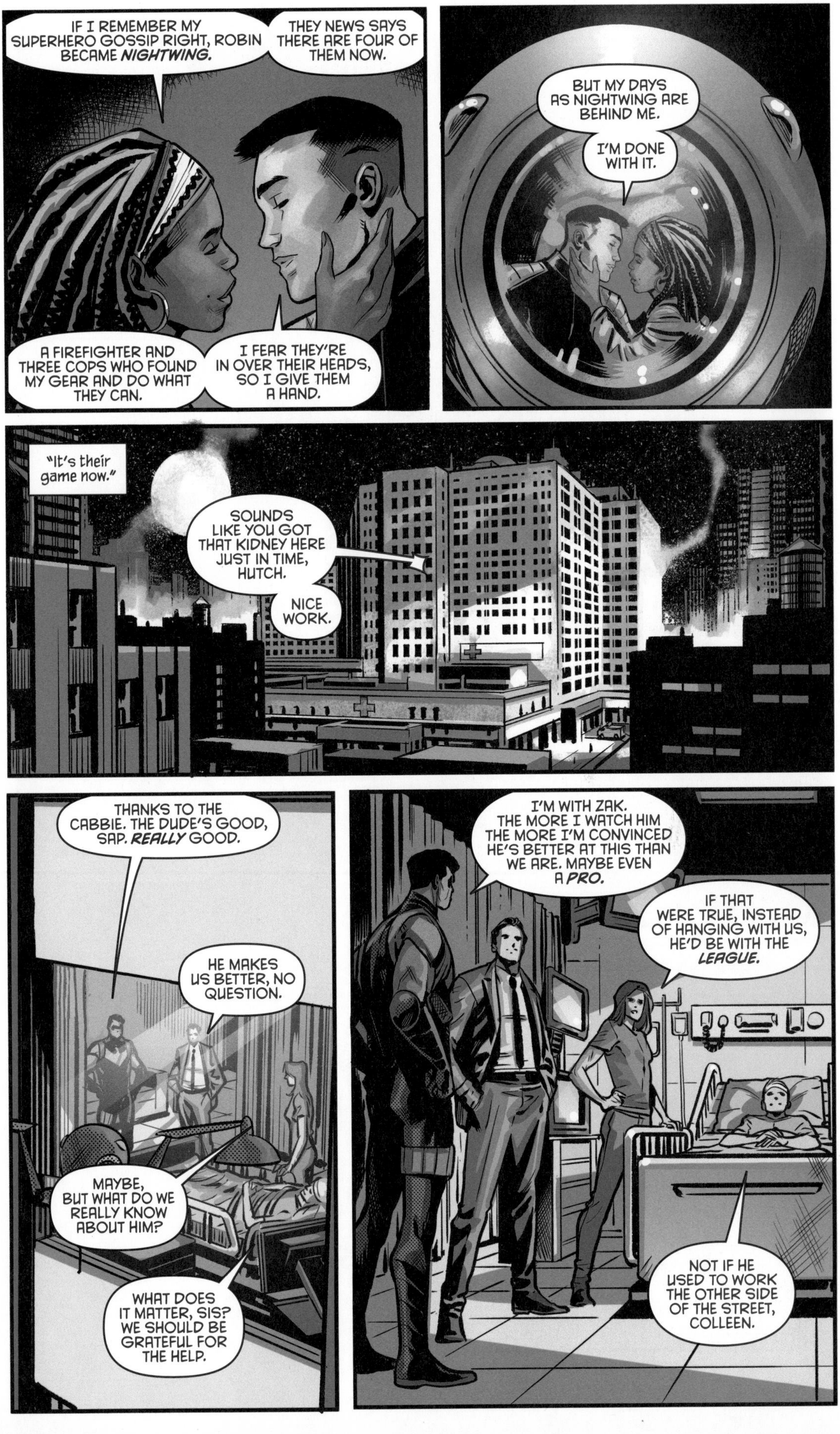
IF I REMEMBER MY SUPERHERO GOSSIP RIGHT, ROBIN BECAME *NIGHTWING.*
THEY NEWS SAYS THERE ARE FOUR OF THEM NOW.
A FIREFIGHTER AND THREE COPS WHO FOUND MY GEAR AND DO WHAT THEY CAN.
I FEAR THEY'RE IN OVER THEIR HEADS, SO I GIVE THEM A HAND.
BUT MY DAYS AS NIGHTWING ARE BEHIND ME.
I'M DONE WITH IT.
"It's their game now."
SOUNDS LIKE YOU GOT THAT KIDNEY HERE JUST IN TIME, HUTCH.
NICE WORK.
THANKS TO THE CABBIE. THE DUDE'S GOOD, SAP. *REALLY* GOOD.
HE MAKES US BETTER, NO QUESTION.
MAYBE, BUT WHAT DO WE REALLY KNOW ABOUT HIM?
WHAT DOES IT MATTER, SIS? WE SHOULD BE GRATEFUL FOR THE HELP.
I'M WITH ZAK. THE MORE I WATCH HIM THE MORE I'M CONVINCED HE'S BETTER AT THIS THAN WE ARE. MAYBE EVEN A *PRO.*
IF THAT WERE TRUE, INSTEAD OF HANGING WITH US, HE'D BE WITH THE *LEAGUE.*
NOT IF HE USED TO WORK THE OTHER SIDE OF THE STREET, COLLEEN.

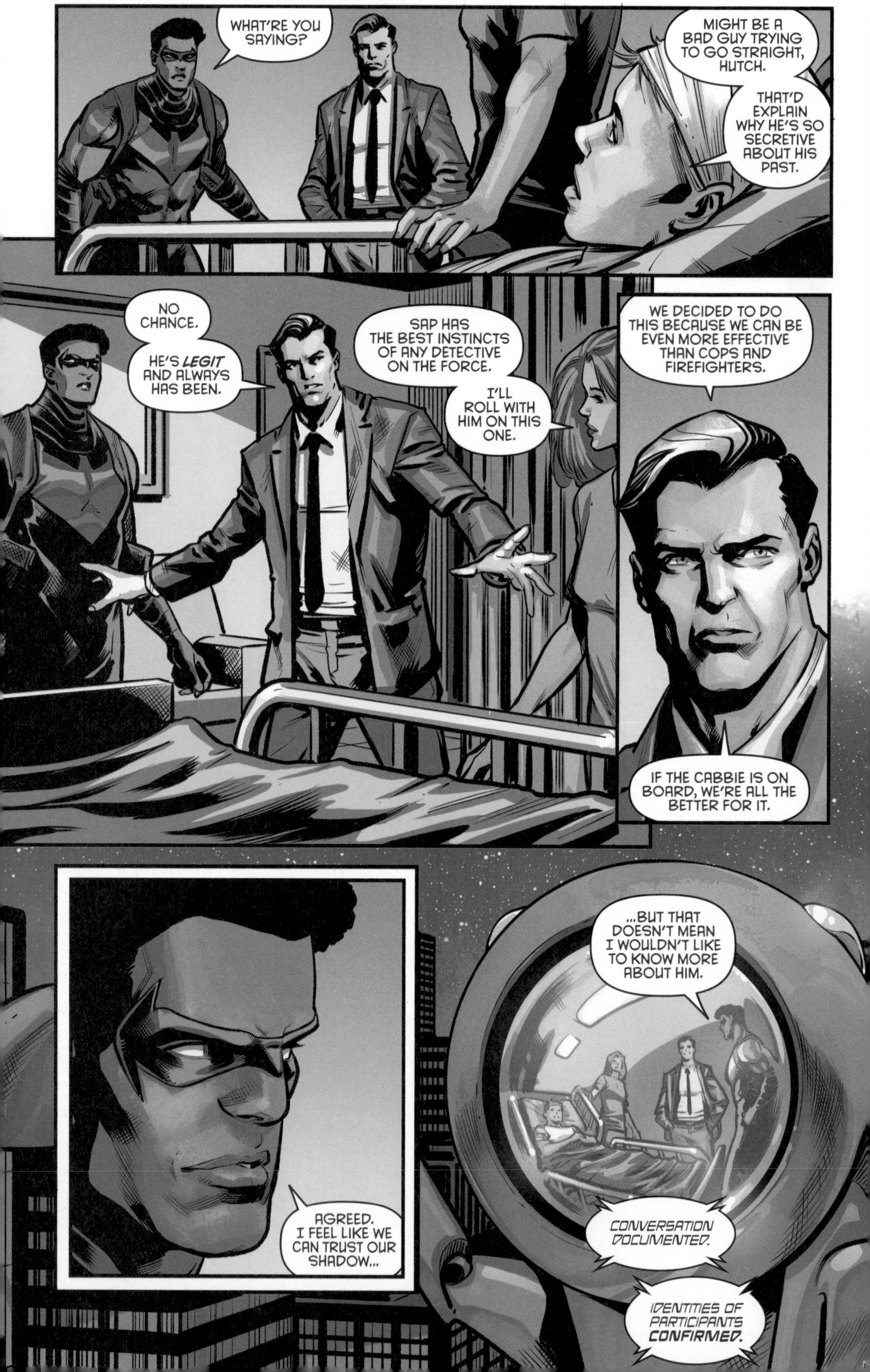
WHAT'RE YOU SAYING?
MIGHT BE A BAD GUY TRYING TO GO STRAIGHT, HUTCH.
THAT'D EXPLAIN WHY HE'S SO SECRETIVE ABOUT HIS PAST.
NO CHANCE.
HE'S *LEGIT* AND ALWAYS HAS BEEN.
SAP HAS THE BEST INSTINCTS OF ANY DETECTIVE ON THE FORCE.
I'LL ROLL WITH HIM ON THIS ONE.
WE DECIDED TO DO THIS BECAUSE WE CAN BE EVEN MORE EFFECTIVE THAN COPS AND FIREFIGHTERS.
IF THE CABBIE IS ON BOARD, WE'RE ALL THE BETTER FOR IT.
...BUT THAT DOESN'T MEAN I WOULDN'T LIKE TO KNOW MORE ABOUT HIM.
AGREED. I FEEL LIKE WE CAN TRUST OUR SHADOW...
CONVERSATION DOCUMENTED.
IDENTITIES OF PARTICIPANTS ***CONFIRMED.***

I don't remember being shot.

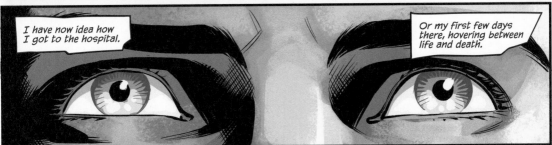

I have now idea how I got to the hospital.

Or my first few days there, hovering between life and death.

I do remember hating it.

The rich man, redhead and butler hovering over me, pushing me to remember.

Smothering me.

They kept telling me how much they cared.

That they loved me.

But you can't return that love to complete strangers.

I had no anchor.

Nothing to keep me there.

So I left.

I'm glad I did, because for the first time since those days...

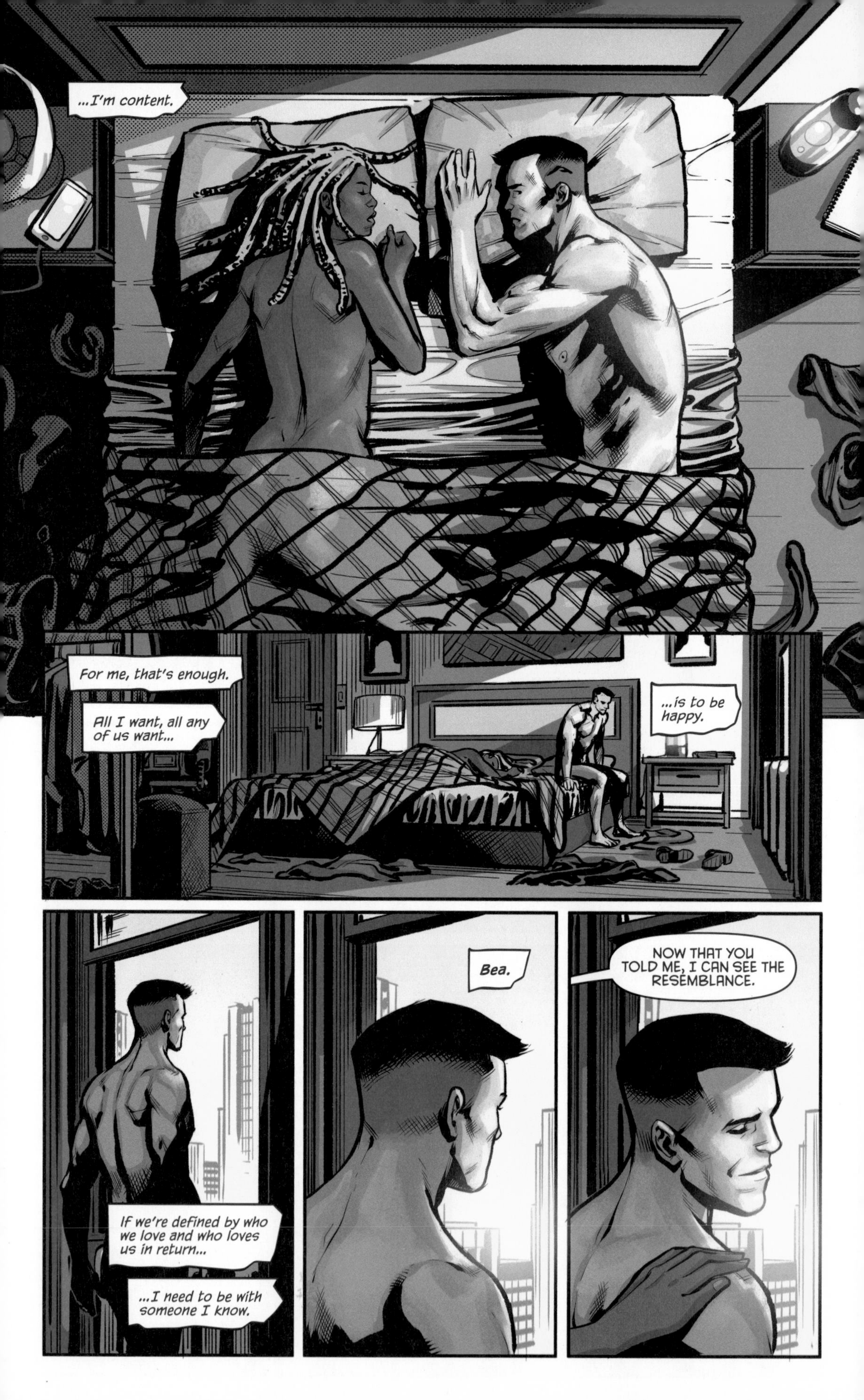
...I'm content.
For me, that's enough.
All I want, all any of us want...
...is to be happy.
If we're defined by who we love and who loves us in return...
...I need to be with someone I know.
Bea.
NOW THAT YOU TOLD ME, I CAN SEE THE RESEMBLANCE.

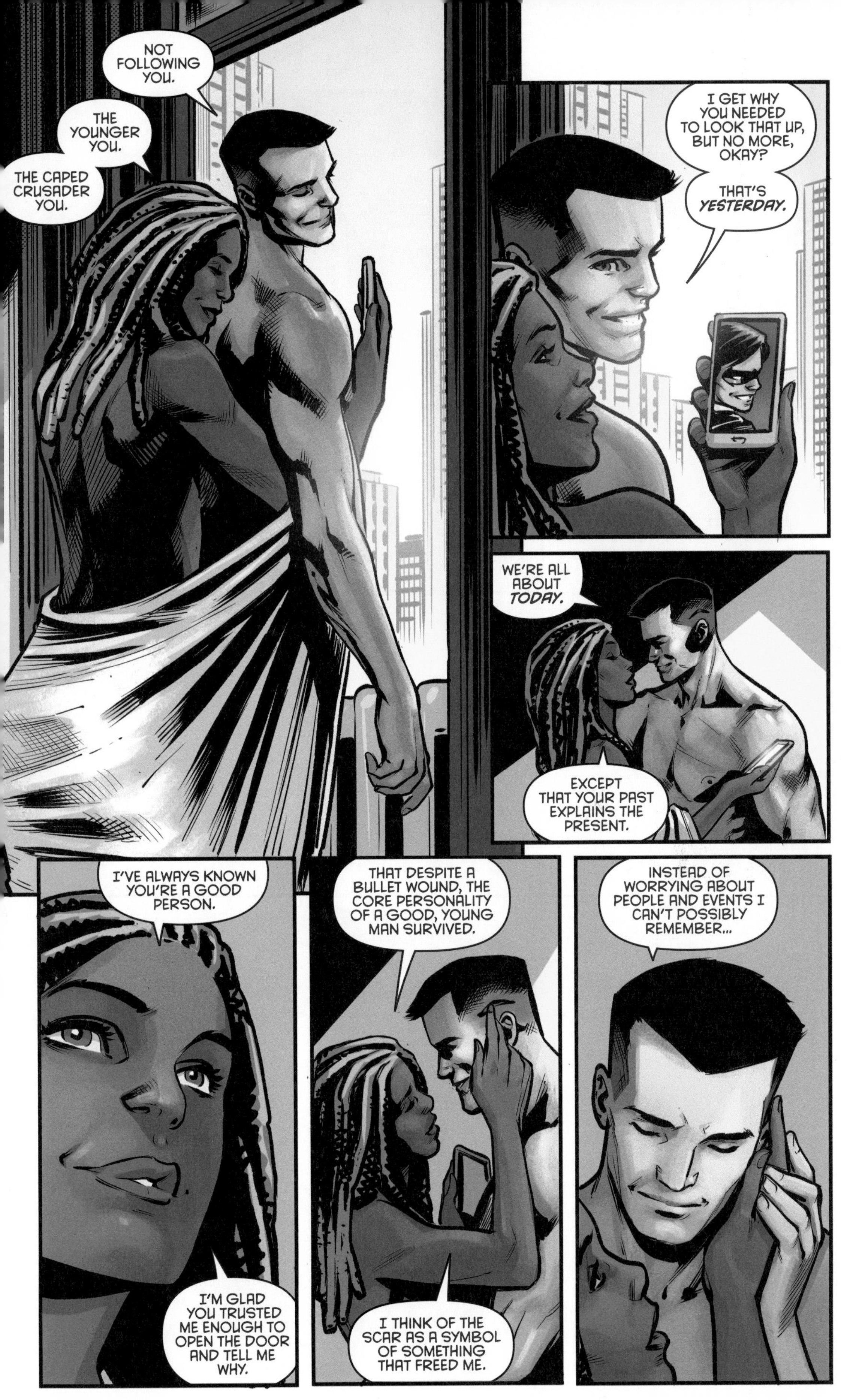
NOT FOLLOWING YOU.
THE YOUNGER YOU.
THE CAPED CRUSADER YOU.
I GET WHY YOU NEEDED TO LOOK THAT UP, BUT NO MORE, OKAY?
THAT'S *YESTERDAY.*
WE'RE ALL ABOUT *TODAY.*
EXCEPT THAT YOUR PAST EXPLAINS THE PRESENT.
I'VE ALWAYS KNOWN YOU'RE A GOOD PERSON.
I'M GLAD YOU TRUSTED ME ENOUGH TO OPEN THE DOOR AND TELL ME WHY.
THAT DESPITE A BULLET WOUND, THE CORE PERSONALITY OF A GOOD, YOUNG MAN SURVIVED.
I THINK OF THE SCAR AS A SYMBOL OF SOMETHING THAT FREED ME.
INSTEAD OF WORRYING ABOUT PEOPLE AND EVENTS I CAN'T POSSIBLY REMEMBER...

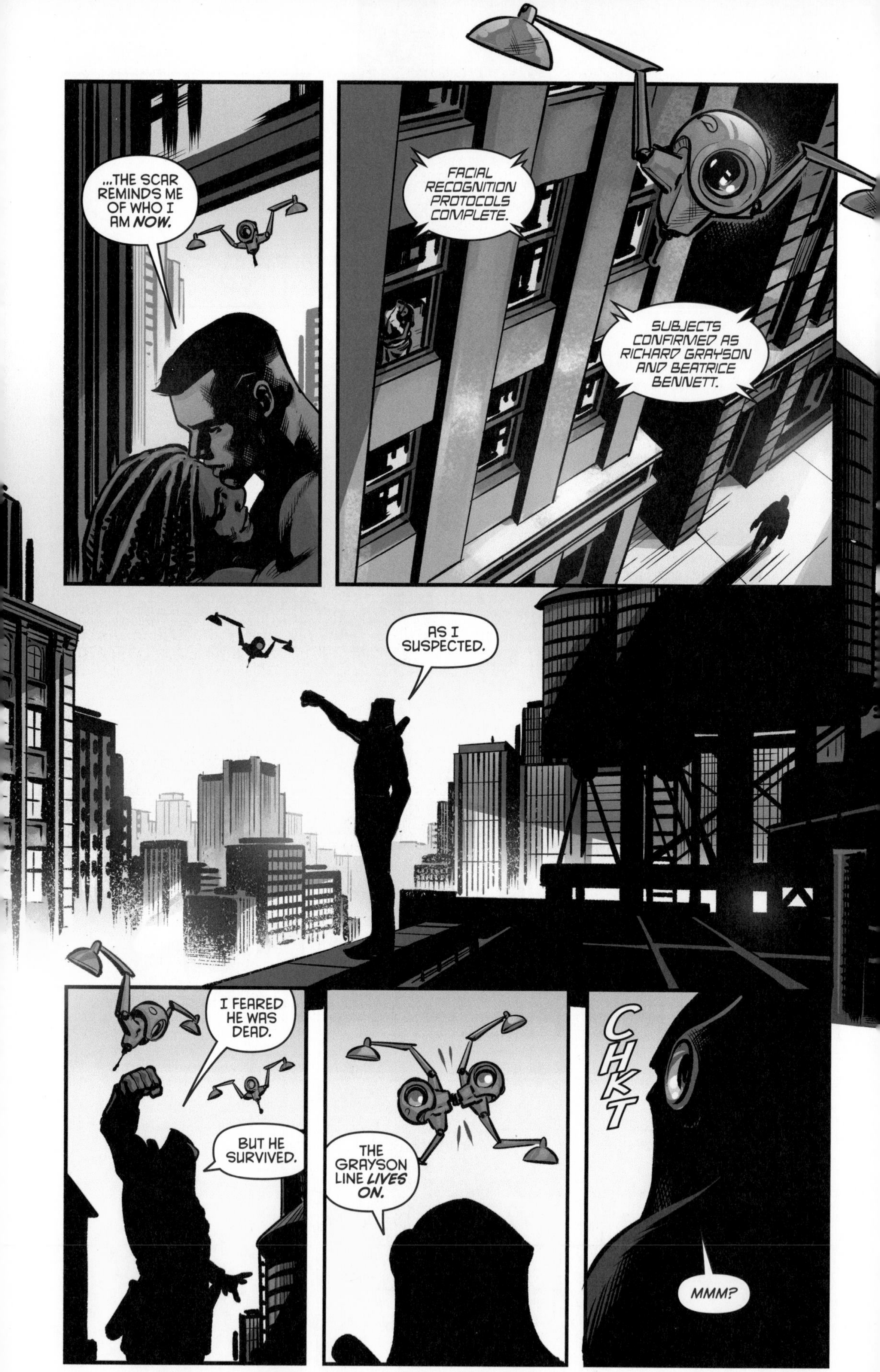
...THE SCAR REMINDS ME OF WHO I AM *NOW.*
FACIAL RECOGNITION PROTOCOLS COMPLETE.
SUBJECTS CONFIRMED AS RICHARD GRAYSON AND BEATRICE BENNETT.
AS I SUSPECTED.
I FEARED HE WAS DEAD.
BUT HE SURVIVED.
THE GRAYSON LINE *LIVES ON.*
CHKT
MMM?

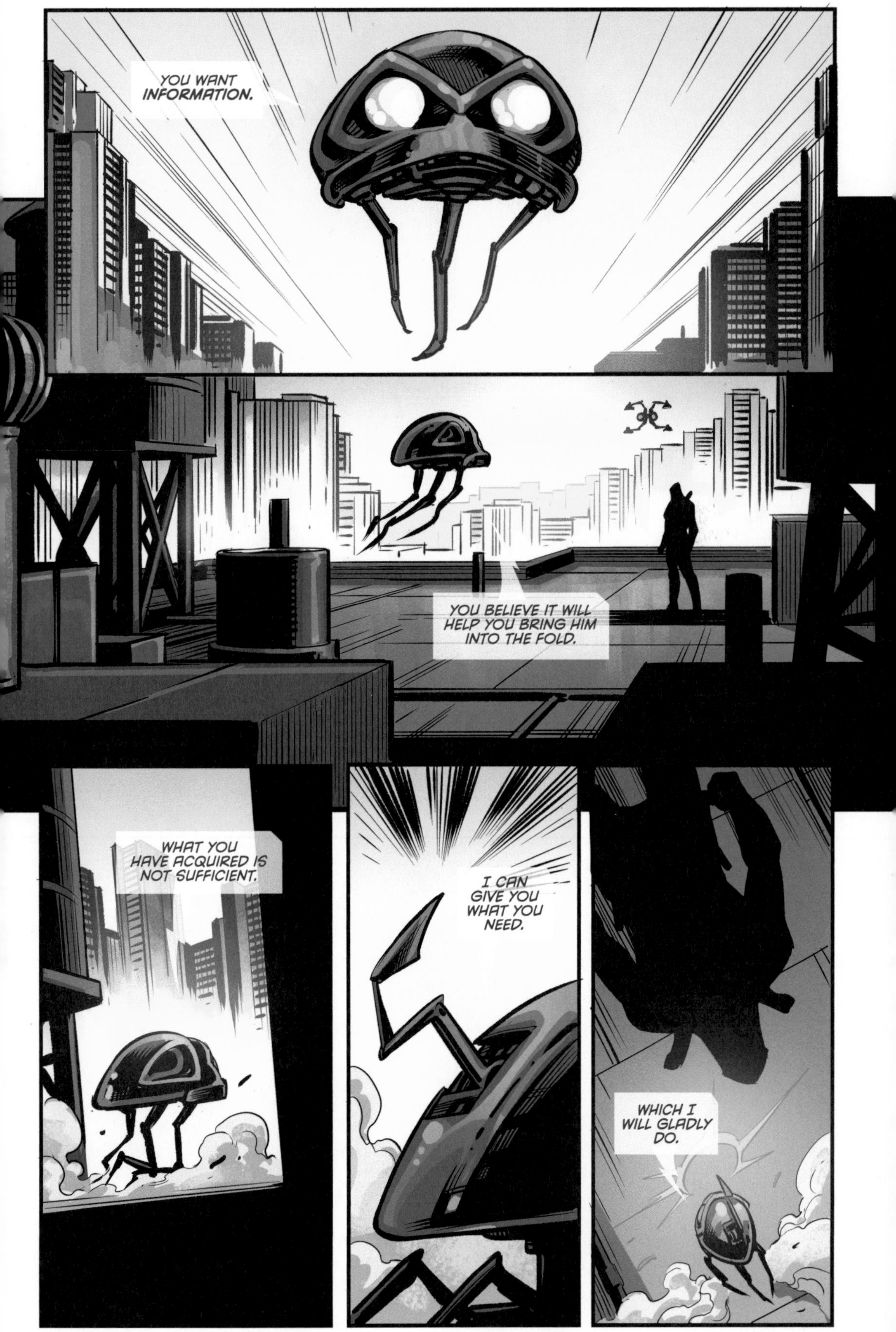

YOU WANT INFORMATION.
YOU BELIEVE IT WILL HELP YOU BRING HIM INTO THE FOLD.
WHAT YOU HAVE ACQUIRED IS NOT SUFFICIENT.
I CAN GIVE YOU WHAT YOU NEED.
WHICH I WILL GLADLY DO.

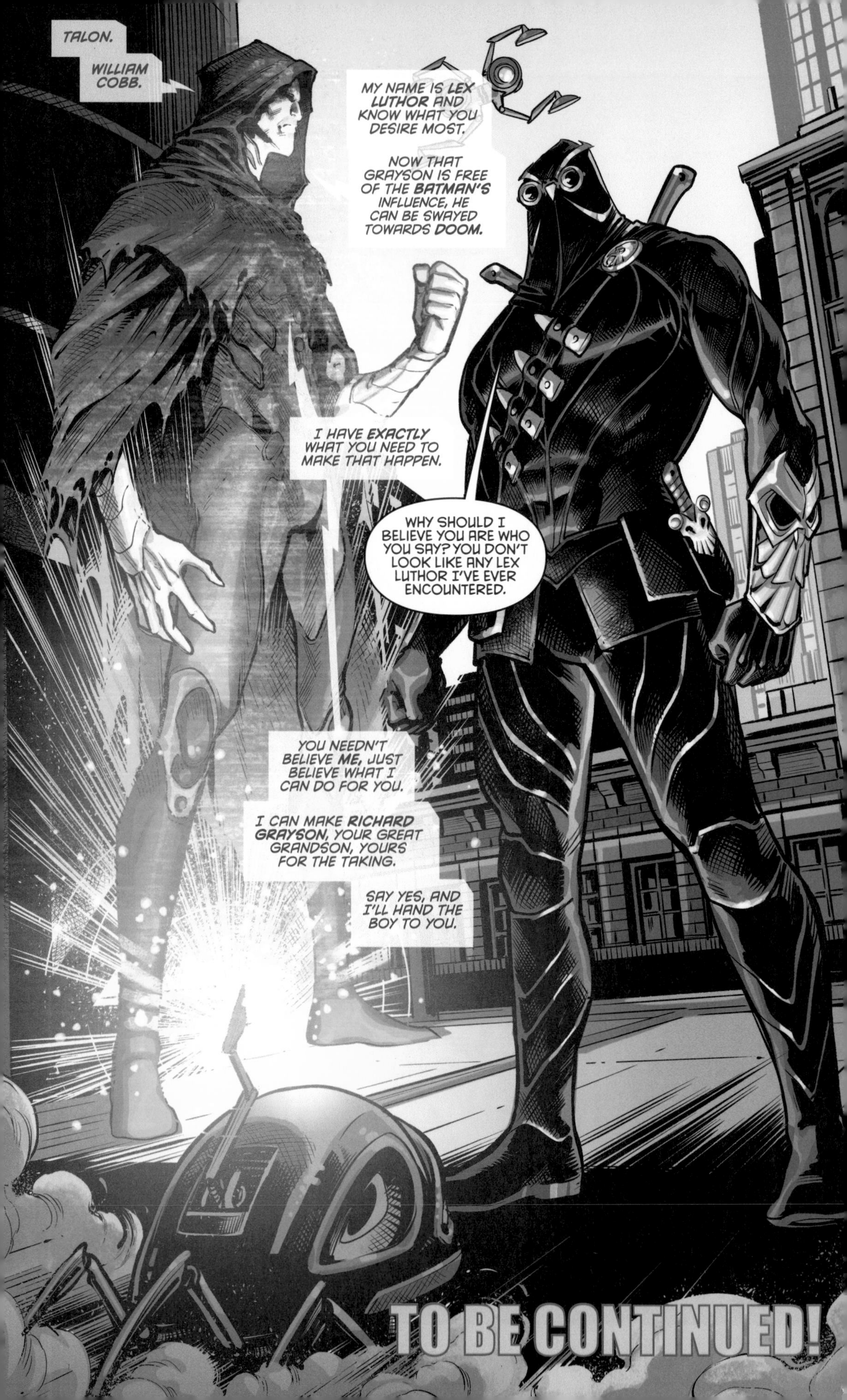
TALON.
WILLIAM COBB.
MY NAME IS LEX LUTHOR AND KNOW WHAT YOU DESIRE MOST.
NOW THAT GRAYSON IS FREE OF THE BATMAN'S INFLUENCE, HE CAN BE SWAYED TOWARDS DOOM.
I HAVE EXACTLY WHAT YOU NEED TO MAKE THAT HAPPEN.
WHY SHOULD I BELIEVE YOU ARE WHO YOU SAY? YOU DON'T LOOK LIKE ANY LEX LUTHOR I'VE EVER ENCOUNTERED.
YOU NEEDN'T BELIEVE ME, JUST BELIEVE WHAT I CAN DO FOR YOU.
I CAN MAKE RICHARD GRAYSON, YOUR GREAT GRANDSON, YOURS FOR THE TAKING.
SAY YES, AND I'LL HAND THE BOY TO YOU.
TO BE CONTINUED!

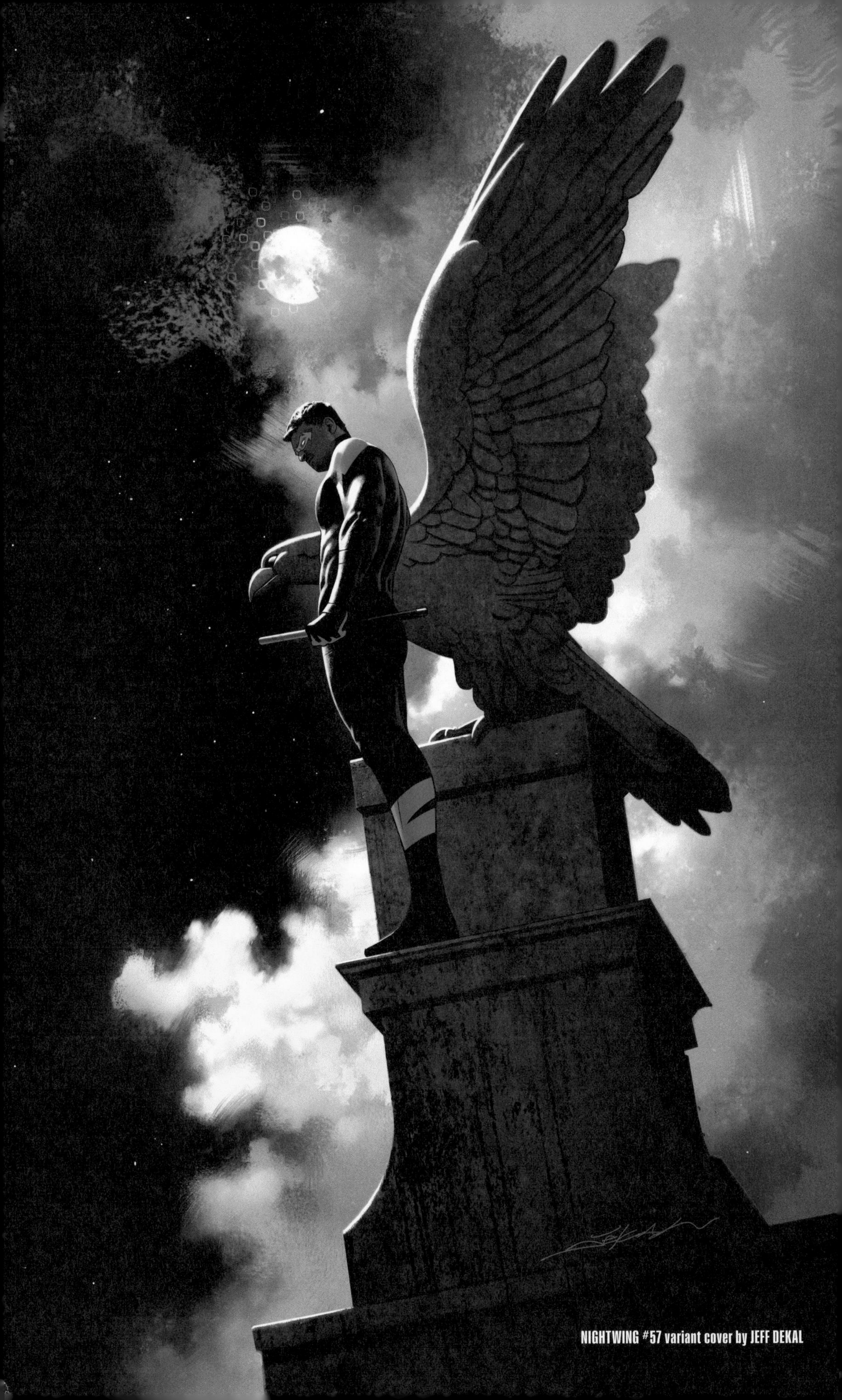

NIGHTWING #57 variant cover by JEFF DEKAL

NIGHTWING #58 variant cover by TYLER KIRKHAM

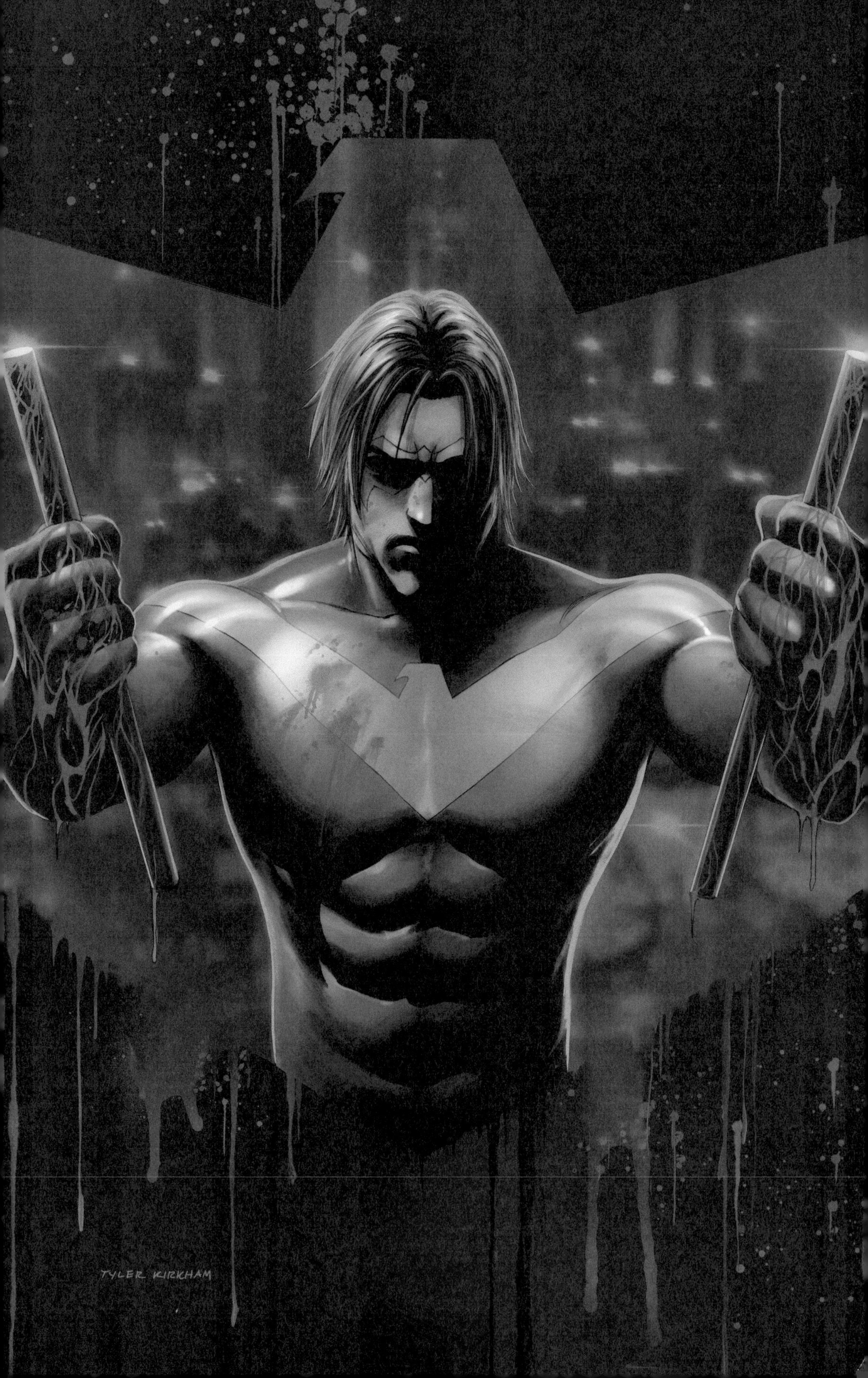
TYLER KIRKHAM

NIGHTWING #59 variant cover by YASMINE PUTRI

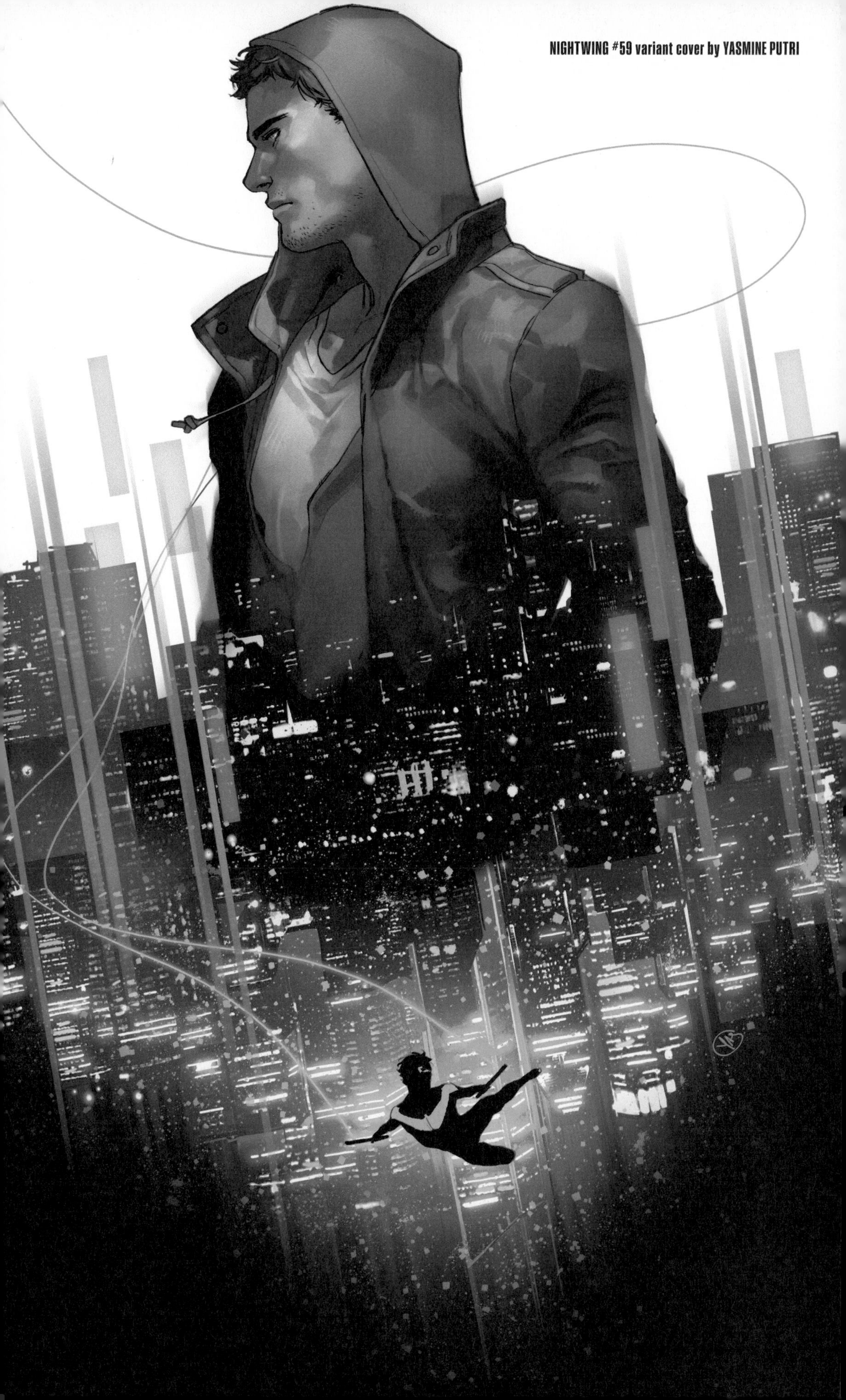

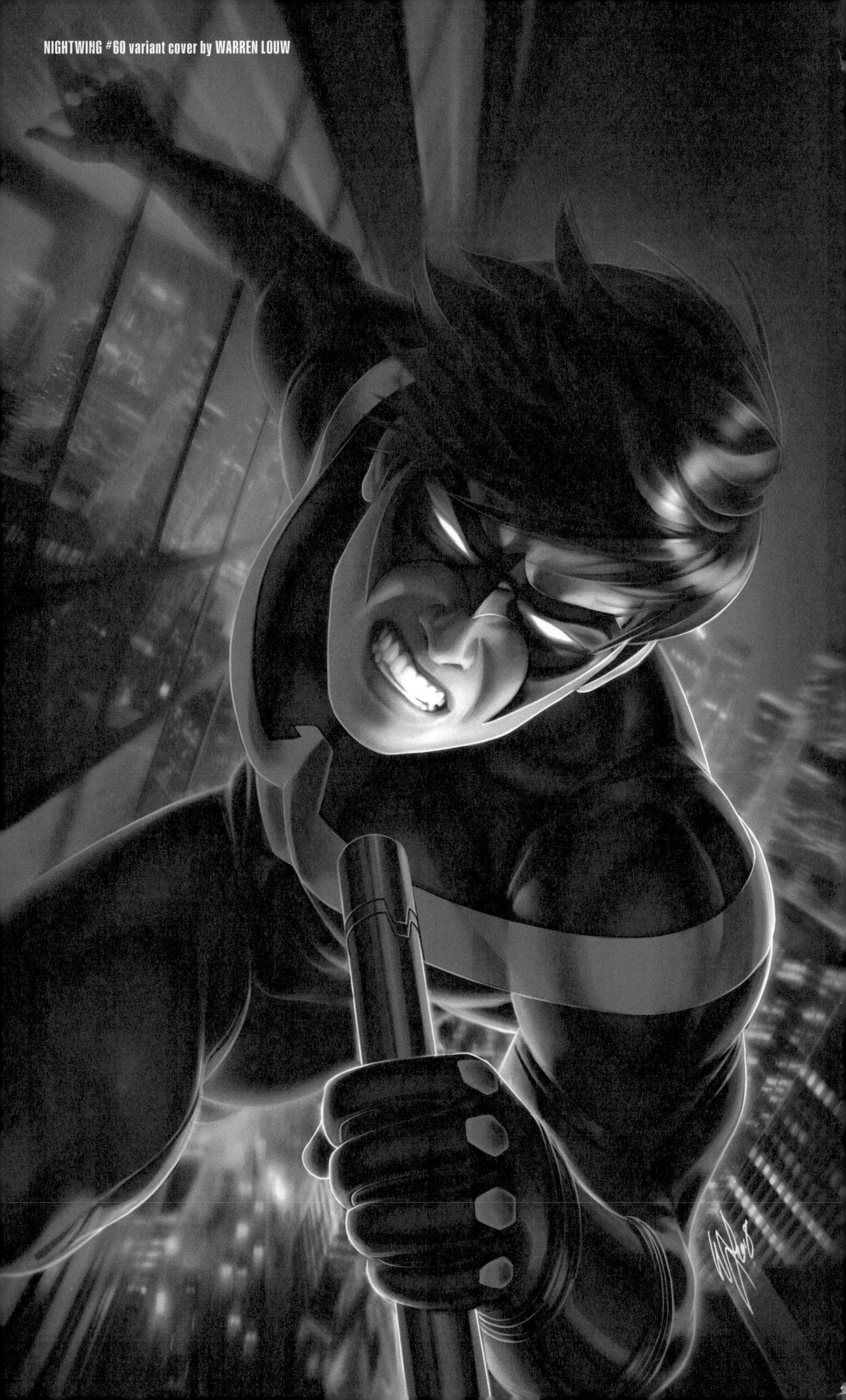

NIGHTWING #60 variant cover by WARREN LOUW

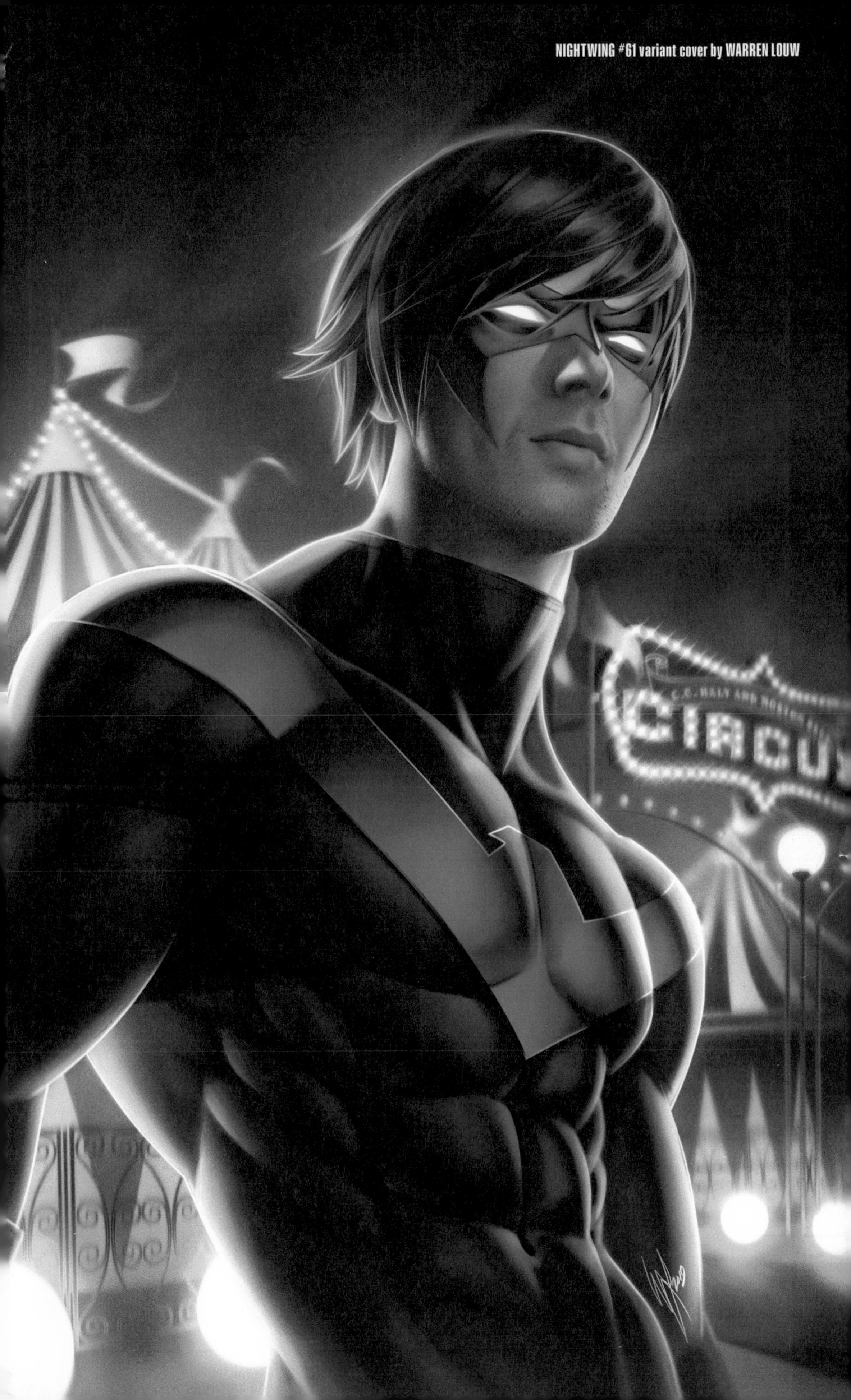

NIGHTWING #61 variant cover by WARREN LOUW

NIGHTWING #62 variant cover
by GREG CAPULLO and FCO PLASCENCIA

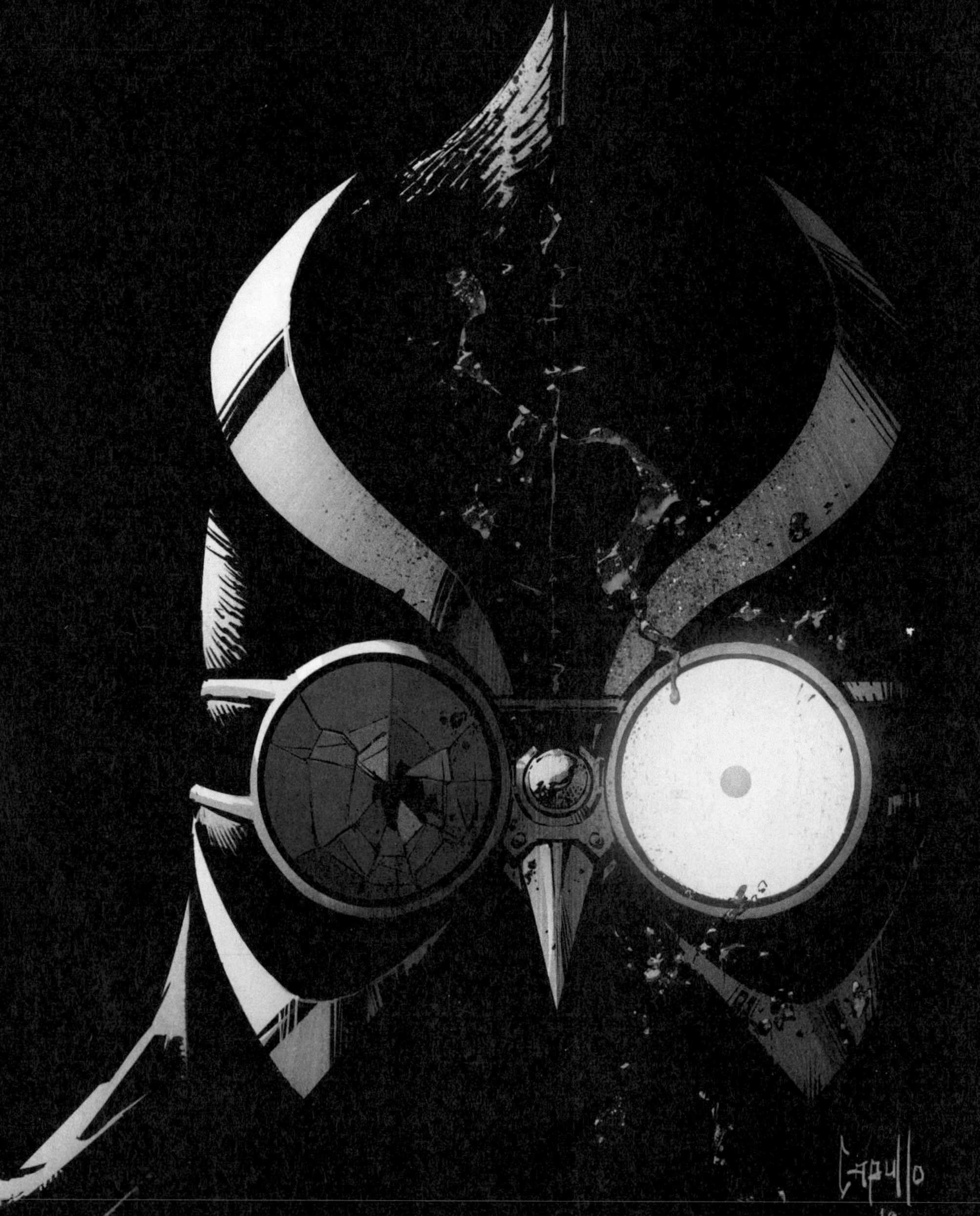
Capullo
19
+fco